S

Happy casting ~
Much success !

Michael Jay
7-2-03

Confectionery
Art
Casting

Confectionery Art Casting

Silicone Mold Making for Pastry Chefs

Chef John Kraus working on a sugar showpiece.

By
Michael Joy

Produced by
The Chicago School of Mold Making and Casting for the Arts

Confectionery Art Casting
Silicone Mold Making for Pastry Chefs
Copyright © 2003 by Michael Joy
All rights reserved

Mailing Address:
The Chicago School of Mold Making and Casting for the Arts
1117 North Harlem Avenue
Oak Park, IL 60302
(708)660-9707

Find us on the World Wide Web at:
http://**www.ChicagoMoldSchool.com**
Comments welcome at **joymold@earthlink.net**

Notice of Liability
The information in this publication is true to the best of our knowledge, without warranty. The author, chefs and any other persons, disclaim all liability to any person or entity with respect to any loss or damage caused or alleged to be caused directly or indirectly by the instructions contained in this book or by the products described herein.

Trademarks
Several products mentioned in this publication are claimed as trademarks by their manufactures. Through out this book where mentioned, the author has respected the trademark with the designation. These and all other product names and services identified throughout this publication are used in editorial fashion only, for the benefit of the trademark owner with no intention of infringement of the trademark.

All photographs were taken by Michael Joy, except the photographs in Chapter 13, credits to **International School of Confectionery Arts**.
Image Manipulation, Design & Layout by Beatrice Schneider, **Better Image Designs, Inc.**
Editorial Credits to Sharon and Andrew Dallstream, Chris Newman and Sigi Schneider.

Publisher's Catalog-in-Publication

Joy, Michael,
    Confectionery art casting : silicone mold making for
pastry chef/Michael Joy.
    p. cm.
    Includes index
    ISBN 0-9740345-0-9
    1. Molds (Cookware) 2. Confectionery. 3. Sugar art.
I.Title.

NK8490.J69 2003   731.4'3
               QBI03-200291

Printed and bound in the United States of America.

CONTENTS

Chef Jacguy Pfeiffer working on a chocolate sculpture.

DEDICATION

This book is dedicated to Jacquy, John, Sebastien, Ewald and Keegan. It is because of their enthusiasm, support and willingness to experiment with new mold making materials and processes that this book was written. I am inspired by chefs like these, who search outside of the food industry to bring new ideas and processes to the forefront of the culinary arts.

A special thank you is also extended to Beatrice Schneider, who single-handedly formatted every photograph, word and element of this book. Without her long hours and clear thinking, this manual would still be trapped in a spiral notebook.

I am grateful to my wordsmiths, Sharon and Andrew Dallstream, Chris Newman and Sigi Schneider for their many years of friendship and support, as well as the significant time and energy they invested into the editorial process of this book. If you stumble across any errors, I am certain they are mine.

INTRODUCTION

Mold making is an exciting and challenging activity that will reward the artist as well as the chef with a surprisingly wide range of creative possibilities. The concepts are straight forward and, when presented as we have in this book, in a step-wise progression from simple to complex, are easily learned and integrated with other ways of making forms.

We have divided the chapters into sections that are devoted to each stage of mold design and casting. Recognizing that many of the terms used every day in mold making are foreign to those in the confectionary arts, we have provided a glossary for terms that are printed in **bold** in the text.

Following the mold making demonstrations, the contributing chefs share how their unique casting methods and artistic skills can be used to create amenities, showpieces and other culinary compositions. We have reserved the last three chapters to illustrate how advanced mold making methods can be used to go beyond traditional duplication of forms to create innovative chocolate sculptures.

We hope that you will be inspired by this book to cast your own confectionary masterpieces. The possibilities using the techniques of molding and casting are endless.

Enjoy, and happy mold making.

-Michael Joy

Making A Silicone Mold Of A Cloisonné Bell

The cloisonné bell illustrates how a basic one-piece mold is made. The bell is a good model to begin with because its smooth, even surface will allow the food grade silicone to be removed easily. When making your first mold, attention should be focused on the proper mixing and use of silicone, not complex mold design issues. Choose a simple model like the bell until you become familiar with handling food grade silicone.

The following section will illustrate a fast and efficient way to make a one-piece silicone mold, also known as an **open face** or **poured block** mold. The term open face refers to a model which is being set face down on the work table while the silicone is poured around it. When the silicone cures, the face area (bottom of the bell) remains open. The open face refers to where the sugar, chocolate or other casting medium is poured into the mold to make a casting.

View of the enameled bell.

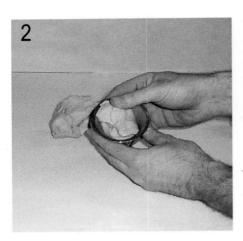

The bell is gently filled with an oil-based clay called Klean Klay. It is soft, affordable and does not contain any ingredients that will affect the curing of the silicone.

NOTE: *Do not use oil based clays that contain sulfur* (you can tell by the strong odor) as they cause a chemical reaction that will adversely affect the curing of the silicone.

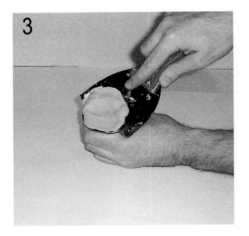

The clay is shaved smooth with a mud knife to ensure a flat, level surface.

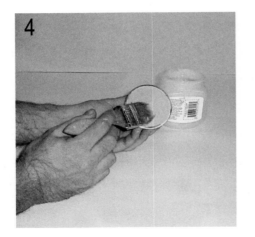

A small amount of Vaseline is dabbed onto the bottom of the clay. Vaseline acts as a temporary glue that seals the model tightly to the **work board**.

NOTE: A work board is any non-porous or laminated surface that you can pour your mold on. A laminated shelf section from a hardware store will make a good work board.

The bell is pushed firmly down on the work board; notice that a paper towel is used to protect the model from finger prints. Use the paper towel to wipe the model clean.

NOTE: Whenever using Vaseline, be careful not to transfer any greasy fingerprints onto the model. The fingerprint texture will be picked up by the silicone and transferred onto your food castings.

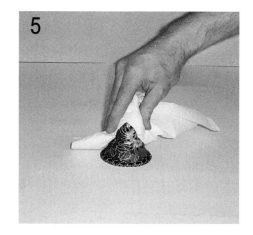

A marker is used to outline a ¼ inch perimeter around the bell. A large metal nut is placed at the tip of the pen to create a spacer for the perimeter outline.

Because the plastic cup's outlined perimeter is about the same size as the bell, it can be used as a **mold box.** The bottom of the cups have been cut off with a razor knife to create an open cylinder.

NOTE: Notice that two cups are stacked together. An individual cup is too flexible and will compress when surrounded with clay.

Oil clay is carefully put around the cup making a watertight seal. To do this, smear the clay at least ¼ inch up the side of the cup and ½ inch around the bottom perimeter of the cup. It is critical that this step be done carefully, as silicone will leak through a pinhole sized opening for over an hour before it begins to cure.

NOTE: All molds must be poured on a level surface. Use **shims** to level the work board if needed.

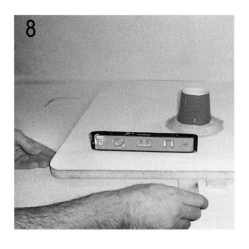

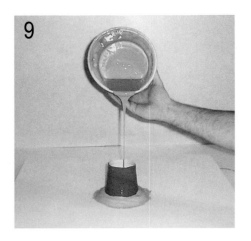

A batch of food grade silicone is poured into the cup. In order to reduce the air bubbles in your mold, the silicone must be poured in a slow, thin stream. Hold the mixing container high above the cup in order to stretch the stream of silicone into a thin line. This is called **needling** the silicone. Needling will cause the air bubbles to stretch and break before entering the mold box. (Refer to the appendix for proper mixing instructions for food grade silicone.)

NOTE: If you do not create a tight and secure clay bond around the base of the cup, it will float up off of the work board. If this happens, do not try to stop it. Scoop the silicone into a container and take a break.

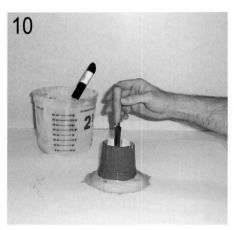

The cup is filled so that the silicone is approximately ¼ inch thick above the top of the bell. Check the depth by setting a knife tip on top of the bell and withdraw the blade to see how much silicone is above the bell.

Remember to make sure the work board is level (page 3, photograph 8) before the silicone begins to cure. Liquid silicone will seek its own level and cure at the same angle of the work board. An unlevel mold will not sit flat when you fill it with chocolate, sugar etc.

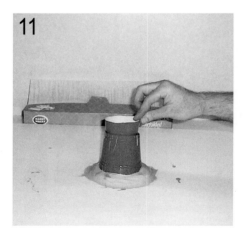

This step is seldom necessary, however, some food grade silicone (such as Silastic L) will not completely cure when it is left open to the air (top surface of the mold). This is known as **air inhibition**. It is easily remedied by placing a piece of wax paper directly in contact with the top surface of the silicone.

NOTE: Since the open end of the cup is too small to put wax paper into, the cut off cup bottom is gently set on top of the silicone. Allow the cup to float on the silicone. Do not press the cup down.

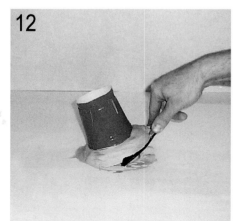

The silicone is allowed to cure for 24 hours. A mud knife is used to pry the entire mold box off the work board.

The cup is removed. Flip the mold and wipe off the Vaseline.

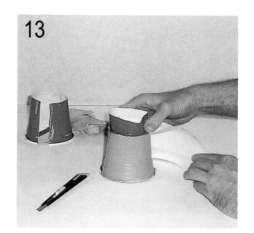

The bell is gently pressed out of the mold.

Manicure scissors are used to carefully trim the **flash** from the edge of the mold. Flash is the term used for silicone that seeps under the model or the mold box. Although it is thin and easy to trim, be careful not to cut into the detail surface of the mold.

The open face mold is completed.

Molding A Decorative Picture Frame And Stand

The picture frame and stand illustrate how a model can be disassembled to simplify the mold making process. Non-food grade silicone will be used to make the molds in this chapter. Many of the molds that I make are made with non-food grade silicone. Using non-food grade silicone is a terrific way to reduce your material costs but should only be used for display or competition pieces. Never use it if there is a chance that the castings might be consumed. When a food grade mold is required, the first (non-food grade) mold can be converted into a food grade mold by making a **master mold**. This chapter provides an example of that process.

This chapter is made up of three sections.
Section 1: Making a non-food grade (NFG) silicone mold of the easel.
Section 2: Making a NFG silicone mold of the frame.
Section 3: Making a NFG silicone mold of three Plexiglas inserts and a master mold of the inserts.

The technique illustrated in Section 3 offers several benefits as molding inserts separately rather than with the frame allows the user much more creative freedom.
   A. The flat inserts can be silk-screened ahead of time without the limitations of screening in a small area inside of the frame.
   B. Transfers can be cut and placed into the insert mold.
   C. The inserts can be cast in a different medium than the frame. For example, if the frame is dark chocolate, the plates could be made of colored sugar and inserted into the frame.

WARNING: NON-FOOD GRADE SILICONE IS NOT COMPATIBLE FOOD GRADE SILICONE.
Food grade silicone will not cure against any surface (clay, work boards, clink boards or models) that has come into contact with non-food grade silicone. The simple rule is: *If liquid, non-food grade silicone touched it, food grade silicone will not cure against it*. Clink boards and work boards must be cleaned with denatured alcohol if you intend to pour food grade silicone where non-food grade has already been used. You must create a separate environment for the two types of silicone or use the master mold system. In order to control the two separate environments these two materials require, only pour food grade silicone into a **Hydrocal** master mold (Hydrocal is a strong plaster). There are exceptions of course, but in general this system works well.

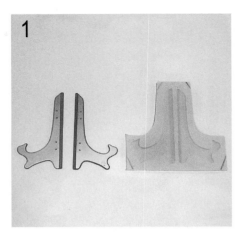

View of the disassembled easel and completed silicone mold. The following sequence will illustrate how this mold is made.

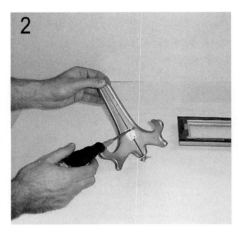

The hinges are removed to disassemble the easel.

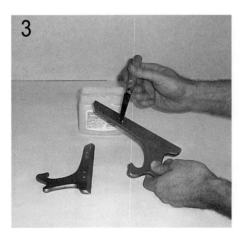

Small dabs of Vaseline are put on the back of the easel.

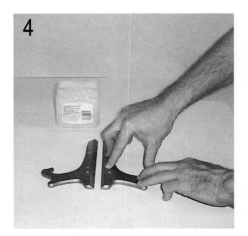

The easel is pressed onto a work board.

A **fettling knife** is used to remove any Vaseline that has squashed out the back.

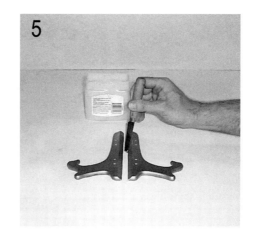

A mold box is assembled around the easel. Four **clink boards** (see page 330) are clamped together. Remember to leave a ¾ inch perimeter from top, bottom and side edges of the easel.

HELPFUL HINT: When assembling the mold box, tack all four outer corners to the work board first. Use two small coils of clay on each side of the corner and pinch them together at the same time. If you try to seal the sides of the mold box before the corners, the whole box will slide on the work board.

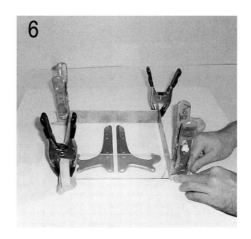

The inside of the clink board is held when sealing the outside edges with clay. This will prevent the boards from sliding, possibly breaking the clay seal at another location.

NOTE: It is not necessary to seal the inside of the mold box with clay, only the outside edges.

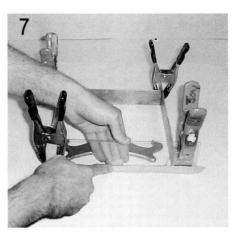

Small slabs of clay are placed inside of the mold box. These clay walls will help reduce the amount of silicone needed to cover the easel.

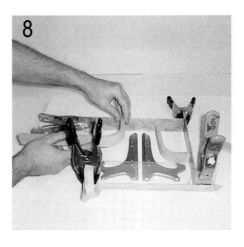

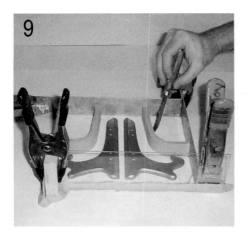

The clay strips must be tightly blended onto the work board. A grapefruit knife with a bent tip is used to press the back edge of the clay onto the board.

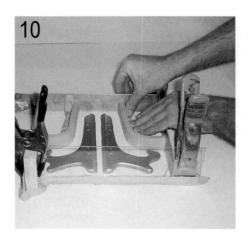

Small coils of clay are pressed behind the clay walls for extra support.

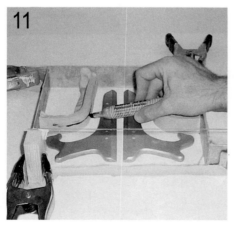

A line, called a **pouring indication line**, is drawn ¼ inch above the top of the easel. This makes it easy to see when to stop pouring the silicone.

Pouring too much silicone increases the thickness of the mold and is a waste of material. A mold that is too thick will be less flexible and can cause a chocolate casting to break during production.

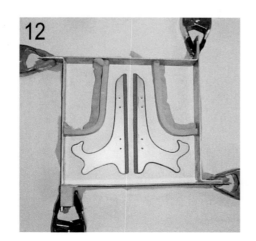

A top view of the model and mold box properly clamped and sealed together.

Level the work board. This is critical for models that are thin and flat. If the board is not level, the mold will cure with a slant on the back. The problem will become evident when you finish the mold and try to fill it with chocolate. The chocolate will not level out in the mold evenly.

To visualize this effect, imagine filling a mold on a tilted table. The chocolate would cast thick at one side and thin on the other.

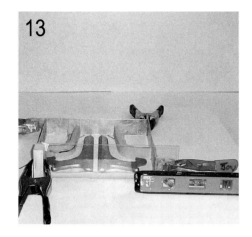

Non-food grade silicone is poured over the model. (See the appendix for mixing instruction).

After the silicone cures, the mold box and clay walls are removed.

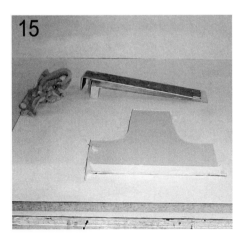

The silicone mold is trimmed.

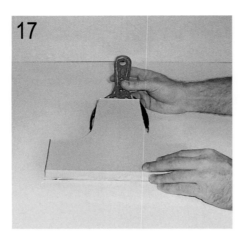

The mold is gently lifted off the work board with a **mud knife**.

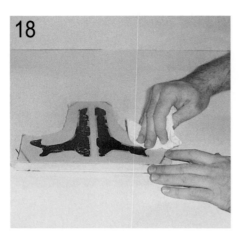

Wipe the excess Vaseline off the model.

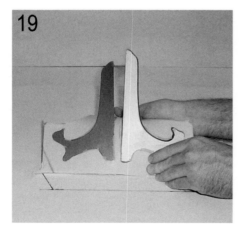

Flex the mold to release the model.

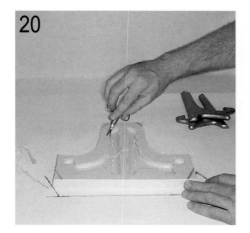

Silicone **flash** on the inside of the mold is removed, being cautious not to over trim the mold.

NOTE: If you cut too much, you cannot fix the silicone gash. Think of it this way, if you cut away too much silicone, the gash created from trimming will cause a raised bump in the finished casting. Each casting will require extra attention at cleanup.

The finished silicone mold and the easel. In order to avoid repetition, I will not show the making of the easel master mold. Master mold techniques will be shown only for the plate inserts. (See page 21 for more information.)

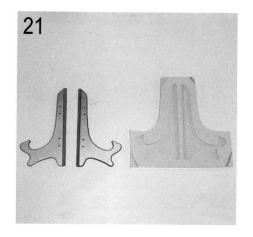

Section 2
Molding the Picture Frame

This picture is shown out of sequence and represents a view of the finished mold that is about to be made.

The frame's backing is removed.

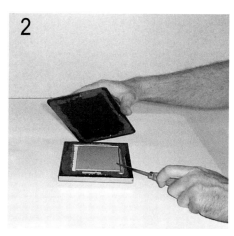

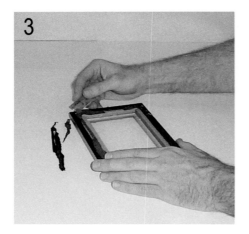

For safety, the glass is removed. A razor blade is then used to shave the felt off the back of the frame.

The glass is placed back in the frame. Oil clay is pressed in the back of the frame to hold the glass in place.

The clay is shaved level with the edge of the frame.

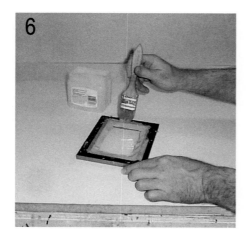

Vaseline is dabbed on the back of the frame.

The frame is pressed onto the work board. Remove any Vaseline that squashed out from the bottom of the frame when it was pressed onto the work board.

NOTE: Remember to wipe any fingerprints off the wood frame.

A ¾ inch guideline is drawn around the frame.

HELPFUL HINT: Use a small piece of flat pine molding from the hardware store as a spacer. Buy several different widths so that they can be on hand for various uses.

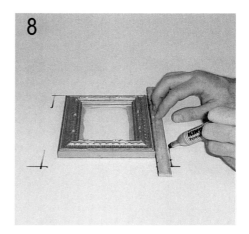

IMPORTANT: **Parting soap** is applied to the frame glass.

Non-food grade silicone will BOND with glass (or any silica/ sand-based material).

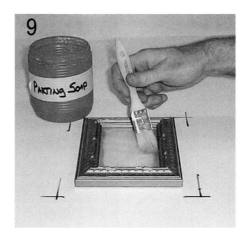

The inside surfaces of the clink boards are lightly coated with Vaseline.

NOTE: Silicone will stick slightly to aluminum clink boards, making it difficult to release the finished mold. It is especially important to coat new **clink boards** the first half dozen times you use them.

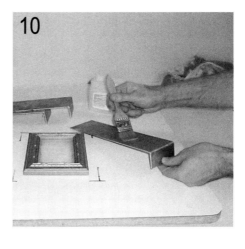

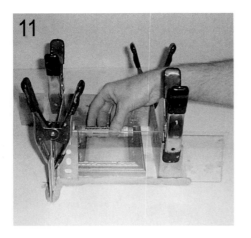

The mold box is assembled. A pouring indication line is drawn inside of the mold box approximately ¼ inch above the top of the frame.

NOTE: It will be difficult to leave a mark on the aluminum if you have put an excessive amount of Vaseline on the clink boards.

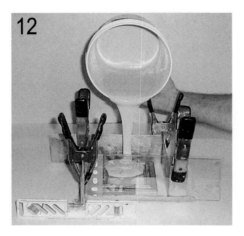

The work board is leveled and non-food grade silicone is poured into the center of the frame, then needled over the detailed surface of the frame.

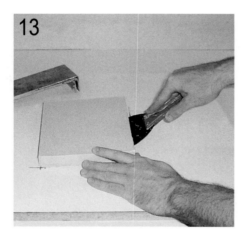

After the silicone has cured, the mold is flipped over by carefully slipping the mud knife under the mold and frame and prying up.

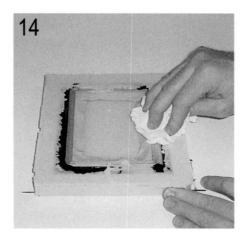

Excess Vaseline is wiped from the frame. Notice how much silicone flashed beneath the frame. This happened because the felt backing prevented a tight seal between the frame and the work board.

The wood frame has been removed and the interior flash is carefully trimmed away.

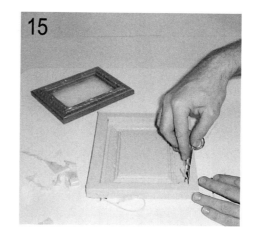

The completed non-food grade silicone mold.

Section 3
Creating Inserts for the Frame

The non-food grade silicone mold and the **Hydrocal master mold**. Both mold processes will be illustrated in the following sequence.

The glass plate was removed from the frame.

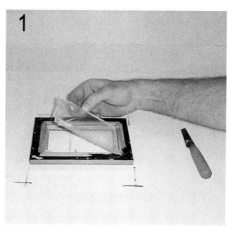

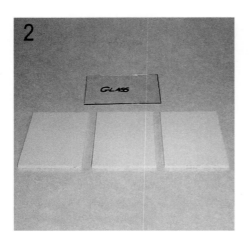

Three identical copies were cut in ¼ inch thick Plexiglas.

NOTE: The Plexiglas inserts have been painted for photographic clarity.

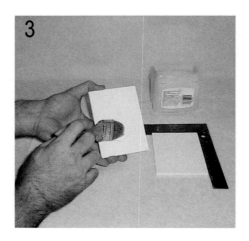

Vaseline is dabbed onto the back side of each Plexiglas insert.

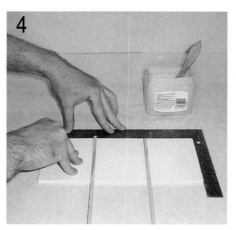

All three inserts are pressed onto the work board. Notice that ¼ inch strips of wood are used as spacers between each insert. A metal square is used to hold the inserts in shape while they are pushed towards the upper right angle of the square. This is an easy way to make the arrangement clean and consistent.

Denatured alcohol is used to clean the inserts.

A small ¼ inch strip of wood molding is used to draw a guideline around the inserts.

NOTE: Only a ¼ inch wide guideline is needed since the Plexiglas cutouts are small and thin.

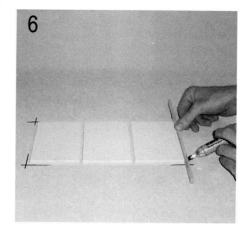

Top view of the completed layout.

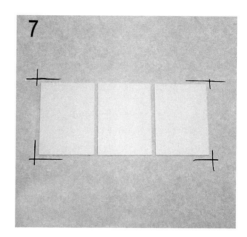

Clink boards are assembled along the guidelines.

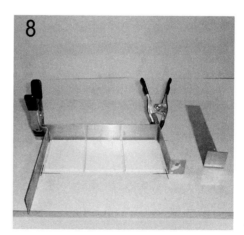

A pouring indication line is drawn in the mold box ¼ inch above the cutouts.

NOTE: Having an accurate pouring indication line is especially important when a master mold is going to be made. Each production (food grade silicone) mold will weigh exactly the same as the non-food grade mold that is now being made. Do not pour a thicker mold than is needed as it will only increase the material costs for each duplicate (food grade) production mold.

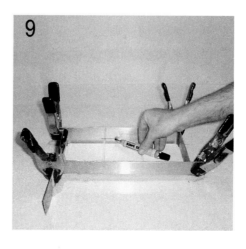

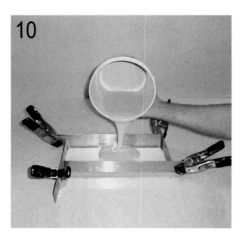

A batch of non-food grade silicone is poured into the mold box.

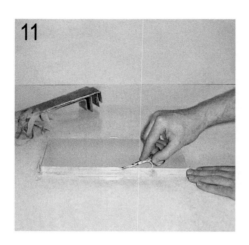

The cured mold is carefully trimmed.

NOTE: Do not trim too much off the back of the silicone as a heavy cut on the back only means that there will be more to carve away in the master mold. (See page 24, photograph 29.)

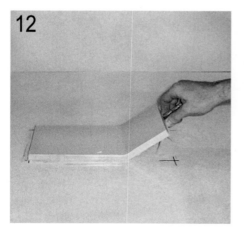

The mold is gently lifted off the work board.

NOTE: Be careful when lifting any new mold off the work board. It is common for silicone to flash beneath the model and adhere to the work board. Flash that is stuck to the work board will stretch and tear as the mold is lifted. It is not a big deal if only the flash tears, but it is a problem if the tear extends into your mold.

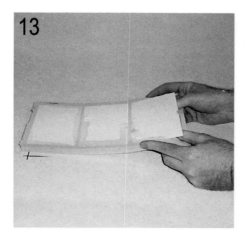

The Plexiglas inserts are removed from the mold. Remember to trim away any extra flash from the mold.

Vaseline is dabbed onto the BACK of the silicone mold. There must be enough Vaseline to glue the mold onto the work board. If the silicone mold is not securely bonded to the work board, it can float when Hydrocal is poured over it. (See page 22, photograph 21.)

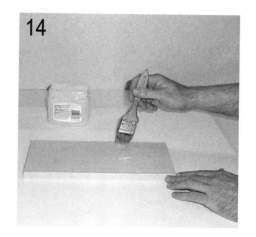

Press the silicone mold firmly onto the work board. Notice the use of a paper towel under the fingers so as not to leave any oily fingerprints on the surface of the mold.

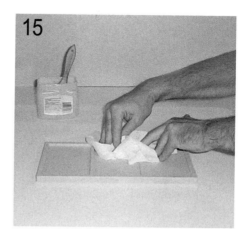

Making The Hydrocal Master Mold

A larger 1 inch guideline is drawn around the silicone mold, while a wider guideline is drawn on the left side of the mold.

NOTE: The extra width on the left side of the mold will be useful because it is the side that the production molds will be pried out to the master mold (See page 24, photograph 27).

Please see page 27 for a detailed explanation of why a master mold is beneficial.

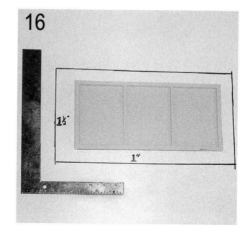

Clink boards are placed on the guidelines.

HELPFUL HINT: Notice that the clink board on top is exactly the same length as the top guideline. Usually, this would mean that the clink board is too short to clamp. In order to extract the extra length needed, flip the clink board over so that the angle is facing inwards.

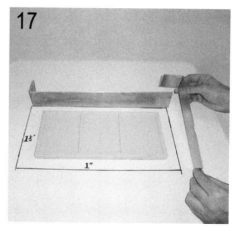

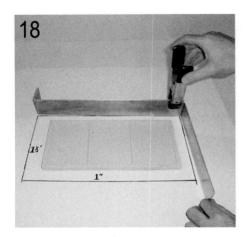

Clamp the clink boards together then repeat the arrangement on the opposite side of the mold box.

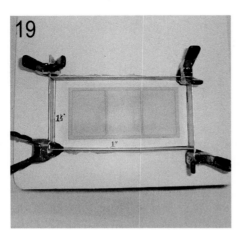

The entire mold box is clamped with the alternative inward position.

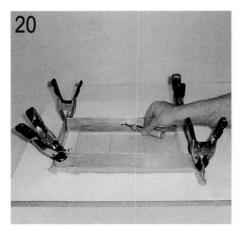

A pouring indication line is put in the mold box and is at least **ONE** inch above the silicone mold.

NOTE: Extra thickness is needed when making a Hydrocal master mold. The thickness will add weight, but it will also add strength.

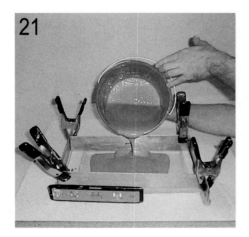

Hydrocal is poured directly into the silicone mold.

NOTE: Make sure the work board surface is level.

Use a brush to gently force the Hydrocal into every corner of the silicone mold.

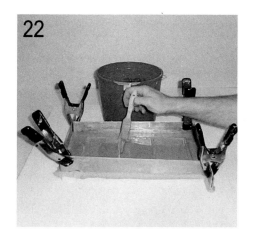

The remaining amount of Hydrocal is poured into the mold box. Make sure to fill the mold to the pouring indication line.

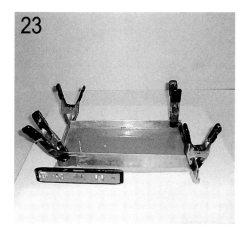

The Hydrocal is allowed to set and the edges are shaved with a **SurForm**™ (rasp).

NOTE: Hydrocal (all plaster) will get warm as it begins to set and then will cool down after setting. Wait an hour for the plaster to cool before continuing. Although Hydrocal can take over a day to completely set, it is strong enough to work within a few hours. Handle it with care.

The master mold is flipped over and the plaster flashing removed with the mud knife. It will pop right off.

Round off the edges with the SurForm™.

A small, one inch wide mud knife is used to pry the non-food grade silicone mold out of the master mold. Do not use a sharp pointed object for this task.

NOTE: Pry from the widest side of the master mold, being careful not to slide the mud knife too far under the silicone. There is only a ¼ inch before you hit the master.

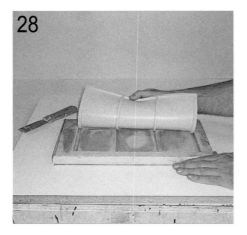

The silicone mold is removed from the master mold.

The interior (perimeter) edges of the master mold are shaved flush with a fettling knife.

NOTE: Trim this as soon as possible as the longer the Hydrocal sets, the stronger it gets.

The non-food grade silicone mold is weighed. Write the amount on the side of the master mold. This will tell you exactly how much food grade silicone is needed to fill the master mold in the future.

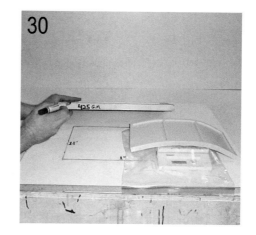

The master mold is sandwiched between two laminated work boards.

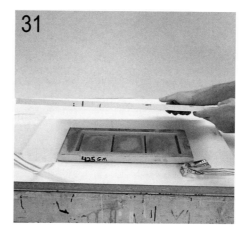

The boards are strapped together.

NOTE: This is a useful, but not critical step as flat plaster molds can warp while drying (2–7 days). The banded pressure will ensure that the master mold dries flat.

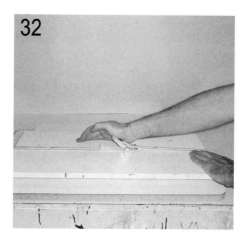

The finished master mold and non-food grade silicone mold used to create it.

NOTE: To use the master mold, fill it with food grade silicone.

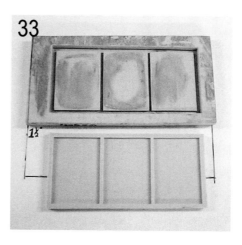

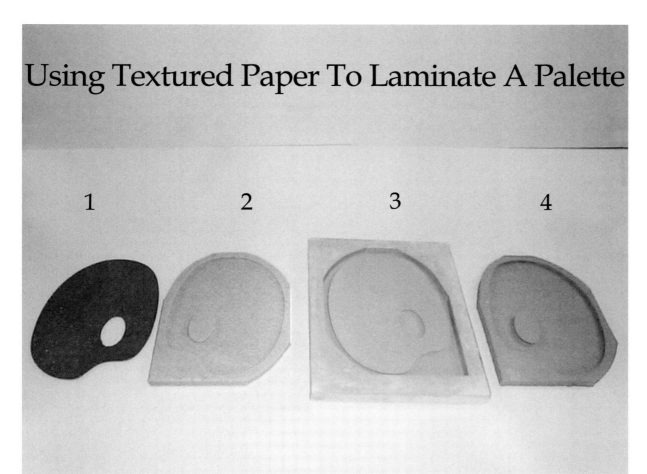

This chapter illustrates how textured wallpaper can be used to laminate a flat surface. Texturing a surface is an easy way to transform a simple shape into an ornamental form.

The photograph above illustrates the four steps it takes to make a food grade production mold.

1. Laminating the model. The process begins with gluing wallpaper onto the Plexiglas palette.
2. Making a non-food grade mold of the Plexiglas model.
3. Making a Hydrocal master mold of the non-food grade silicone mold.
4. Making a food grade **production mold**. This is done by pouring food grade silicone into the master mold.

Section 2 will show one method for making a master mold (introduced in the last chapter). If you will recall a master mold is a rigid mold that makes a duplicate silicone mold. Master molds are commonly made of Hydrocal (a strong plaster) and will enable you to make duplicate silicone molds 75% faster. Master molds take more time to make but will pay for themselves very quickly. If you need to produce at a production level, a master mold is the way to go. Remember, silicone molds do not last forever and they can be lost or damaged over time. Having a master mold is a good way to archive your models and to protect your investment.

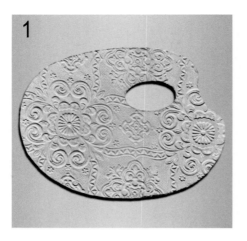

The textured wallpaper used in this chapter does not print well in a black and white photograph. Therefore, this preview of the finished model has been enhanced to show the wallpaper detail more clearly.

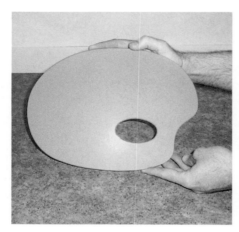

View of the Plexiglas palette. (Purchased at an art supply store).

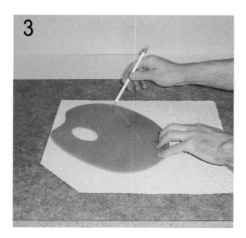

The palette shape is traced onto the wallpaper.

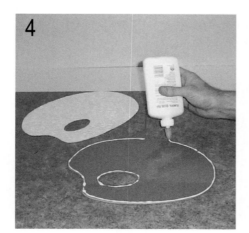

Craft glue is applied to the perimeter of the palette. It is important to create a tight seal between the paper and the Plexiglas along the entire perimeter of the palette.

NOTE: It is important not to put too much glue on the palette as excess glue will saturate the paper and make it wrinkle.

A small brush is used to smooth the glue along the perimeter.

NOTE: Without a good seal along the perimeter of the shape, silicone will flash between the paper and the palette.

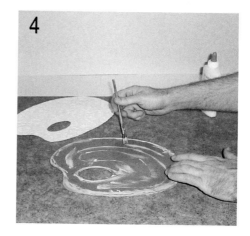

The wallpaper is gently pressed onto the face of the palette. Do not press down very hard as excessive pressure can collapse the embossed texture on the wallpaper.

Turn the palette over so that the wallpaper is face down on the work board and gently place a second work board on top of the palette.

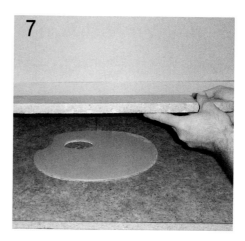

The weight of the second work board will make the wallpaper dry flat and evenly. Allow the glue to dry.

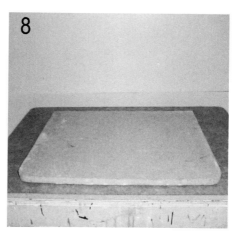

Paint the palette with several layers of gloss spray paint. The gloss surface from the spray paint will be transferred onto the silicone mold.

Remember, if the model has a glossy surface, the mold will have a glossy surface. A glossy surface in a mold will make a glossy surface in the casting.

NOTE: Do not try to get a glossy surface with just one heavy coat. This will cause the paint to pool on the model. Apply additional layers over several hours. (All spray painting should be done outside.)

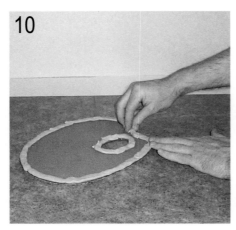

To increase the thickness of the palette, a coil of clay is placed around the perimeter. Make sure that the coil forms a tight seal against the palette. If it does not, silicone will seep under the clay during the mold making process.

NOTE: Use very soft clay for this step. To make the clay soft, warm it in a microwave oven for one minute before applying it to the palette.

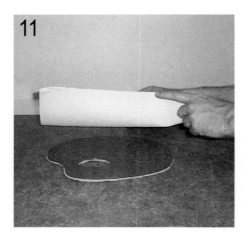

Set the palette, clay side down, onto the work board. A paper towel is put on top of the wallpaper so that the paint will not be scratched during the next step.

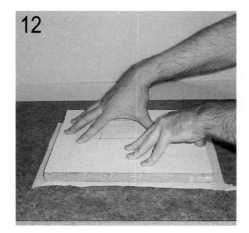

Place a piece of laminated wood on top of the paper towel. The wood will create an even pressure on the palette when pushing down.

NOTE: Pressing down on the palette squishes the clay tightly onto the work board. The intention is **NOT** to flatten the clay, but to create a tight seal.

The perimeter of the palette is filled out with additional coils of clay. Remember, working with oil clay is easier when it is warm rather than cold.

NOTE: The purpose of this is to create a solid edge around the palette. The edge will be trimmed down in the next step.

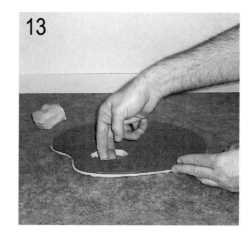

A sculpture tool with an angled tip is used to shave away excess clay. Do not try to shave off all of the clay in one pass. Use several passes, shaving a little bit at a time and patch any holes in the coil with more clay.

Notice that a paper towel is used to hold the palette steady. Working clean like this will prevent oily fingerprints from getting on the model.

NOTE: Beveling (shaving at an angle) the clay slightly beneath the palette creates a more pleasing and delicate look. Leaving the edge flat would make the edge look thick and heavy.

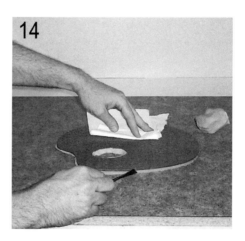

A mold box is assembled around the palette with a ½ inch space between the edge of the palette and the mold box. A batch of non-food grade silicone is poured over the model.

NOT SHOWN: A pouring indication line was drawn in the box ¼ inch above the palette.

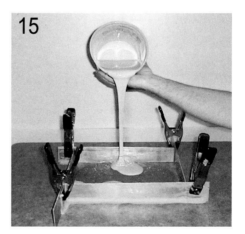

The cured silicone mold is cleaned up.

The mold is gently lifted off the work board with a mud knife.

NOTE: Pry from all four sides before lifting. Be careful not to tear the mold.

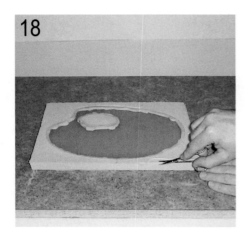

The mold is turned over and the flash is trimmed away from the edges.

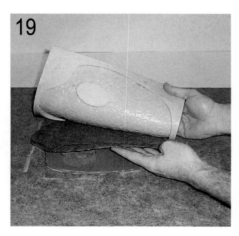

The mold is flexed to release the palette. It is common for spray painted surfaces to stick slightly to the silicone.

NOTE: Using parting soap on the painted models prior to pouring silicone will reduce sticking. However, the soap can dull the glossy finish of the paint.

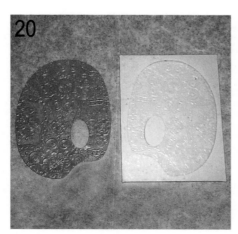

View of the finished non-food grade mold and palette.

HELPFUL HINT: Paint residue can be cleaned out of the mold by casting fast-setting urethane plastic into the mold. When the plastic cures, it will bond to the paint residue but not to the mold. (See page 190, photograph 11 for more details.)

NOTE: It is nearly impossible to clean paint out of the mold by scratching at it with a tool. This can damage the mold and affect the glossy surface.

Section 2
Making a Master Mold

This is a photograph of the master mold that will be made in the following sequence.

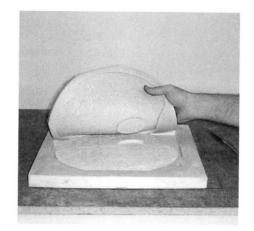

A line is drawn ½ inch outside of the palette's perimeter.

NOTE: The lower right hand corner is left intact. This is where the mold will be pried out of the master. (See page 35, photograph 11.)

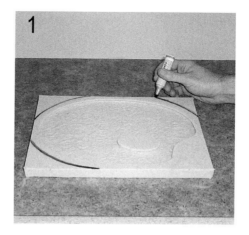

The excess corners are trimmed off of the mold. Trimming the mold at this point will reduce the amount of food grade silicone that it takes to fill the master mold.

NOTE: It was easy to build a square mold box around the round palette. However, a square mold box requires extra silicone to fill it. If only making one mold, that is acceptable. If making many production molds, a square shape wastes material.

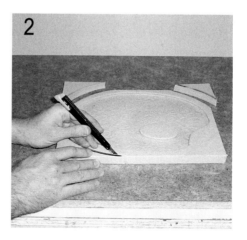

Even though the glue bond was good between the wall paper and the palette, some silicone still flashed. Flex the mold to expose the flash and cut it cleanly off with a razor knife.

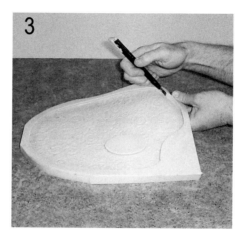

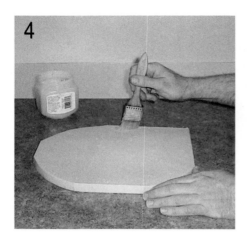

Stipple the back of the mold with Vaseline, making sure to use enough so that it will stick securely onto the work board.

NOTE: Stippling (up and down) will create a heavy textured surface that when compressed creates suction between the silicone surface and the work board. Merely brushing Vaseline onto the back of the silicone mold will not create enough suction to hold the mold securely in place.

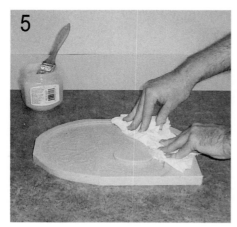

The mold is pressed (detail surface up) onto the work board. Use a paper towel when pressing down so that no fingerprints will be left in the mold.

NOTE: If the mold is not securely stuck onto the work board, it will float up when Hydrocal is poured over it.

A guideline is drawn around the silicone mold. Notice that the guideline on the right side of the palette is wider than the other sides. Extra plaster is needed on this side since it will be the area from which the food grade silicone molds will be pried. (See page 35, photograph 11.)

NOTE: The large open spaces at each corner are of no concern. These areas will be filled with (inexpensive) Hydrocal, not silicone.

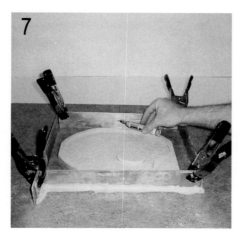

A mold box is assembled along the guideline, next a pouring indication line is drawn one inch above the silicone mold.

Overview of mold box.

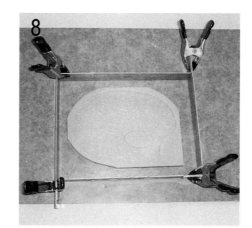

A batch of Hydrocal is transferred into a small cup for easy handling. Use a brush to ensure that plaster is forced into every detail of the mold. Be very thorough so that there is no chance for air bubbles to remain trapped on the surface of the silicone mold.

Use a carpenter's level to make sure the work board is perfectly level. If the master mold is not level, the production molds will not be level.

NOTE: An unlevel mold is equivalent to having a soup bowl on a slanted table. You will never be able to fill the bowl, because soup will spill over the low side first.

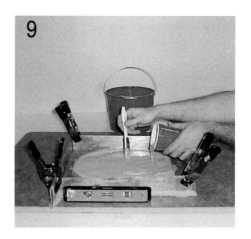

The plaster is allowed to set for two hours. The edges are then rounded with a SurForm™ rasp.

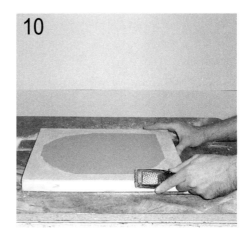

The master mold is flipped over and the silicone mold is carefully removed. Be careful not to push the mud knife too far under the silicone mold as pushing too far can damage the detail surface of the master mold.

Notice that the silicone mold is being pried out at the widest side of the master mold. This side has the most strength and will be least likely to crack under pressure from the mud knife.

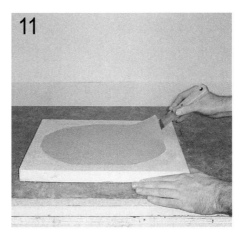

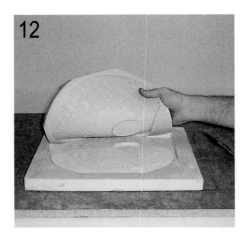

The silicone mold is gently lifted out of the master mold.

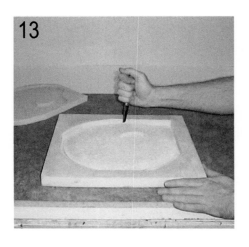

The sharp edges along the interior of the master mold are shaved with a fettling knife. Do this immediately as the longer the Hydrocal sets, the more stone-like it becomes.

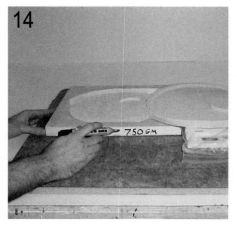

The exact weight of the non-food grade mold is written on the side of the master mold. This will remind you how much silicone it takes to fill the mold the next time you pour.

HELPFUL HINT: Keep the digital scale clean by placing it in a Ziplock® bag.

Within hours of making the master mold, a work board is placed on top of it. Plaster molds that are flat and thin have a tendency to warp while they are drying.

The work board is strapped down on top of the master mold. Keep the master mold strapped down for a couple of days. When the Hydrocal mold is dry, it will no longer feel cold to the touch.

NOTE: The master mold could be used right away before it is dry and without strapping it down. However, if the Hydrocal mold were bigger than the one shown, the chances of it warping (without strapping) would increase.

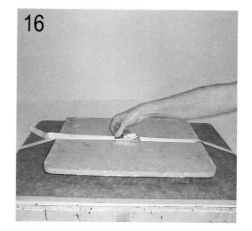

In order to make food grade production molds, a 750 g batch of **FOOD GRADE** silicone is poured into the master mold. Make sure that the master mold is level with the worktable.

NOTE: Much less silicone will be used to make this mold because the square corners where removed from the first silicone mold.

WARNING: Never pour non-food grade silicone into your master mold as it will contaminate the master mold and create a chemical reaction that makes it impossible for food grade silicone to cure. Remember, food grade and non-food grade silicones are incompatible and must be used in separate environments. (Review Chapter 2 introduction.)

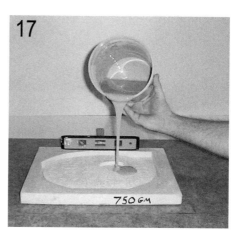

A sheet of wax paper is gently placed over the newly poured silicone. Do not push the wax paper down into the silicone.

NOTE: Some silicones such as Silastic L have a tendency to remain partially uncured on the surface. This is known as **air inhibition**. It just means that the back of the silicone mold will remain **tacky** while the rest of the mold has cured. The wax paper trick solves the problem.

Another method for dealing with air inhibition is to fill the master mold and leave the surface open to the air. Let the silicone cure overnight and then remove the silicone mold. The open face of the mold will be still be tacky. Place the tacky side of the mold on a flat sheet of wax paper. It will cure in a few days. Both methods work well.

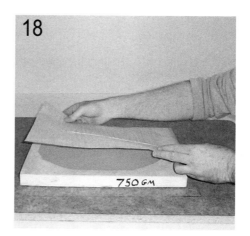

The silicone is allowed to cure overnight and the wax paper is removed. A mud knife is used to carefully pry the mold out of the master. Notice that it is being lifted at the only corner that was not trimmed off the original mold (See page 33, photograph 1.) The extra silicone in this corner is useful as a handle to pull the mold out of the master.

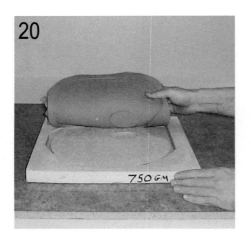

750 GM

Carefully peel the production mold out of the master mold.

IMPORTANT: Large surface areas such as the interior side walls of the master mold should be lightly coated with Vaseline each time before the master mold is filled. The Vaseline will allow the food grade silicone to peel out of the master mold with less stress.

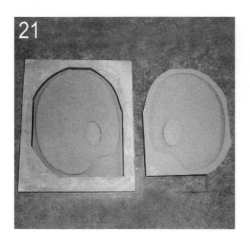

A view of the completed Hydrocal master mold and a food grade production mold. Putting the food grade mold in an oven at 38° C/100° F for a few hours will help finish the cure. Wash the production mold with mild detergent before use.

NEVER HEAT THE FOOD GRADE SILICONE ABOVE 275° C/527° F. AT 350° C/662° F THE SILICONE WILL GIVE OFF TOXIC FORMALDEHYDE.
(It is critical to read the manufactures safety data sheet to confirm temperature thresholds.)

TROUBLE SHOOTING TIP: I have found that many of first time mold makers share a similar mold making problem. The problem is this:

When filling a master mold with food grade silicone for the first time, some areas of the silicone do not cure against the surface of the Hydrocal master mold. In simple terms, the food grade mold remains gummy in some areas. This happens because the Hydrocal is absorbing oils and catalyst out of the silicone mix, causing irregular curing.

If the gumminess is slight, put the mold in an oven at a low temperature 38° C/100° F for several hours. The heat will help to cure out the gummy areas. If the gumminess does not cure, discard the mold.
NEVER USE A MOLD THAT HAS UNCURED GUMMY AREAS TO CAST FOOD PRODUCTS.

Why does this happen?
1. The Hydrocal is overly porous due to improper (water to Hydrocal) mixing ratio.
2. The liquid Hydrocal was poured too early and the plaster was not able to cure to full strength or density.

What are the solutions?
1. Before pouring food grade silicone into a master mold, brush a LIGHT coating of Vaseline to the interior surface. Melt the Vaseline into the Hydrocal with a hair dryer or heat gun. The intention is to create a slight gloss surface on the inside of your master mold. Do not apply so much Vaseline that brush marks are visible. Wipe out any excess Vaseline with a paper towel. Use only enough Vaseline to seal the porous surface of the master mold. If too much Vaseline remains on the inside of the master mold, the excess Vaseline will inhibit the cure of food grade silicone.

2. If you have already poured a food grade mold in the master mold and it is gummy, remove it and pour another one into the same master mold. (Do not clean out the master mold in between pours.) The second batch will "cure out" the gummy material on the surface of the master mold. Additional silicone pours (3rd, 4th etc.) into the master mold should work because the porosity of the Hydrocal has already been sealed with the oils from the food grade silicone (during the first pour).

Making A Production "Gang" Mold Of A Jewel

This chapter will illustrate numerous methods which can be used to make production quality candy gang molds. **Gang mold** is a term used to describe a mold that has numerous cavities which allow several castings to be made at the same time.

This chapter is divided into five sections.

> Section 1. Making a silicone mold of a small resin jewel.
> Section 2. Making ten fast-setting urethane duplicates.
> Section 3. Making a non-food grade gang mold of the resin duplicates.
> Section 4. Making an open face master mold of the gang mold.
> Section 5. Using the master mold to make food grade production molds.

This chapter will highlight how to use the silicone available from Ewald Notter's International School of Confectionery Arts. This particular silicone is very soft and is ideal for small shapes. A unique property of this silicone is that it will not bond to glass.

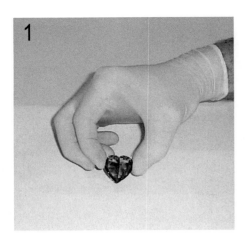

View of the glass jewel.

Notice that I am wearing rubber gloves so as not to get fingerprints on the jewel. Usually you can wipe off prints, but this jewel is too small to handle once mounted to the work board.

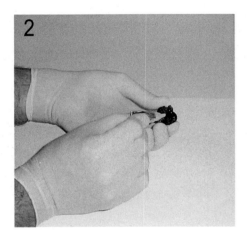

A drop of super glue is put on the flat side of the jewel.

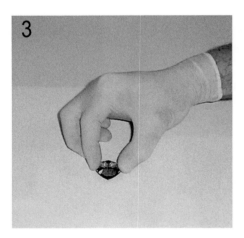

The jewel is glued to the work board.

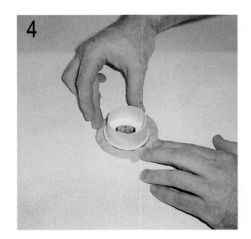

Three small paper cups are cut and stacked together to form a mold box. (Three cups are used so that the paper has more strength when clay is sealed around it.) A small coil of clay is gently placed AROUND the perimeter of the cup to hold it round.

NOTE: Do not press the clay against the cup as it will deform the cup.

A second coil of clay is placed ON TOP of the first. It is used to hold down the lip of the paper cup.

NOTE: The first coil (last image) is meant to keep the base of the cup *round* while the second coil holds the cup *down*.

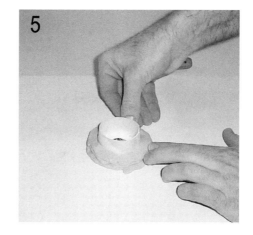

The bottom of the coil is smeared onto the work board while the top is smeared upwards against the side of the cup.

NOTE: This instruction may seem tedious, but if the cup is not sealed to the work board, it will float when filled with silicone. Cups make great mold boxes, but they also can be frustrating to first time user.

The cup is filled with non-food grade silicone and allowed to cure for 24 hours.

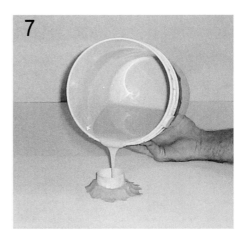

The cured mold is lifted from the work board.

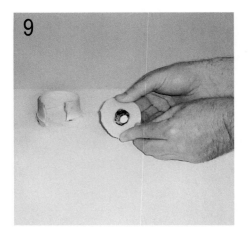

The cups are removed and the jewel is flexed out of the mold. It should not be necessary to slice the mold to release the jewel.

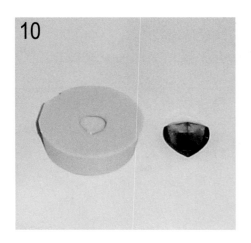

A view of the completed non-food grade silicone mold and jewel.

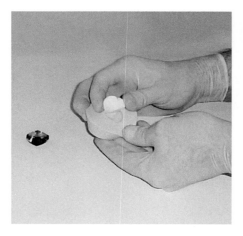

Section 2
Casting Resin Duplicates

The following sequence will show how fast-setting urethane is used to make duplicate castings of the jewel.

WARNING:
Do not do this or any other mold making process in your kitchen. The chemicals used are not food safe.

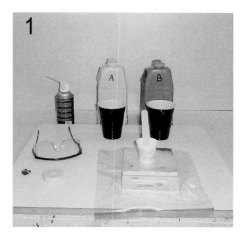

Fast-setting **urethane resin** is an extremely valuable material for model making but compared to most things that might be in your work environment, it is a hazardous material. This material is widely used in the gift ware industry and can be used safely with proper handling and care. It requires special safety instruction.

NOTE: Always wear rubber gloves, apron, safety goggles and work outside or in a ventilated area. A ventilated area means one where you smell fresh air, not the slight odor of the resin.

Pour a half cup of Part B and a half cup of Part A into individual plastic cups. Mark each cup A and B so that they do not get intermixed. Recap the large container immediately after use. (The resin is poured into the cups for easier handling. Final measuring will be done in the small paper cups.) Do not weigh resin in a Styrofoam™ cup, it will dissolve the cup quickly.

NOTE: The resin is sold in two components Part A and Part B. When mixed together in equal amounts, it cures into a hard plastic in only a few minutes.

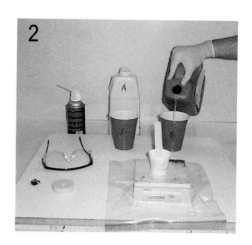

Ten grams of Part A are poured into a small cup on the scale.

Notice that the digital scale is placed in a Ziplock® bag to protect it from spills.

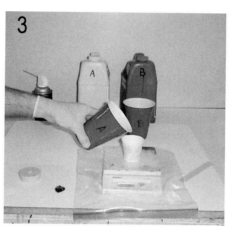

Next, ten grams of Part B are poured into the same cup. Be very careful to pour equal amounts of A and B.

NOTE: The resin will still set even if the measurements are not perfectly equal.

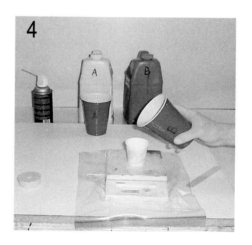

Pick up the cup and begin mixing immediately. Mix for about 30 seconds until you feel the mix beginning to get warm.

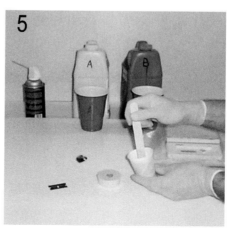

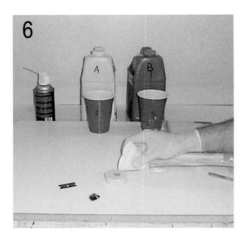

Pinch the cup lip to make a spout and pour the liquid resin into the jewel mold.

Gently squeeze the jewel mold so that resin flows into all areas.

NOTE: When casting a larger mold, use a brush to push the resin into the detail. Large amounts of resin will set much faster than small amounts.

A razor blade is used to scrape the excess resin off the mold making it level with the top of the mold.

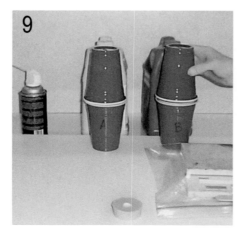

Clean, empty cups are set on top of the A and B cups in between each pour in order to reduce the amount of fumes that are escaping from the resin.

NOTE: Do not leave the uncured resin in the plastic cups for more than thirty minutes. The resin components will dissolve the bottom of thin plastic cups. Do not use Styrofoam™ cups.

The resin jewel is de-molded and the process is repeated ten times. Duplicates could have been poured in plaster, however it would have taken a lot longer and the plaster would not have captured the sheen of the polished jewel surface.

NOTE: Hydrocal is my preferred casting medium. However, small highly detailed or geometric shapes cast better in resin.

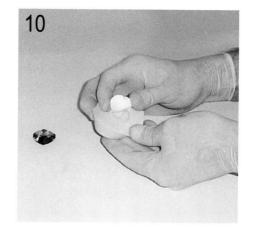

HELPFUL HINT: Have other silicone molds nearby when pouring resin. Pour the excess material into the other molds as resin will bond to itself layer upon layer.

All of these pieces were cast at the same time as the jewels.

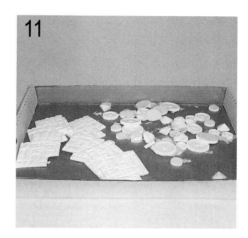

HELPFUL HINT: When cleaning the work board with a mud knife, wrap your fingers around the handle as shown in the photo. This is the safest way. Do not extend your finger tips towards the work board, as the thin pieces of resin can suddenly pop off the work surface and be pushed under your finger nail.

When you are finished casting, pour the remaining resin back into the proper storage container. Make sure to pour the B cup into the B container and the A into the A container. An accidental cross mixing will spoil the entire lot.

NOTE: Remember, do not leave the unmixed resin in the plastic cups. The cups will dissolve and the resin will spill everywhere.

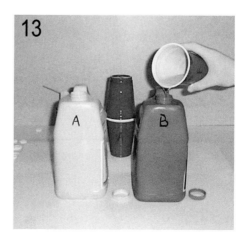

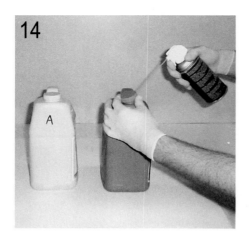

To make the urethane resin last a long time, spray **Xtend-It™ (nitrogen air blanket)** into the containers. Holding the lid of the jug slightly open, spray into the container for a few seconds and then close the lid. Xtend-It™ is a nitrogen air blanket. Because nitrogen is heavier than air, a microscopic layer of it will settle directly on top of the liquid resin. This film will prevent any moisture from the air in the container from contaminating the uncured resin. Without a nitrogen air blanket, resin will only last a few months. Urethanes are moisture sensitive and will harden if exposed to humidity.

HELPFUL HINT: Before spraying, wipe the containers mouth clean with a paper towel. Otherwise residue around the mouth will dry like glue. Re-opening will be difficult.

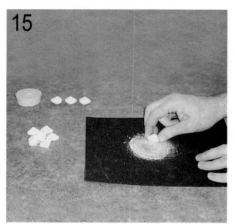

The flat side of each resin casting is sanded smooth. A circular motion on fine grade sandpaper works well. For best results, sand on a flat, laminated work board.

NOTE: Do this outside and wear a dust mask.

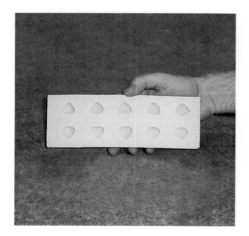

Section 3
Making a Gang Mold

This is a picture of the gang mold that is going to be made in the following sequence.

A **gang mold** is a mold that allows you to pour several castings at the same time. An ice cube tray is a gang mold, allowing you to make many cubes at once.

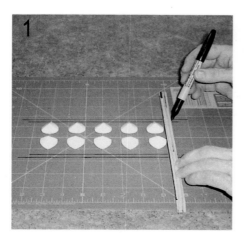

Lay the resin castings on a cutting mat (Available from a hobby store).

The castings are then glued (with a fast-setting glue) ½ inch apart from one another, using the mat's grid lines as a template. Next, a ¾ inch boarder is drawn around the jewels.

Remember to lightly coat the clink boards with Vaseline.

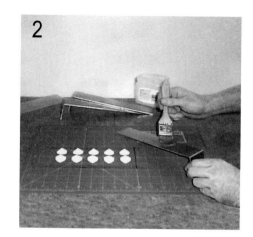

Section 3

Making a
Gang Mold
of the Resin
Models of
the Jewel

Remember to seal the clink boards at the corners first so that the mold box does not slide out of position.

NOTE: A Plexiglas clink board is used for photographic clarity.

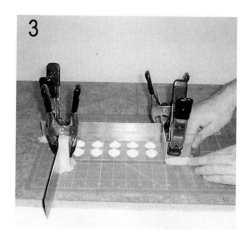

Remember to seal the vertical corners with clay.

Seal all of the bottom edges.

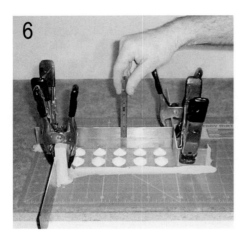

A miniature ruler is used to visually approximate the silicone pouring level.

NOTE: These rulers are available at hardware stores.

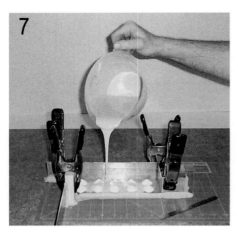

Non-food grade silicone is needled into the mold box.

IMPORTANT NOTE: Once non-food grade silicone has been poured onto this mat, it can never be used for pouring food grade silicone onto because the mat is slightly porous and cannot be thoroughly cleaned. Food grade silicone will not cure on the tin contaminated surface. Reserve a separate mat for pouring food grade silicone.

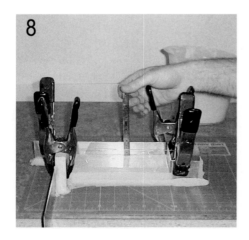

The miniature ruler is dipped into the bottom of the mold to check for depth.

NOTE: Leave the ruler in the mold long enough for silicone to flow around it. This will give you a more accurate reading.

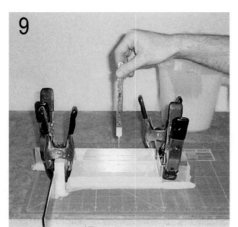

The ruler is lifted out to read depth of silicone. If it is lower than your original intention, add more. If it is too full, use a small paper cup or spoon to ladle silicone out. Be careful not to disturb the resin models.

The silicone is allowed to cure. Remember to make sure the work board is level in all directions.

NOTE: Notice the mud knife (on left) being used as a shim to level the work board.

Section 3

Making a
Gang Mold
of the Resin
Models of
the Jewel

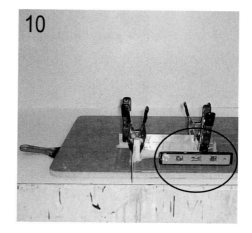

After the silicone has cured for 24 hours, the clay seal can be easily removed with a mud knife.

NOTE: Keep the clay free of debris so that it can be reused.

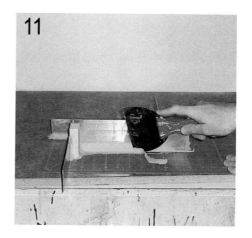

Carefully trim the flash from the bottom of the silicone mold.

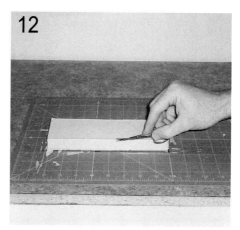

Lift the mold from the cutting mat. The resin models will come up with it.

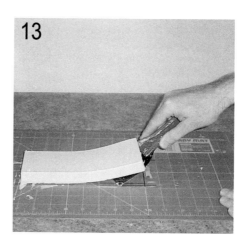

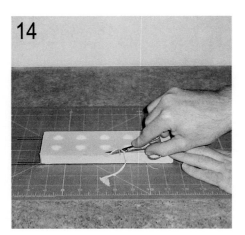

Trim the flash from the top of the mold.

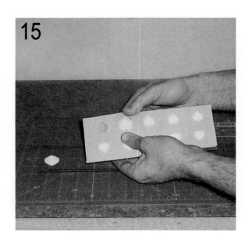

Flex the mold to remove the resin jewels.

NOTE: Save the resin castings in case part of the process needs to be repeated at a later date.

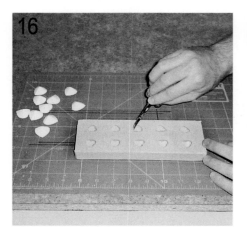

The flash around each "mouth" or opening of the mold is carefully trimmed. It is critical to do this well as the flash looks a lot like the mold. Think before you cut.

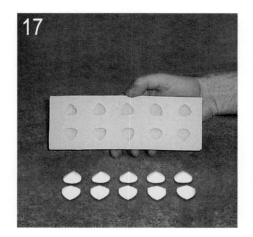

The finished mold with resin castings.

Section 4
Making an Open Face Master Mold

This is a picture of the open faced master mold that will be illustrated in the following sequence.

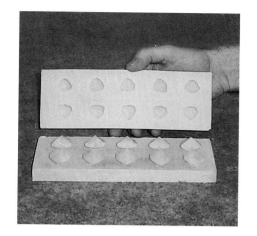

The silicone gang mold is placed **FACE UP** on the work board. A mold box is assembled tightly around the gang mold and is sealed with oil clay.

Be careful not to put too much pressure on the sides of the mold box as the gang mold is flexible and can be easily distorted.

NOTE: Do not expect the clink boards to form a perfect seal around the silicone gang mold. The mold will flash, but it can be cleaned up later.

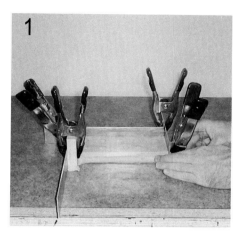

Hydrocal is poured into the silicone gang mold, making sure to fill the mold box at least 1 inch above the silicone mold.

NOTE: Fast-setting resin could be used in place of Hydrocal.

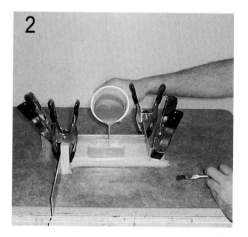

Use a small brush to push the plaster into each mold cavity.

NOTE: Remember, a master mold must have perfect detail, or it is worthless.

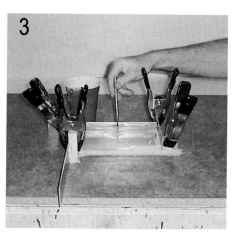

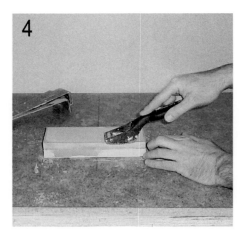

The Hydrocal is allowed to set and the mold box is removed. Shave the sharp edges with a SurForm™.

Remove the flash from the sides of the mold.

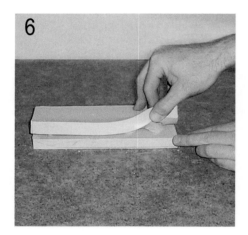

The silicone mold is gently pulled off the master mold.

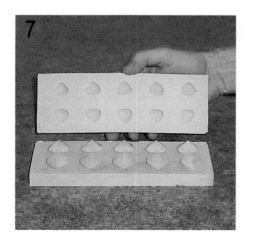

The view of the open face master mold and the gang mold.

The sharp edges on the master mold are shaved away with a trimming **tool**.

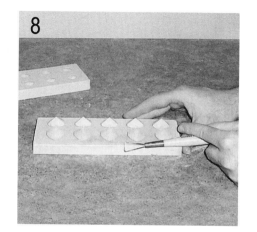

Section 5
Using the Jewel to Make a Food Grade Production Mold

This is a picture of the production mold that will be illustrated in the following sequence.

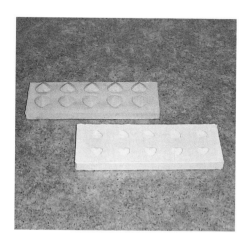

A light coat of Vaseline is put on the *flat* surface of the master mold. DO NOT brush Vaseline onto the jewels.

NOTE: This special preparation is required on this particular master mold because of the jewels unique shape. Each jewel has a slight angle, called an undercut, that "cuts" beneath it.

Vaseline will help the silicone release from the master mold. In addition to the Vaseline, an extremely soft food grade silicone will be poured. The soft silicone will easily peel from under the base of the jewel.

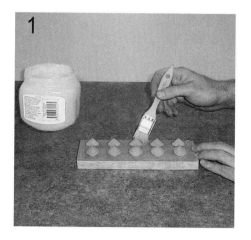

Use a paper towel to wipe off the excess Vaseline from the master mold.

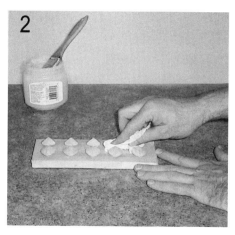

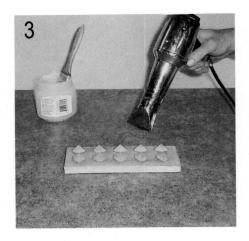

Use a heat gun to melt the Vaseline into the Hydrocal as this smooths the Vaseline into a glaze. Wipe away any pooling beneath the jewels.

NOTE: Silicone will not bond to Hydrocal, but it will grip it slightly. The Vaseline reduces the grip and allows the silicone to be removed without much force.

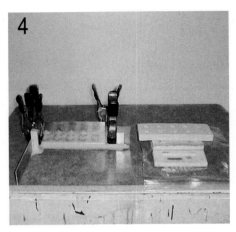

Weigh the original gang mold so that the second mold can be poured without waste.

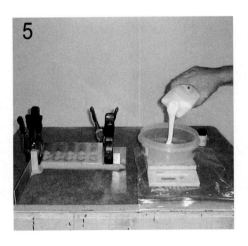

The appropriate amount of food grade silicone base (400 g) is weighed out.

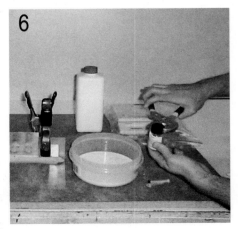

Pliers may need to be used to open the jar of catalyst.

NOTE: Catalyst will dry into a tough glue if left on the rim of the jar. Avoid this by wiping the lid clean after each use.

Chef Keegan Gerhard Casts Chocolate And Sugar Amenities

This chapter shows how Chef Gerhard of the Four Seasons Hotel Chicago uses molds to create exquisite display amenities. Several casting methods are shown in order to highlight the use of the molds made in preceding chapters. Chef Gerhard explains, "A tremendous benefit of working with molds is that several different amenities can be designed by using the same molds in various ways to create completely new displays."

Chef Gerhard demonstrates a few of the methods he is currently using in the hotel. Molds allow him to create impressive amenities efficiently and with consistently high quality.

Section 1
Casting the Cloisonné Bell

Chef Gerhard begins the amenity castings by preparing melted **Isomalt** sugar.

Chef Gerhard has pours a pan of melted Isomalt into the bell mold.

Isomalt Formula:
1000 g Isomalt
  100 g Water (heat both to 165° C/329° F)
Add colorant if desired (mix into batch)

Let the Isomalt cool to 125°C/257° F before pouring into the mold. If the Isomalt is poured too hot, it will continue to cook and bubble in the mold. The lower the pouring temperature, the clearer the casting.

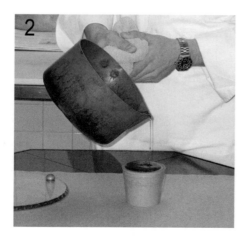

Fill the mold to the top in a single consistent pour. This is very important to do. If the mold is only partially filled or swirled by hand to cover the rest of the mold detail, the wall thickness will not be consistent. It is also possible that a visible line will remain in the finished casting at the exact point where the pouring of the sugar was stopped.

Allow the Isomalt sugar to sit undisturbed in the mold for 15 minutes.

NOTE: Be careful not to drip any sugar on the edges of the mold. It will make for extra clean up later.

Invert the mold and drain it back into the pot. A thin, even coating will remain inside the mold.

Chef Gerhard uses scissors to trim off the excess sugar. This must be done immediately after the mold is drained while the sugar is still soft and pliable. He then uses his fingers to fold any excess sugar flaps back into the casting.

NOTE: If part of a casting slumps away from the mold wall, it should be gently pressed back against the mold wall before it cools.

Let the casting cool in the mold for at least an hour. (A cast of a larger object will require longer to cool.) Chef Gerhard carefully loosens the edges of the mold by gently prying it away from the sugar bell.

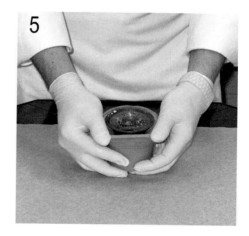

The bell is carefully removed from the mold.

NOTE: Make sure to wear gloves when handling the sugar casting so that fingerprints will not be transferred onto the casting.

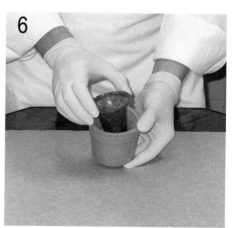

Chef Gerhard uses a small brush to apply a light dusting of non-toxic metallic dust to the surface of the sugar bell. The application is delicate and is intended only to highlight the surface detail of the casting. Applying too much metallic powder will conceal rather than emphasize the bell's detail.

A second method for applying metallic powder is to use a small foam sponge to gently wipe the powder onto the surface of the bell.

A finished view of the two bells. One is cast in sugar, the other in chocolate.

Section 2
Casting the Wooden Frame and Easel

The following casting sequence illustrates how Chef Gerhard casts perfectly seamless, multi-colored chocolate picture frames.

Chef Gerhard casts the insert mold by piping white **coating chocolate** into the mold. He is careful not miss any corners, which would result in air pockets.

NOTE: The insert mold can be seen on page 17, Section 3.

Chef Gerhard uses a piping bag to fill the insert mold. After the mold has been filled, he levels the it by pulling a large palette knife across the top of the mold.

NOT SHOWN: The mold was placed on a small work board so that he could tap the back of the mold on the work board. Tapping the mold allows air bubbles to rise to the top of the mold.

NOTE: The chocolate is allowed to cool in the mold for 30 minutes before de-molding.

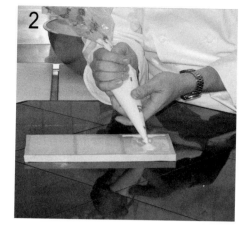

After the white chocolate inserts have cooled, they are removed. Chef Gerhard has placed a silk-screen frame over one of the chocolate inserts. A small amount of dark cocoa paste is pooled above the screen image.

NOTE: Cocoa paste is an ideal material to silk-screen with because it makes a clean, sharp print.

Chef Gerhard carefully pulls the squeegee over the back of the silk-screen. The squeegee forces the cocoa paste through the screen where it has not been blocked by the pattern applied to the screen.

NOTE: The squeegee should be pulled firmly, in a single, even pass across the screen. It is not as easy to do as it looks.

A second method for putting an image on the insert is to set a **transfer sheet** into the silicone mold prior to filling it with white chocolate. When the chocolate insert is de-molded, the transfer sheet is peeled off the casting leaving the image on the chocolate.

Next, Chef Gerhard fills the easel mold (seen front left) with dark coating chocolate. Using the same bag, he then pipes chocolate into the frame mold.

NOTE: The frame mold should only be partially filled with chocolate. Use only enough chocolate to fill the "outer ring" of the frame. The level of chocolate is not allowed to flow over the center of the frame.

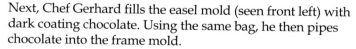

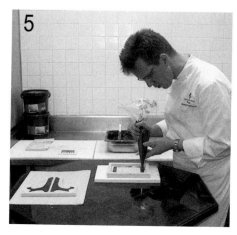

Chef Gerhard taps the mold (on a work board) against the edge of the table. The vibration will level the chocolate and shake out any air bubbles.

NOTE: The same process was repeated for the easel.

Chef Gerhard adds a little more chocolate so that it is perfectly level with the top edge of the center section.

NOTE: The center of the frame mold must remain clean and free of any chocolate, so the mold is not overfilled.

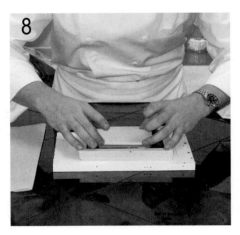

The silk-screened insert is set (image side down) onto the flat center section of the frame mold. It is important to place the insert squarely in the mold. If the insert is positioned at an angle, the finished product will not look right.

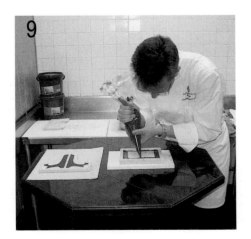

With the insert properly positioned in the mold, Chef Gerhard completely fills the rest of the mold by piping chocolate around and over the insert.

NOTE: The intention is to completely encapsulate the white chocolate insert. If the insert is not completely covered, viewers will be able to detect that the frame was made in two sections.

Any low spots are filled with a final application of chocolate.

After the chocolate has cooled for 30 minutes, the frame is de-molded. The result is a white chocolate insert with a seamless fit into a dark chocolate picture frame.

NOTE: The easel sections are de-molded at the same time.

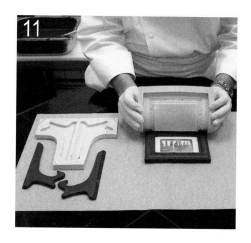

To assemble the easel, Chef Gerhard uses a paper cone filled with liquid coating chocolate to pipe a small bead of chocolate along the edge of the easel.

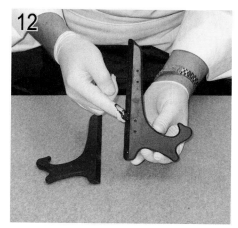

The two halves of the easel are quickly attached by holding them together tightly for about a minute.

NOTE: It is important to measure the width of the easel prior to assembly. If the easel is too narrow, the picture frame will not rest in it properly.

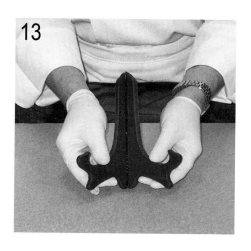

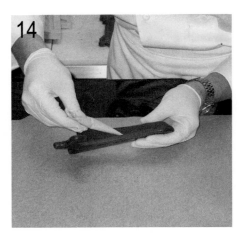

A second bead of chocolate is piped along the inside edge of the easel for added strength.

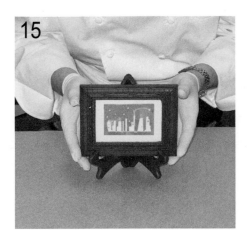

The silk-screened chocolate frame is test fitted on the easel.

The easel can support a frame vertically or horizontally.

As a finishing touch, Chef Gerhard applies a light dusting of non-toxic metallic powder to the surface of the frame. The presentation is quick and clean.

The second frame is dusted and ready for final presentation.

Casting With Sugar

The same molds can be used to cast the frame in hot sugar. A beautiful effect can be achieved by casting two colors of sugar into the molds. In this picture, Chef Gerhard is using a torch to melt down an edge on a cast sugar frame.

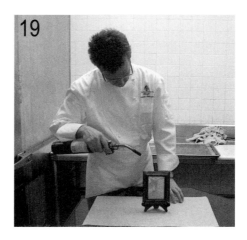

The finished multicolored sugar frame.

Chef Gerhard uses the chocolate frames to add a personal touch to the many unique amenities he creates for guests at the Four Seasons Hotel Chicago. He personalizes each frame with an appropriate message for individuals, weddings, anniversaries or other special events.

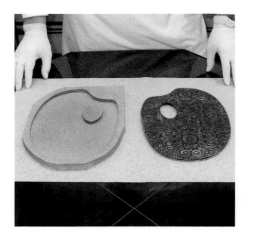

Section 3
Casting the Palette

In this section Chef Gerhard shows how he uses the silicone mold of a textured palette to create a variety of amenities.

Chef Gerhard is filling the mold with colored Isomalt sugar.

NOTE: The sugar is melted and allowed to cool to 125° C/257° F before pouring.

Care is taken not to pour sugar over the raised plug in the center of the mold.

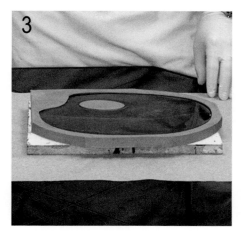

The casting is allowed to cool at room temperature. Do not place the sugar casting in the refrigerator because it will cause condensation to form on the casting and make the sugar sticky.

NOTE: When pouring this mold in chocolate, the casting can be cooled in a refrigerator set at 16°–18° C/60°–65° F, but only cool the casting for a short time.

The third palette is glued into position. It took careful planning to make sure that the palettes would be stable and provide good support. Chef Gerhard makes this look easy.

The finished view of another successful amenity.

Chef Gerhard has demonstrated that with some creativity, a chef can create several amenities that are completely different, even though they are based upon the use of the same mold.

Section 4
Casting the Jewels

The Four Seasons Hotel Chicago created a custom room amenity that coincided with a local museum's historic RMS (Royal Mail Steamer) Titanic exhibit. Chef Gerhard chose to create heart shaped candies to accent the amenity display.

Using the production gang mold, several sugar jewels were cast at one time. The sugar was pigmented blue and marbled with white pigment.

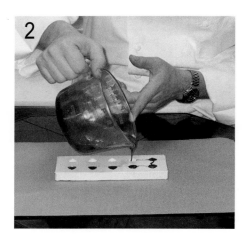

Each heart candy is carefully poured.

The sugar is allowed to cool for about 30 minutes before the candies are de-molded.

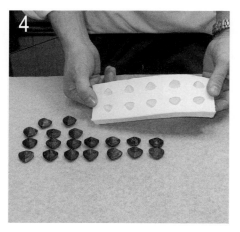

The gang mold design allows Chef Gerhard to cast 10 jewels at a time.

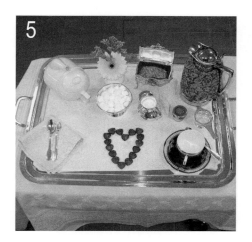

The heart shaped sugar candies added a nice touch to the tea amenity.

The candies have been positioned in a heart pattern to look like the famous necklace seen in the movie *Titanic*. The tea set included faithful ceramic reproductions of an actual tea cup and saucer that were used in service on the ship.

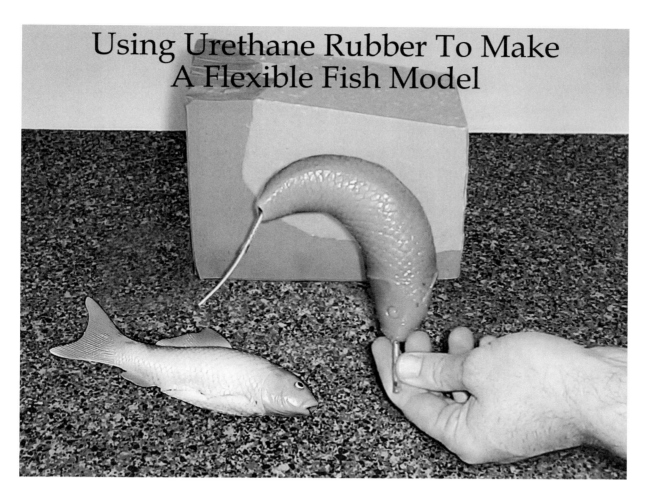

Using Urethane Rubber To Make A Flexible Fish Model

This chapter illustrates an uncommon but very useful process. Making a flexible model allows the user to transform the original object into a pliable model. For example, the plastic fish shown above had good detail but the posture was static and uninteresting. Casting the fish in urethane rubber with an aluminum wire imbedded in it will allow the posture of the fish to be reshaped in anyway the chef chooses. The benefit of this process is that the model (fish) can be reshaped without loosing any of its original detail.

Given enough thought, this process can be used to give any shape a new and dynamic gesture. Imagine all of the simple models that can be recast and altered to look completely different.

The fish will be the first of three molded components to be used by Chef Jacquy Pfeiffer and Chef John Kraus to create a sugar show piece.

The chapter is divided into three sections.

> Section 1: Making a silicone mold of the plastic fish.
> Section 2: Casting urethane rubber into the silicone mold.
> Section 3: Making a two-piece, silicone mold of the altered (bent) urethane fish.

View of the unaltered plastic fish.

NOT SHOWN: The hollow fish was filled with plaster.

NOTE: The model must be filled with plaster so that it does not float in the mold when silicone is poured over it.

The tail and fins are cut off of the toy and will not be molded.

The fins will be hand created (in sugar) by Chef Pfeiffer. The process will be shown in detail at the end of Chapter 9.

A small hole is drilled through the work board.

A drywall screw is pushed through the work board and a piece of tape is placed over the end of the screw. The tape will create a seal around the screw.

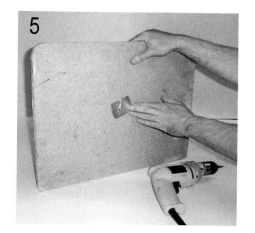

The plastic fish is twisted down onto the screw, until the fish is suspended 1 inch above the work board.

NOTE: Twisting a model onto a screw will hold better than pushing it onto a nail. If your model is filled with plaster, pre-drill a hole so that it twists into the model easily.

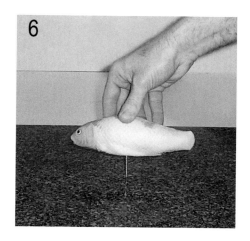

An $\frac{1}{8}$ inch hole is drilled into the mouth of the fish.

The drill bit is removed from the drill and repositioned in the hole. The bit is allowed to extend $1\frac{1}{2}$ inch beyond the mouth of the fish.

NOTE: When the mold is finished, the bit will create a hole in the silicone mold. The hole will provide a fitted channel that the aluminum wire can fit into. (See page 80, Section 2.)

A **reference line** is drawn beneath the belly of the fish directly on the work board. The line will transfer onto the finished silicone mold, indicating where to cut the mold open.

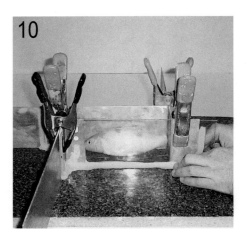

A mold box is assembled around the fish.

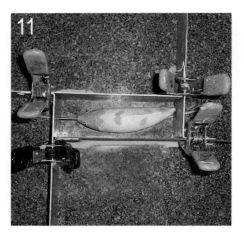

The top view of mold box.

NOTE: The tail of the fish is touching the clink board on the right. This is where urethane will be poured into the finished mold. Notice the extra space in front of the fish head for the length of the drill bit.

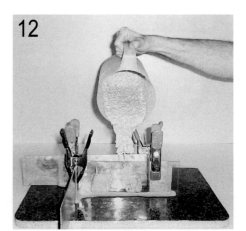

Non-food grade silicone is poured into the mold box.

HELPFUL HINT: Notice the lumpy texture of the silicone, it is due to the **regrind** in the mix. Regrind is recycled silicone that has been reclaimed by grinding up old silicone molds. Up to thirty percentage of regrind can be added as filler to a regular batch of silicone. It is a great money saving method.

Whenever making a **single use** (a mold you only use once, usually for model making) or a mold that is extra thick, a large percentage of regrind can dramatically cut the material cost.

The silicone is allowed to cure for 24 hours, after which the flash is trimmed off the mold.

Twist the mold off the work board.

NOTE: The reference line has been transferred onto the silicone mold. This is where the mold will be cut open.

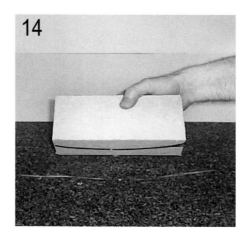

A special **groove knife** is used to cut the mold open.

NOTE: The knife shown in the photograph has a special blade attachment. The blade on this knife has been bent so that it has a small arch in it. As the blade is pulled through the mold, it cuts a half round groove into the silicone, creating a **registration key** in the mold.

It is not a good idea to cut a mold open with a straight razor. The two halves will not register well because a razor cut is too clean and smooth. If you must use a razor knife, cut the mold open in a zig zag pattern to increase accuracy of the registration.

The plastic fish is carefully de-molded.

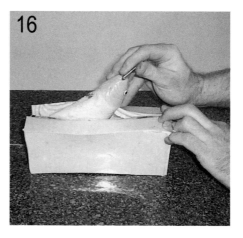

A view of the one-piece silicone mold and the plastic fish.

Section 2
Making the Urethane Rubber Casting

An aluminum wire (¹/₈ inch thick) is cut a few inches longer than the mold and is bent to match the reference line on the belly of the mold. The position of the wire is important because if it is not centered, the wire may tear out of the urethane fish when bent.

NOTE: The wire has the same diameter as the drill bit and will fit into the hole at the bottom of the mold. (To better visualize this, imagine a pole vaulter. The vaulter must plant the pole into a fitted pocket on the ground in order to hold the pole in place.)

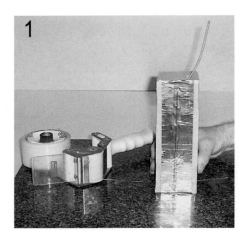

The mold is completely sealed with tape. A strip of **aluminum tape** runs vertically from under the mold up to the top while the sides are held together with clear packing tape. Since tape will not stick to silicone, it is necessary to wrap the tape completely around entire mold. If you do not do this, the urethane will leak out.

NOTE: Aluminum tape, not duct tape, is the best for this process. Aluminum tape is an extremely adhesive foil tape, available at most hardware stores.

Liquid **urethane rubber** is poured into the silicone mold and allowed to cure overnight.

NOTE: Urethane rubber is used because it will not stick to silicone. DO NOT pour liquid silicone into this mold, it will stick.

Allow the urethane to cure for 24 hours. The tape is cut away from the mold.

The fish is de-molded.

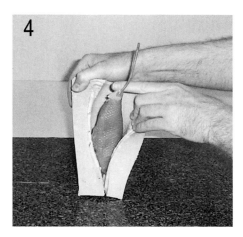

View of the completed urethane rubber casting and silicone mold. Notice the aluminum wire running through the entire fish. The wire will act as a flexible skeleton when reshaping the fish.

The fish is bent to create a more dramatic gesture.

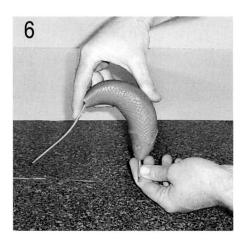

Notches are cut out wherever a fin has been removed.

NOTE: The notches will be useful when attaching the sugar fins onto the sugar fish.

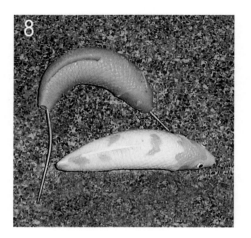

The reshaped rubber fish next to the original plastic fish.

Section 3
Making a Two-Piece Mold

This section will illustrate how a two-piece silicone mold is made.

Start by drawing a dividing line down the middle of the fish. The line is continued along the belly of the fish.

NOTE: The aluminum wire has been cut off at the mouth and tail, making it easier to mold.

Wax paper is put on the work board and the fish is positioned so that the tail does not hook forward over the head. An oil clay dividing wall is begun by securing the fish into position.

REMINDER: Oil clay is temperature sensitive. Cold clay will be hard to work with whereas warm clay will be soft and pliable. Use a space heater or heat lamp to soften the clay.

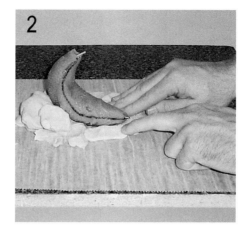

The clay dividing wall is built up along the ink dividing line on the fish, extending outwards about ¾ inch from each side of the fish.

NOTE: The wax paper allows the entire fish (with clay) to be easily rotated on the work board. Without using wax paper, it would be necessary to rotate the entire work board. Moving the board around sounds easy, but on a table full of materials, it is very cumbersome.

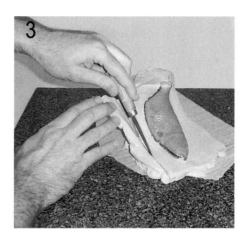

A small wire loop **tool** is used to cut a linear groove key (also known as a zipper key) into the clay dividing wall approximately ¼ inch deep around the perimeter of the fish. (See page 87, photograph 18 for the results.)

NOTE: In the finished mold, the groove will provide the registration for the second mold section. A wire loop tool is a necessary part of your mold making tool kit.

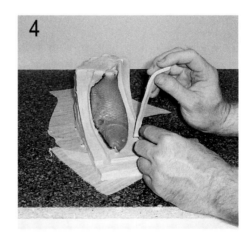

A small piece of plastic pipe is placed on top of the tail. Adding this pipe is an easy way to make a **pouring gate**. A pouring gate is the open area at the top of a mold. It must be large enough to allow the casting medium (chocolate, sugar) to flow easily into the mold.

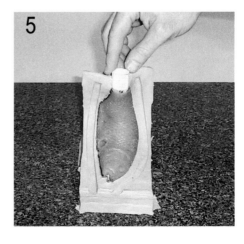

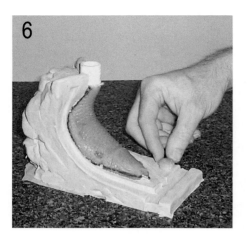

A small wooden plug (**snap key**) is placed in one corner of the mold as another registration technique. Snap keys are unique because they snap together, preventing two mold sections from pulling apart. At this moment, the snap key is a piece of wood but in the finished mold, the key will be in silicone. Remember, everything that is being made in clay (plastic pipe and wood) will be covered with silicone. This means that a groove will become a raised silicone ridge, a wood plug will become a small silicone hole etc. (See pages 86–87, photographs 16, 18 and 19.)

NOTE: The linear groove key has been cut in front of the fish head as well as along both sides. The wooden plugs used for making a snap key can be bought at a hardware store.

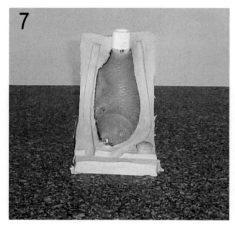

The clay dividing wall is complete.

NOTE: The clay dividing wall has been extended up to the top of the plastic pipe (pouring gate).

A mold box is assembled around the fish, so that the clink boards fit snugly against the clay dividing wall.

NOTE: Remember to seal up high along the vertical corners of the mold box.

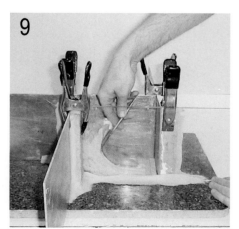

A small knife is used to blend the clay into the clink boards. If the seal is not water tight, silicone will leak behind the clay dividing wall.

NOTE: It is not critical if silicone leaks behind the dividing wall, it is just a waste of material.

A batch of non-food grade silicone (with regrind) is poured into the box.

NOTE: The silicone is poured 1½ inches below the top of the plastic pipe. The following sequence shows an easy way to reduce the amount of silicone needed to cover a model. The savings are minor in a small mold like this one, but in a large mold, the savings are significant. Overall, using this method with regrind reduced the material costs by 50%. (See the appendix for more information on using regrind.)

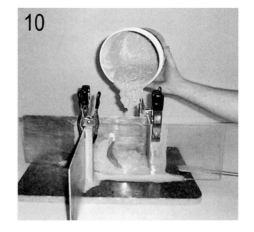

The entire work board is propped at a steep angle so that the silicone will flow back covering the plastic pipe, reducing the amount of silicone needed to cover the model. The mold is left at this angle overnight to cure.

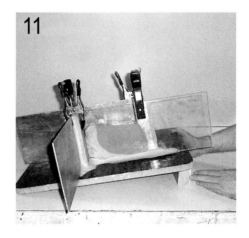

The silicone has cured and the work board has been set level. Notice that the silicone cured at the angle at which it was previously tilted.

A temporary plaster plug is made by filling the mold box level with plaster. The temporary plug is necessary because the mold must be able to sit flat when it is turned upside down to make the second silicone section.

NOTE: It may look like a lot of work to reduce the amount of silicone in this mold, yet in real time it only took 20 minutes to complete.

The mold box is disassembled and the flash is cut away.

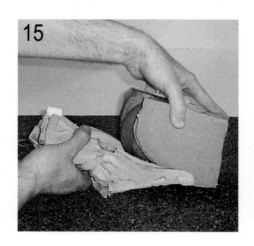

The clay dividing wall, plaster plug and plastic pipe stub are removed. (Save the plaster plug and plastic pipe stub).
DO NOT REMOVE THE FISH FROM THE SILICONE SECTION. Be careful not to flex the mold when removing the clay as this can break the seal between the fish and the silicone.

NOTE: If the seal is broken, even a little, silicone from the next pour will seep behind the urethane fish and stick to the mold, ruining the detail of the mold. If the fish had come loose, it would have been necessary to remove it completely and cover the entire interior surface of the mold with Vaseline. The layer of Vaseline would prevent any new silicone from bonding to the first mold section.

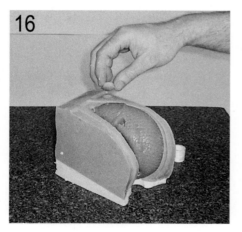

The wooden plug is removed.

NOTE: There is now a small hole where the wooden plug used to be. This is the first half of the snap key.

The entire silicone section is coated with Vaseline.

NOTE: Remember to lift the mold off of the plaster and Vaseline the bottom. This is necessary because the silicone from the next pour will seep everywhere.

Making A Giant Press Mold Of A Palm Frond

This chapter will illustrate how to make a large two-piece **press mold**. A mold of this size would be impractical to most chefs, however, for those interested in competitions or large centerpiece displays, this type of mold would give unprecedented freedom.

In Chapter 9, Chef Kraus will use the mold to press a variety of sugar shapes. The pressed sugar will be used in the creation of a sugar showpiece. The beauty of pressing small pieces in a large mold is that each pressed piece can have a completely different pattern. Pressing sugar near the base of the palm where the pattern is very tightly grouped or pressing near the top where the pattern is much more broad and fan-like will yield two completely different patterns. Other uses of the mold include pouring a single massive frond or casting dozens of perfectly fluted single strands.

We would like to give a special thank you to Chicago's Garfield Park Conservatory. The generosity of their staff is the only reason we were able to obtain such a beautiful palm frond in the middle of winter.

The palm frond was originally over 5 ft. by 7 ft. long (not including the stem). It has been cut into a specified shape.

NOTE: The palm frond has large wavy contours. Although the contours are attractive, they are not necessary to capture in the mold.

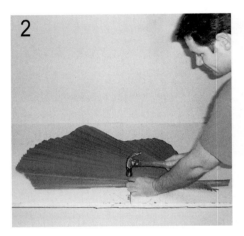

Small nails are set through the stem of the frond in order to flatten the contours.

Small squares of packing tape are used to hold the exterior perimeter flat on the table.

NOTE: Only four or five areas along the perimeter needed to be secured with tape.

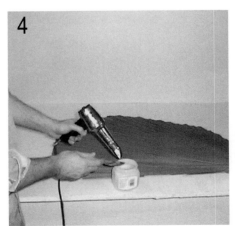

Vaseline is melted with a heat gun before being applied to the frond.

NOTE: Melted Vaseline is easier to apply than when it is gelled.

The Vaseline is brushed into every area on the palm, being careful not to apply an excessive amount. Too much release will fill in the fibrous texture on the frond.

Use the heat gun a second time to melt the Vaseline into the fibers of the palm. This has two positive effects. The first is that Vaseline will flow into all of the detail. The second is that melted Vaseline will create a slight gloss to the surface of the frond. The gloss will be transferred into the final mold.

Top view of the prepared palm frond.

A clay dividing wall is built around the base of the stem.

NOTE: The stem could not be nailed down onto the table top without causing damage or distortion to the frond. Therefore, a clay dividing wall is necessary to fill in the area below the upturned stem.

Close up view of the clay dividing wall.

A small batch of fast-setting (non-food grade) silicone is applied over the perimeter of the frond. Let the silicone flow from the frond onto the table. The silicone will cure, thoroughly bonding the frond to the table.

NOTE: For more information on **fast-setting silicone,** please **see** the appendix.

Allow the fast setting silicone to cure. Next, pour a second batch of (**regular setting**) non-food grade silicone is applied to the frond. The second batch has a higher **durometer** than the first. The high durometer silicone is more rigid. If a soft silicone is used for the press mold, the high ridges will be soft and may fold down when the mold is compressed. In order for the press mold to work, the ridges of the palm frond must be stiff enough to push into the sugar.

NOTE: Durometer is the term used to measure the flexibility of rubber materials. A high durometer is more rigid than a low durometer.

Brush the second layer of silicone over the entire surface of the palm frond. It is not necessary to cover the frond completely as the intention is to fill only the deep ridges of the palm frond.

NOTE: The two layers of silicone have been pigmented for photographic clarity.

Allow the silicone to cure for 24 hours. The fast-setting silicone that flowed onto the table (page 94, photograph 10) is trimmed flush with the perimeter of the palm frond.

NOTE: Trimming away the fast-setting silicone will not loosen the palm frond from the table. The frond is still securely attached to the table because much of the fast setting silicone seeped under the palm frond, as desired.

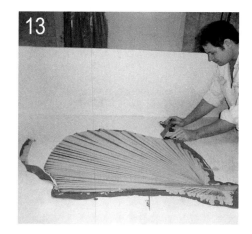

Top view of the palm frond with first two applications of silicone.

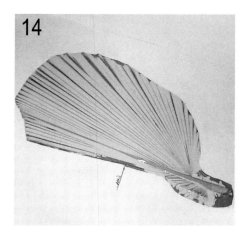

Although the frond is securely affixed to the work table, there are numerous open gaps beneath the ridges of the palm frond (one opening per ridge). These gaps must be covered with a batch of **thickened silicone.** (See appendix for information on thickening silicone.)

NOTE: In an upcoming step, a large amount of silicone will be poured over the entire frond. If there are open gaps beneath the ridges, the liquid silicone will flow under the palm frond. A small amount of silicone beneath the frond is acceptable, but a large amount of silicone will make it difficult to flip the mold over.

The same batch of thickened silicone is applied over the stem at the base of the palm frond. A ¼ inch thickness of silicone is sufficient.

NOTE: Covering the stem is necessary because it is the highest point on the model. In an upcoming step, a batch of silicone will be poured over the entire frond. It does not make sense to waste material just to cover a few small high points. (See page 97, photograph 23.)

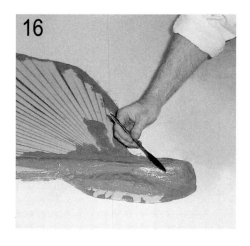

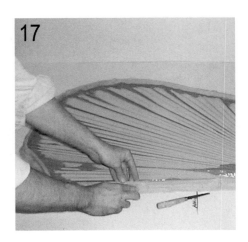

A continuous strip of oil clay is assembled tightly around the perimeter of the frond. The clay must be securely blended onto the tabletop (watertight).

The clay wall will be the mold box and must be tall enough to contain the level of silicone needed to cover the frond and the plaster **mother mold**.

NOTE: See page 97, photograph 23 and 24 for more information.

A large batch of non-food grade silicone with regrind is poured over the palm frond.

When silicone contains regrind, it does not flow easily. Therefore, several pools must be spread over the frond.

Use a small mud knife to pull the silicone over the entire frond.

Regrind will never be completely smooth, and will cure with a gravel-like surface. This is because the regrind chunks do not always settle beneath the liquid level of silicone. To minimize this effect, use a large mud knife (in a chopping motion) to gently push the surface layer of regrind beneath the liquid level. This also helps force out unwanted air bubbles. Be careful not to damage the frond below the silicone.

Allow the regrind batch to cure for 24 hours.

HELPFUL HINT: After the regrind batch cures, the top surface will not be smooth. Using a razor from a retractable blade, shave the high points off the surface as a bumpy texture can compromise the registration of the mother mold.

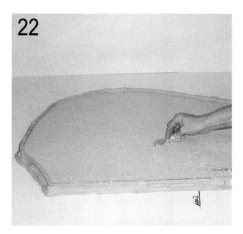

A batch of **No. 1 Molding Plaster** is poured on top of the cured silicone. It is not as strong as Hydrocal, however, it is lighter in weight and easier to work. To increase the strength of the moulding plaster, **chopped glass strands** have been added as reinforcement. A hundred years ago, horse hair would have been added to the plaster, but today, chopped glass is used. Adding chopped glass reduces the amount of plaster needed to achieve the same strength. Adding wood glue to the liquid plaster also makes it stronger.

A mud knife is used to pull the plaster over all areas of the mold.

If you have never worked with plaster before, this is a tricky step. A batch of plaster is mixed with chopped glass strands. Just before the batch is about to set, the thickened plaster is smeared over the surface of the first layer of plaster.

The two mixes were applied one right after the other, so there was no trouble with the plaster bonding to itself. (See the appendix for more information about mixing plaster.)

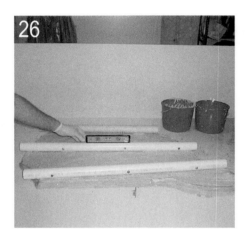

In order for this step to make sense, it is important to know that the mold is being built upside down. The top of the plaster mother mold is actually the area that will sit on the table when the mold is finished. If the plaster surface is not even, it will rock on the work table when it is used. To make the mold stable and flat, a **mother mold support frame** must be attached to the mother mold.

To make this mold frame, three sections of plastic pipe are cut to length. The pipes are leveled by placing small amounts of clay beneath any low areas of the pipe. Drill holes through the pipe and insert large bolts through the holes in the pipe. The next few photographs will help explain the process.

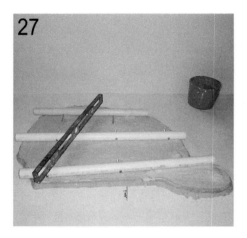

A large carpenter's level is used to verify that the pipes are level in all direction. Notice the long bolts extending through the pipes.

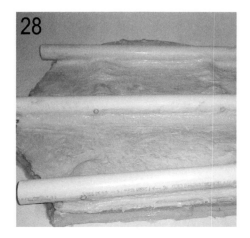

A batch of thick plaster is mixed and applied over the extended bolts. Pushing plaster under the length of the pipes will provide extra reinforcement.

NOTE: Do not put any plaster on top of the pipes. The idea is to create a smooth and level cradle for the mold to rest on. (See page 103, photograph 48.)

The top silicone liner is placed on the lower mold liner. Notice the color differences in the silicone. The areas where I used fast-setting silicone are darker.

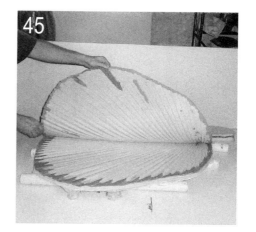

The top liner is trimmed so that the edges are flush with the bottom liner.

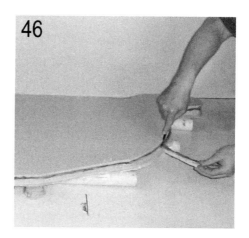

A marker is used to outline the new perimeter of the silicone mold. This line will provide a quick reference point when **seating** the mold in the mother mold.

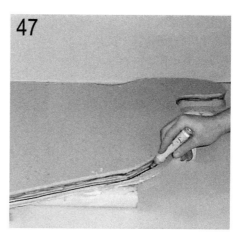

The finished palm frond press mold. After carefully washing any impurities that stuck to the mold from the original frond, the mold is ready for use.

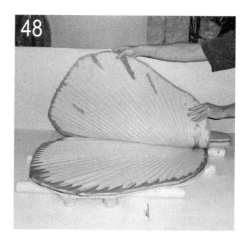

Using A Mold To Rework
A Chocolate Ring Carving

For this chapter, Chef John Kraus carved a solid chocolate ring. As many of you know, a smooth surface is difficult to achieve when carving chocolate. In order to perfect Chef Kraus's model, a silicone mold and subsequent plaster casting were made. Plaster is a much more forgiving medium than chocolate when it comes to smoothing out a surface. Once the plaster model is cast, any imperfections on the surface can be easily patched, sanded and polished. Without using a mold to cast a duplicate plaster model, a smooth surface would be difficult to achieve.

The first section of this chapter shows how to make an open-faced silicone mold using recycled silicone. Following that is a brief instruction on how to finish a plaster casting.

The final section illustrates how a thin layer of **silicone paste** is used to cover the new plaster model. The process continues on to illustrate how to make a two-piece silicone mold with a two-piece plaster mother mold. A **mother mold** is a rigid shell on the outside of the silicone mold. Without a mother mold, a thin layer (liner/blanket) of silicone cannot hold its shape. Covering a model with a thin layer of silicone and then supporting it with a plaster mother mold is one of the most efficient ways of using silicone. Making a thin silicone **liner** is much less expensive than covering a model with a block of liquid silicone.

Although the large number of photographs does not reflect it, the method shown for making a two-piece silicone mold is quick. This mold design is simple and efficient for a models that have a perfectly horizontal **parting line**. (See page 110 photograph 2 or the glossary for more details.) Models that have an irregular parting line, like the fish in Chapter 6 and later in Chapter 10 the figurine, must be separated with a time consuming clay dividing wall.

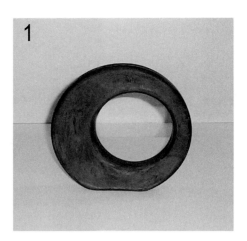

A front view of the chocolate carving.

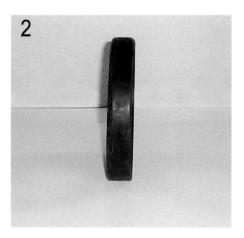

A side view of the chocolate carving.

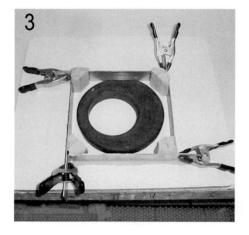

A mold box is assembled around the chocolate ring.

NOTE: Leave at least a 1 inch open perimeter around the ring, as the extra width will create thicker side walls in the mold. The thick walls will be less likely to flex (bulge out) when the mold is filled with plaster. (See page 108, photographs 11 and 12.)

Notice the blocks of clay that have been put in the corners of the mold box. The clay plugs reduce the amount of silicone needed to fill the mold box.

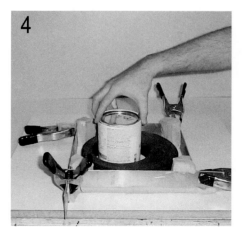

A small paint can is put in the center of the ring. The can will have the same material reducing effect that the clay plugs do.

NOTE: Remember to put Vaseline on the paint can so that it will be easily released from the silicone mold.

Build a mold box around the ring and LEVEL the work board. Then pour a small batch of plaster into the mold box. Do not fill above the parting line that was drawn on the plaster ring in photograph 2.

NOTE: The bottom of the plaster ring is pressing against the side of the clink board. This will be the **pouring gate**. (See page 122, photograph 50.)

Section 2

Making a
Two-Piece
Silicone Mold
with a Plaster
Mother Mold

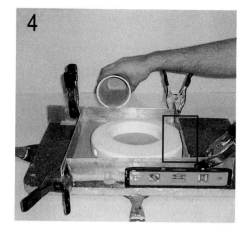

Top view of the mold box. The thin plaster dividing wall has been pigmented for photographic clarity.

Allow the plaster dividing wall to completely set.

Not shown: Wooden **snap keys** are soaped and then adhered to the plaster dividing wall with Vaseline.

NOTE: When using wooden snap keys for the first time, soap them with parting soap before use as it will prevent the silicone from sticking to them.

Top view of mold box with snap keys placed around both sides of the ring.

NOTE: See page 121, photograph 44 and page 122, photograph 49, for better understanding of how the snap keys will work on this mold.

A small batch of silicone is needled over the ring, completely covering the snap keys.

NOTE: Do not use a brush for this. Cover the entire ring only by needling the silicone.

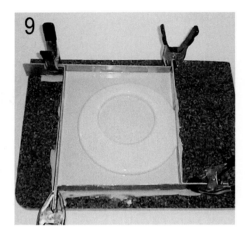

A top view of the mold box.

NOTE: The snap keys are completely covered and the plaster ring is glazed with a thin layer of silicone. Do not disturb for 24 hours. Allow the silicone to cure just as it is.

NEXT DAY: A small batch of thickened silicone (slightly darker) is applied with a small spade tool.

NOTE: A layer of **thickened silicone** (paste) is applied along the vertical sides of the ring FIRST. Make sure to build up enough silicone to create a ramp–like draft along the side of the ring. A proper **draft** will allow the plaster mother mold to easily pull off the silicone section. (See page 121, photograph 45.)

(The front clink board has been removed for photographic clarity.)

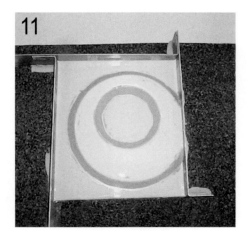

A top view of the plaster ring with thickened silicone around the sides.

NOTE: This part of the process is called **frosting** the mold. Frosting is a term used to describe covering a model with thickened silicone. Frosting a mold is much more efficient than covering a model with liquid silicone. This mold section could have been poured with a large amount of silicone, but it would have been expensive.

Continue frosting the mold. Use the same batch of silicone to cover the top of the ring. Applying thickened silicone is not easy. A good technique is to only pick up a small amount (the size of a grape) of silicone on the spade and push it forward onto the model. Do not try to spread the silicone out too far. Pull forward only a ½ inch or so, making sure that each dab of silicone blends into the previous one. Try not to trap air pockets.

NOTE: When applying silicone this way, it is common for beginners to apply it too thin. The appropriate thickness for a frosted mold is ¼ inch thick. When applying a second layer of silicone, pigment it with **red iron oxide** as the color change will help you see proper coverage.

Section 2

Making a
Two-Piece
Silicone Mold
with a Plaster
Mother Mold

Continue frosting the mold until the entire surface of the ring is covered. It is not necessary to add any more silicone over the snap keys.

NOTE: A layer of silicone is pulled up (½ inch above) the bottom of the ring. This thickness will create a **lip** in the finished mold.

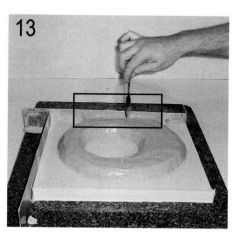

In order to make silicone registration keys, use the same batch of thickened silicone to fill several small plastic (female) natches. (I call them mouse bowls.)

NOTE: Plastic natches are used in the ceramic industry (in a different way) to make mold keys for plaster molds. Any small plastic cup shape would work.

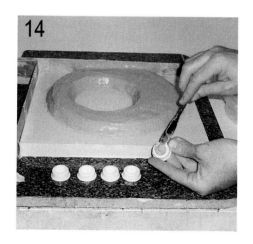

While the silicone is still sticky, place the natches (silicone side down) onto the ring. The silicone will bond perfectly to itself.

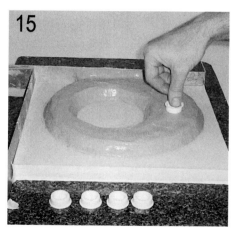

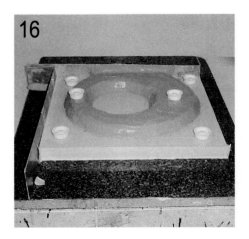

Six natches are placed on the silicone blanket. They will stick to any silicone surface, including the silicone outside of the ring, which was poured the day before.

The silicone is allowed to cure overnight. The plastic natches are removed to expose their silicone interior. The silicone cured inside the plastic natches in the shape of a small dome. These domes will act as registration keys for the plaster mother mold section that will be poured over the silicone liner.

A mold box is assembled around the ring mold and a pouring indication line is put in the box. If you use this method, make sure your clink boards are tall enough for the entire mold.

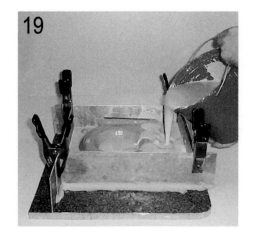

A batch of plaster (does not have to be Hydrocal) is poured directly over the silicone liner. The plaster should cover the entire silicone blanket, but not go above the top of the lip shown on page 113, photograph 13.

While the plaster is still liquid, I use my hand to "**jog**" the plaster level. A slight back and forth movement should be enough to do the trick. Wash your hands as soon as possible. (Do not let the plaster set on your skin as it will stick to small hairs on your hand.) If you are going to handle wet plaster, wear gloves or grease you hands with Vaseline.

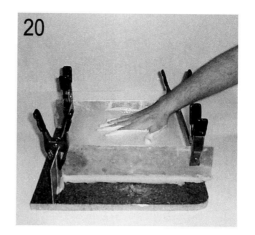

Section 2

Making a
Two-Piece
Silicone Mold
with a Plaster
Mother Mold

The plaster is allowed to set and the edges are shaved down.

The entire mold (in one piece) is flipped over. Although it may happen on its own, do not try to separate the plaster mother mold from the silicone blanket beneath.

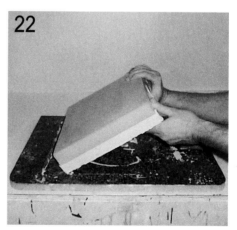

The mold has been flipped over and the plaster dividing wall is now on the top surface of the mold.

The plaster dividing wall is now removed and discarded. It is very easy to separate from the silicone and the ring.

NOTE: If the plaster dividing wall sticks to the ring, more parting soap was needed.

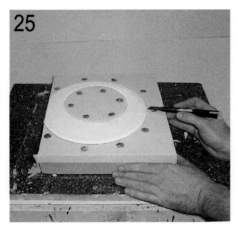

A razor knife is used to carefully trim away flash that seeped between the plaster dividing wall and ring. (There should be minimal flash.)

Remove the snap keys from the silicone section.

NOTE: If parting soap had not been put on the snap keys prior to molding, they would have been difficult to remove.

Make the second half of the silicone mold.

Put a small amount of Vaseline on your finger and smear the inside of the snap keys. Be thorough, as the next silicone layer will bond with any area that has not been coated with Vaseline.

Brush Vaseline on to EVERY surface of the silicone.

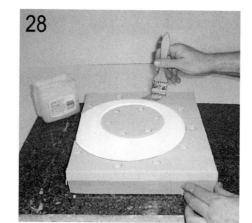

Section 2

Making a
Two-Piece
Silicone Mold
with a Plaster
Mother Mold

Don't forget to brush Vaseline on the sides of the silicone mold as well.

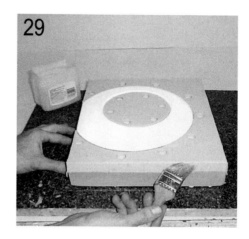

HELPFUL HINT: Use your hand to smear the Vaseline smoothly onto the silicone. You will feel any areas that were missed with the brush.

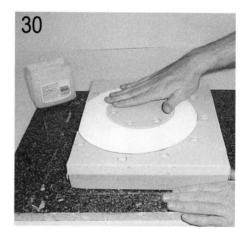

Use a paper towel to remove any Vaseline smudges on the plaster ring. The plaster ring should be as clean and smooth as possible.

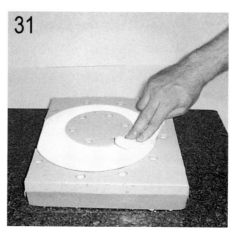

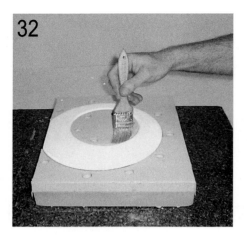

A final application of Vaseline is carefully brushed along the **EDGES** of the silicone near the ring.

NOTE: Keep the ring surface clean. Do not let the brush slip onto the ring.

Fill any large gaps between the ring and the clink board with clay.

NOTE: Leaving open gaps will allow silicone to flash between them.

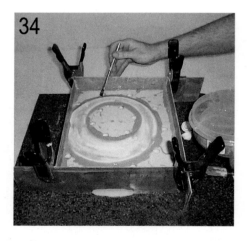

A small amount (200 grams) of fast-setting silicone is brushed along the perimeter of the mold box and the perimeter of the plaster ring. The fast-setting silicone is used to seal areas that are likely to flash.

NOTE: The fast-setting silicone has been pigmented for photographic clarity.

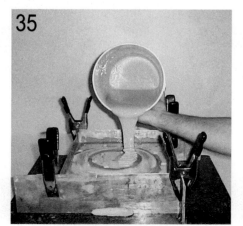

Let the fast-setting silicone set for 30 minutes or until tacky.

Enough regular setting silicone is poured into the mold box to cover the ring by ¼ inch.

NOTE: Because this mold section is flat, it makes more sense to pour silicone over it rather than frosting it with thickened silicone.

After the liquid silicone levels itself, gently set a (male) natch into the surface. The plastic natch will settle part way into the silicone. Due to the design of the natch, it won't sink.

The registration key is created when the silicone cures around the natch. When the natch is removed from the cured silicone the negative impression remains. This impression will be the registration key for the second mother mold section.

NOTE: The natch that was used in photograph 14 was a female (recessed) natch. This step uses the male (raised) natch.

Section 2

Making a
Two-Piece
Silicone Mold
with a Plaster
Mother Mold

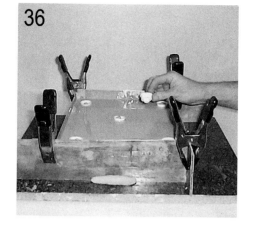

This is a close up view to illustrate the shape of a male natch.

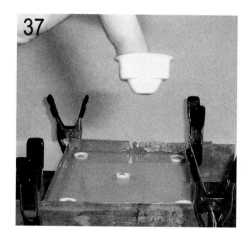

Top view of mold box.

NOTE: Small bits of clay have been placed inside the back of the natches. The clay helps the natch float upright while the silicone is curing.

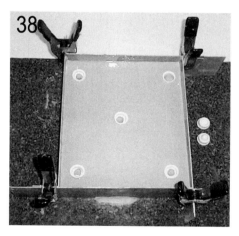

Allow the silicone to cure for 24 hours, then remove the plastic natches.

Overview of the mold with negative registration keys in the surface of the silicone.

Next, the second mother mold section is made by pouring one inch of plaster over the silicone mold.

NOTE: No release agent is necessary between the silicone and the plaster.

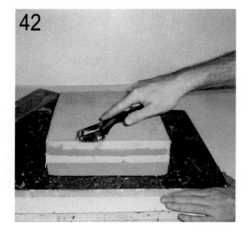

Allow the plaster to set for about an hour.

The clink boards and clay are removed and the plaster edges are then rounded out with a SurForm™.

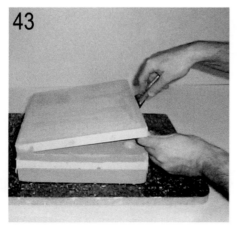

Next, the mold is disassembled. The top mother mold section is lifted off the silicone with a mud knife.

The silicone liner beneath the mother mold is peeled off of the plaster ring.

NOTE: This is a good view of the snap keys at work.

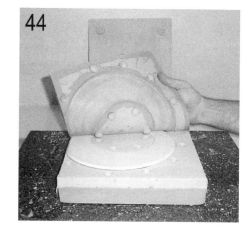

Section 2

Making a
Two-Piece
Silicone Mold
with a Plaster
Mother Mold

The second silicone section is lifted out of the bottom mother mold section.

NOTE: The first half of the mold is seen in the background.

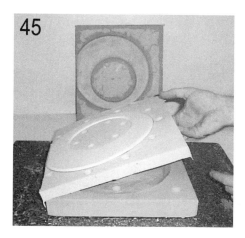

The plaster ring is removed by flexing the silicone liner.

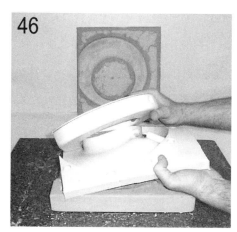

Overview of the completed mold. Each silicone liner is resting (seated) in its individual mother mold section.

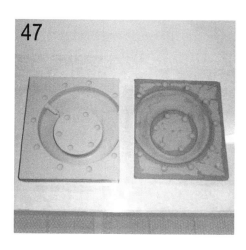

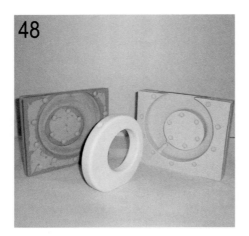

A view of the finished silicone mold and plaster model.

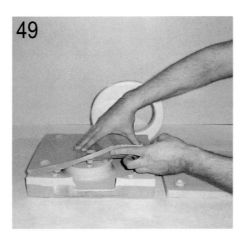

The mold is reassembled (seated).

NOTE: Putting a small amount of Vaseline in each snap key (before assembly) will make the mold fit together more easily.

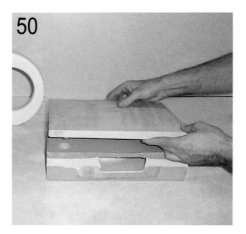

The mother mold section is set in place on top of the silicone.

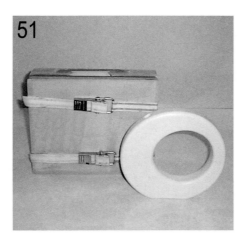

The entire mold is strapped together and is ready for casting.

Chef John Kraus And Chef Jacquy Pfeiffer Cast A Sugar Showpiece

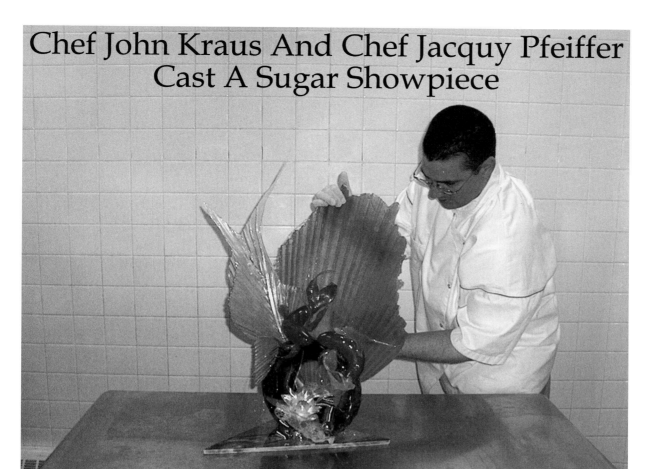

This chapter illustrates Chef Kraus and Chef Pfeiffer using several different molds from the preceding chapters to cast and assemble a sugar showpiece. These molds can be used to cast an endless variety of compositions using the same three basic elements of the fish, the ring and the palm frond.

Chef Kraus comments, "Having a library of different molds allows me to experiment with composition and structure. It's great to be able to create a completely new sculpture each time simply by rearranging the position of the same cast objects." Another benefit he appreciated was the production consistency that the molds allowed. When it was necessary to produce several of the same displays, Chef Kraus was able to pre-cast numerous elements and then assemble several similar displays at the same time.

Chef John Kraus demonstrates how to cast a multicolored sugar base for a showpiece with an aquatic theme.

NOTE: Shown in the photo is the silicone mold of the ring and a cast sugar ring.

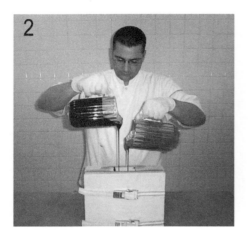

Chef Kraus prepared two pitchers of melted Isomalt containing different colors. When he pours both colors into the mold simultaneously, the two colors mix randomly inside the mold and create a beautiful translucent marbled look.

NOTE: Always wear latex gloves when working with melted sugar to prevent unwanted finger prints. More importantly, if some material is spilled, the gloves can be removed quickly to avoid a serious burn.

To prepare Isomalt for casting, heat it to 165° C/329° F and then let it cool to 125° C/257° F before pouring. Additional coloring information is provided later in this chapter.

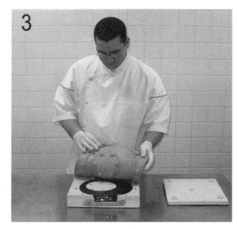

Chef Kraus allows the mold to cool overnight before de-molding. This is necessary because the ring is thick and silicone insulates the heat within the mold. Together, these characteristics require a long cooling time.

NOTE: The first silicone liner is removed while the mold lies on its side.

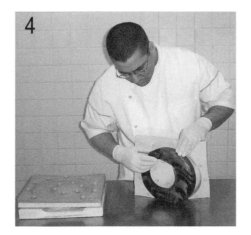

Chef Kraus removes the second half of the mold while the ring is standing upright. Removing the silicone liner in this position reduces the amount of stress placed on the casting and allows him to gently push the center of the mold through the ring.

Chef Kraus displays the completed cast base.

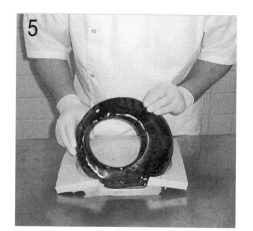

Chef Kraus uses a propane torch to melt the bottom of the ring onto a marble tile. The marble will provide the showpiece with additional support and allow him to carry the showpiece to another location.

NOTE: When melting the sugar base onto the marble tile, it is important to heat the marble with the torch as well. If the marble is cold, a hot sugar piece will not stick.

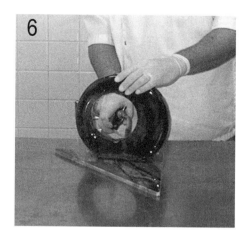

Section 2
Casting the Fish and Fins

This section illustrates how Chef Jacquy Pfeiffer casts the fish mold with Isomalt sugar and attaches them to the base of the showpiece.

The two-piece fish mold.

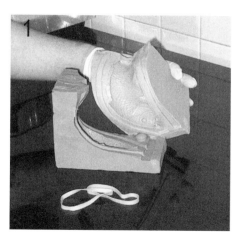

Working With Isomalt Sugar

Chef Pfeiffer uses an induction stove to prepare the melted Isomalt. 1000 grams of Isomalt mixed with 10% water and is heated to 165° C/329° F. Then water-based colorant is added to the batch and allowed to continue to boil for a short time.

NOTE: Whenever adding colorant to Isomalt, it is necessary to bring it to a quick boil so that water in the colorant is cooked out.

Chef Pfeiffer allows the Isomalt to cool to 125° C/257° F before pouring the fish mold. If the Isomalt is poured at a higher temperature, it will continue to cook because the silicone mold will insulate the heat. Also, over heated Isomalt will create air bubbles in the casting as well as damage some types of silicone molds. Most non-food grade silicones are easily burned by temperatures over 204° C/400° F.

The fish mold has been positioned at a slight angle to help ensure that air will rise from the mold.

REMEMBER: Always wear latex gloves when pouring hot sugar. If material is spilled on your hands, the glove can be removed quickly to avoid a serious burn.

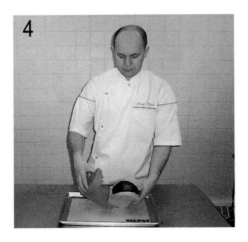

The solid Isomalt fish is allowed to cool for several hours before de-molding. Thick castings can take a very long time to cool because the silicone insulates the heat inside of the mold. De-molding too early will result in a casting that is still liquid in the center.

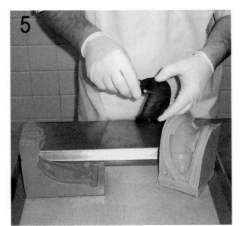

Chef Pfeiffer uses a sharp knife or razor to clean the seam lines on the fish.

NOT SHOWN: A decorative effect can be created on the fish by airbrushing the surface at this time. The airbrushed color will show through the clear coating of Isomalt created in the next photograph and result in a translucent layering of color.

In order to create a shiny "water-like" surface on the fish, Chef Pfeiffer prepares to coat the fish with a layer of clear Isomalt.

A second pot of clear Isomalt is boiled and allowed to cool to 125° C/257° F. If the Isomalt is too hot, it will remelt the fish casting.

NOTE: Always were rubber gloves when working with hot sugar as sugar burns can be serious and debilitating.

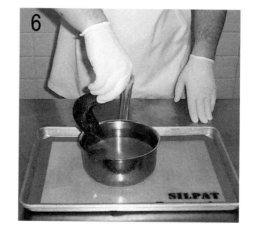

Holding the tip of the tail, Chef Pfeiffer carefully dips the fish into the Isomalt. The pot is tilted slightly to ensure that the fish is completely covered.

NOTE: The dipping should be a quick in and out. Do not allow the fish to sit in the hot Isomalt.

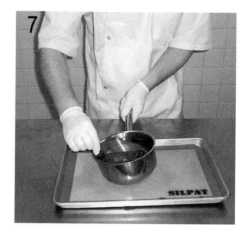

Allow the maximum amount of hot Isomalt to drain off the fish. Lift and roll the fish upwards as the last amount of Isomalt drips off the fish. The rolling motion will cause the final drips to be absorbed into the surface of the fish.

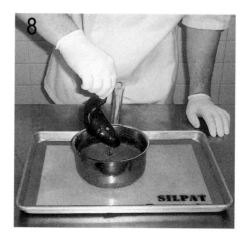

Chef Pfeiffer places the coated fish in front of a fan immediately after dipping. The fan cools the surface of the fish so that it hardens quickly.

NOTE: Without the use of a cooling fan, the heat from the clear Isomalt will soften the fish and cause the shape to distort.

Chef Pfeiffer applies a small amount of clear Isomalt to the display base. The clear Isomalt will be used as a glue to hold the fish in place.

The fish is attached to the base.

NOTE: An acrylic pitcher is used as a temporary support to hold the fish in place while the attachment point hardens.

Chef Pfeiffer attaches the second fish in the same manner.

Making The Fins

Chef Pfeiffer preheats a silicone mat in the oven for few minutes at 100° C/212° F.

NOTE: The silicone mat has a pin stripped texture on the surface.

A small pool of colored Isomalt is poured onto the warm silicone mat.

With one motion, Chef Pfeiffer uses a spatula to spread the Isomalt into a thin sheet.

The process is repeated several times so that there will be enough pieces for all of the fins.

After the fins have cooled, they are transferred onto a Silpat® mat.

NOTE: The textured side of the fins is placed face down.

The fins are reheated (**flashed**) in the oven at 100° C/212° F just long enough to make the Isomalt pliable.

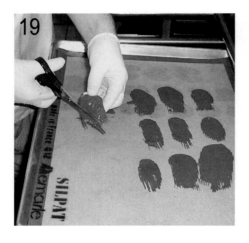

Chef Pfeiffer uses scissors to trim the fins so that one end is pointed. After the fins have been trimmed, they are reheated in the oven.

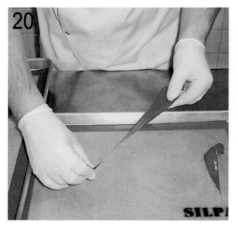

After the fins have been reheated for a few minutes, Chef Pfeiffer pulls the end of the fin to the desired length. The pulling should be done in one, steady motion. After pulling the fin, he bends the fins to the desired shape. The process is repeated for all the fins.

NOTE: It was necessary to reheat the fins a few times in order to stretch them all before they cooled.

Chef Pfeiffer uses a propane torch to flash heat the base of a fin. The intention is to slightly melt the back of the fin so that it can be attached to the fish.

NOTE: An alcohol lamp can be used in place of a torch.

Chef Pfeiffer attaches the fin to the fish body. The Isomalt fin must be held in place by hand (for 20–30 seconds) while it cools.

Note: Chef Pfeiffer bends his body around the sculpture during assembly. The fins that are closest to the Chef's chest are attached last to prevent accidental damage to the sculpture by his leaning into the piece during assembly. (The sculpture could also be placed on a turntable for mobility during assembly.)

Chef Pfeiffer tests the position before attaching the fin.

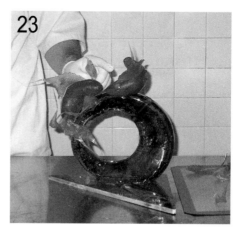

He continues to attach the fins.

Chef Pfeiffer holds the last fin in position while it cools.

Section 3
Casting "Coral" Using the Large Palm Frond Press Mold

Chef John Kraus demonstrates how he press-molded numerous sugar forms. The forms will be attached to the (partially assembled) sugar showpiece seen previously.

Chef Kraus lays out Neoprene strips on a Silpat® mat. He uses small metal weights to hold the strips into the desired shapes.

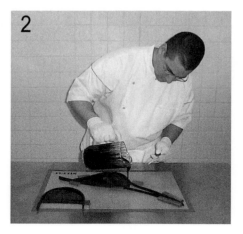

Chef Kraus pours colored Isomalt into the Neoprene forms to a ¼ inch thickness. He then allows the Isomalt shapes to cool for an hour.

NOTE: He pours the Isomalt from a heavy duty, heat safe plastic pitcher. A pitcher provides more pouring control than a pot.

Chef Kraus has removed the Neoprene strips and placed the sugar forms on a baking pan. He warms (flashes) the sugar at 71° C/160° F until it becomes malleable again. To test how soft the sugar is in the oven, one side of the Silpat® is lifted. If the sugar follows the contour of the Silpat®, the shape is ready to be press molded.

NOTE: Pre-forming shapes with Neoprene strips will provide a clean shape for Chef Kraus to press into the frond mold. Pouring a large amount of hot sugar directly into the mold would not yield a clean controlled shape. (Please view the color gallery page 350 at the back of the book to see how Chef Kraus piped hot sugar directly into the press mold in order to make individual fluted strips.)

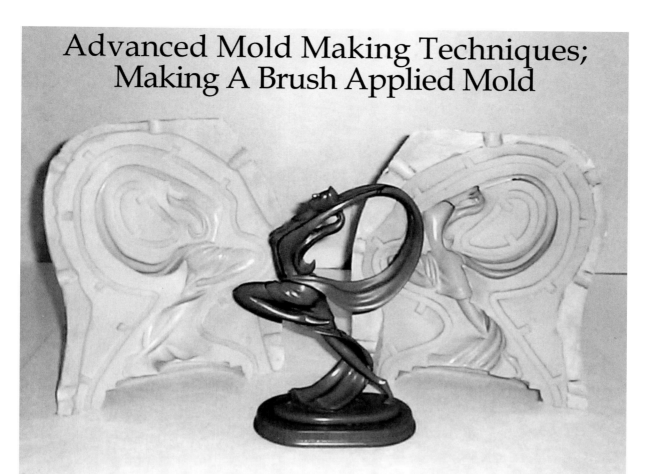

This is a time consuming and expensive mold to make. At the time of this book's publication (2003) a professional mold maker could charge $1,600.00 to make this mold. The price is based on time and materials. Expect to pay between $50.00–$65.00 per hour for labor (about the same amount a fine wood worker will charge). Due to the high cost, many people involved with culinary arts will never be able to use a mold like this. A common exception is the person who needs a totally unique item for promotional reasons, competition or display. Another exception would be the manufacturer who needs to produce numerous finished (tallow, sugar, chocolate, etc.) castings in a short time. A manufacturer considers a mold to be a piece of equipment. Therefore, the up-front mold cost is divided by the amount of saleable objects it can produce. Casting a sculpture that sells for $100.00 will enable them to recoup mold charges very quickly and it will not be long before the mold is making money instead of costing money.

The mold shown above is commonly referred to as a **brush applied** mold. Brush applied (also known as frosting the mold) is a term used to describe applying thickened silicone paste with a brush, trowel or spade knife. Every brush applied mold will demand some variation in mold design. In order to design a mold successfully, it is important to understand how the finished mold will be handled during casting. Every casting medium (i.e. chocolate, sugar, water) has different properties that need to be considered.

The mold design must complement the casting medium. For example, a mold designed for casting chocolate should be made with very soft silicone, whereas a mold for pressing hot sugar must be rigid enough to hold up to the pressure. Another casting consideration is how well the casting material will flow through the mold. Water will flow through narrow passages in a mold very easily while allowing air to escape. Hot sugar is completely different, it is thicker and can chill on the cool surface of a mold, causing it to cool slower in thick areas and fast in thinner areas. Uneven cooling makes it difficult for trapped air to escape from the mold. These are a few considerations to keep in mind when molding a complex shape. Having said this, read on for a glimpse into the challenges of creating a brush applied mold.

Right profile of model.

Left profile of model. Notice the oval space between her arms and back. It is called a "**window**."

NOTE: This sculpture has many windows. There is a second window at the base of the sculpture between the right foot and drapery.

The significance of the windows will become more apparent as the process unfolds.

A parting line is drawn on the model. The parting line is the visual reference point where the mold will be divided into halves. Choosing the best location for the parting line is not as easy as it looks.

As a basic mold design principal, follow the silhouette of the figure to establish the parting line. The silhouette is easy to find by placing the model in front of a spotlight. The light will illuminate the front of the model by creating a shadow on the back side of the model.

Trace the perimeter of the shadow onto the model. Do not be concerned if the lines are not perfect, as they can be corrected later.

The model is positioned horizontally on the work board. Notice that bits of clay have been put beneath the model, making the parting line parallel with the work board.

NOTE: **It is critical to place wax paper beneath the model before starting to make the mold.** Place the wax paper under the model so the model can be turned easily and moved around freely on the work board.

Build The Clay Dividing Wall

The next step is to build a clay dividing wall that raises up to the parting line on the model. (See page 140, photograph 11 for more details.) Building a dividing wall entirely out of clay requires a lot of material. Using blocks of wood as filler is a great way to reduce the amount of clay needed to build the wall. This is called "blocking up a mold." Secure the wood blocks in place with bits of clay.

NOTE: The parting line is not perfectly straight. There will be low areas that should not have blocks near them. The blocks must be lower than the parting line on the model.

Make A Bottom For The Mold

A large clink board is set tightly against the bottom of the sculpture. Make sure that the clink board is at least two inches taller and wider than the base of the model. The clink board is held in place with a large amount of clay behind it.

NOTE: A large piece of laminated wood or Plexiglas could be used in place of a clink board. (See page 146, photograph 2 to understand why a bottom is added to the model.)

Clay Up The Mold

Numerous small coils of clay are quickly placed on top of the wood blocks. This step should not take a long time to do. The only rule at this point is not to clay above the parting line on the model. Do not waste time by being detail oriented.

HELPFUL HINT: Warm the clay in a microwave for a minute or place it in front of a space heater prior to working with it. Soft clay is easier to work with.

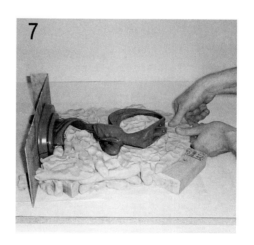

A top view of the "rough" clay dividing wall.

The dividing wall extends two inches beyond the perimeter of the model. Keep the clay wall perpendicular to the model. A common mistake is building a clay wall that is flush against the parting line (on the model) but slopes steeply down to the work board away from the model. (See page 142, photograph 18.)

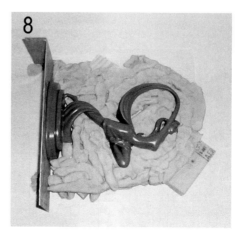

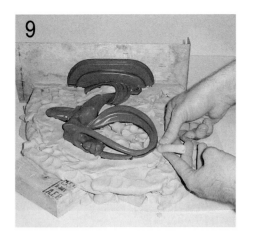

Create A Tight Seal Against The Model

Feed small (½ inch thick) coils of clay up to the parting line. The goal is to create a narrow but clean mini dividing wall around the model. Don't be concerned that the coil doesn't extend the whole width of the dividing wall.

NOTE: This step demands that the clay coils be pressed tightly against the model. If the coil does not mirror the contour of the parting line, the mold will not have a tight seal.

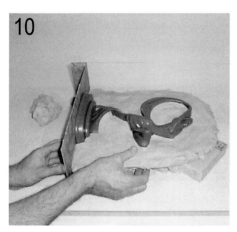

Even Out The Dividing Wall

Add more coils around the first coil. Keep doing this until the entire dividing wall is level by blending the coils together with your fingers. It should not be necessary to use any tools at this point. Be careful not to disturb the inner coil. Building a dividing wall with coils is very fast. Lay one coil down and move on. Do not keep reworking the same surface area again and again. This step should not take more than 15 minutes.

NOTE: Do not disturb the coil of clay that is touching the model.

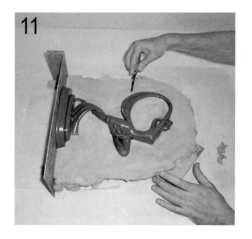

Scrape The Dividing Wall Smooth

Use a **fettling knife** to shave down the lumpy surface of the dividing wall. Do this in several passes.

NOTE: This fettling knife has been altered for this use; the blade has been shortened and the tip blunted.

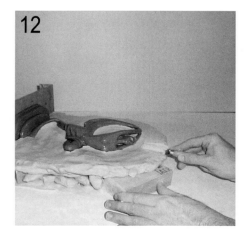

Shave Down The Dividing Wall

Do not expect the dividing wall to be totally flat. Do the best you can, remember, the smoother the better.

Compress The Dividing Wall

Use the flat edge of the fettling knife to press the clay surface smooth. The blunt tip of the knife is pushed against the model to create a tight seal.

NOTE: The two inch width of the clay dividing wall is less than the length of the knife blade, allowing the knife to be pulled over the clay surface without dragging the handle into the clay.

Clean Up The Dividing Wall

Use a triangle trimming **tool** to smooth and blend the clay area closest to the model. A trimming tool will shave small amounts of clay much cleaner than the knife. Stay focused on the area nearest the model.

NOTE: Using the trimming tool to shave the entire clay surface will create more scratch lines than it is worth.

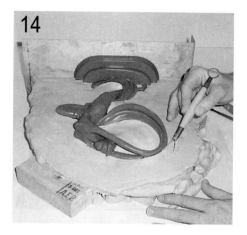

Use A Detail Tool To Reach Small Areas

This figurine has several nooks that are too small for the fettling knife or the trimming tool to fit into. Use the sharp point of a detail **tool** to make a tight seal between the model and the clay.

NOTE: This tool is perfect for this task because its tip is bent upwards like a spoon. This is a necessary tool for a mold maker.

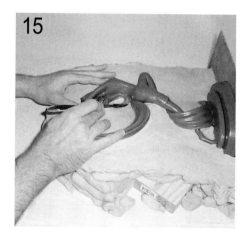

Fill In The Window At The Base Of The Figurine

A large loop **tool** is used to scrape out excess clay from the small window. A loop tool is different than a trimming tool, in that it has a curved piece of wire at the end whereas the trimming tool has a triangular blade.

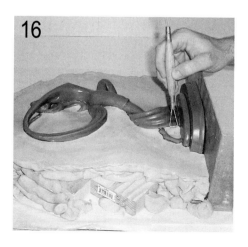

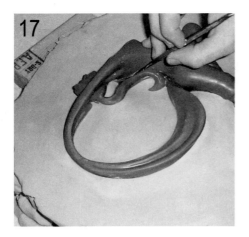

Use the detail tool to make a clean seal in the small window inside of the figures hair.

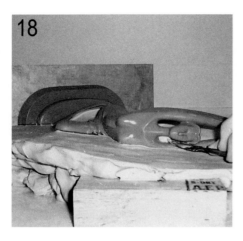

There are three window around the head. Fill in the bottom window with clay, making sure to create a tight seal. Do not fill in the other two windows yet.

NOTE: This photograph is a good illustration of a level dividing wall.

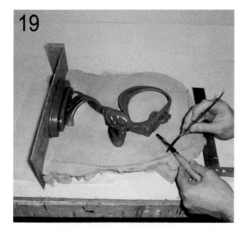

Shape The Perimeter Of The Dividing Wall

Trim off the excess width of the dividing wall, as it does not need to be more than two inches wider than the perimeter of the model. An outline can be quickly made by using the knife blade as a spacer and the detail tool as a pen. Hold the knife tip against the edge of the model and scratch the clay under the handle of the knife. Do this at numerous points around the model until you have a dotted line around the statue.

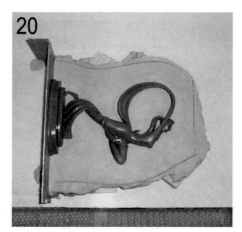

A top view of the dividing wall with the perimeter outline completed.

The excess edge is trimmed off of the dividing wall.

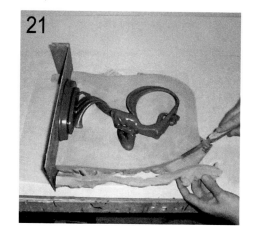

Clean The Model

A cotton swab is used to remove small bits of oil and clay along the very edge of the model.

NOTE: The cleaner the parting line, the tighter the mold seam. The tighter the mold seam, the smaller the flash between mold sections. The less flash on a casting, the less clean up time to remove it on the finished casting.

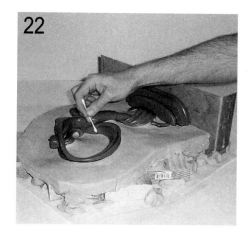

Remove Any Oil Residue From The Model

A lot of oil clay has been handled while making this dividing wall. Make sure that the model is wiped free of any fingerprints. If there is a fingerprint on the model, it will show up in the mold.

Shim The Last Two Windows Around The Head

A **shim** (or fence) is a thin piece of material that covers the back side of a window. Shims are needed wherever there are open windows. (The other windows were divided with the clay dividing wall.) The new shim is created by sticking a piece of clear packing tape behind the two windows near the head. (See page 142, photograph 18). Tape is the perfect shim for this model because it will stick neatly to the resin statue.

NOTE: The purpose of a shim is to create a "floating" dividing wall. The shim will allow the silicone to split open inside of a window. Although this is a very brief explanation, it should make more sense after viewing the entire chapter.

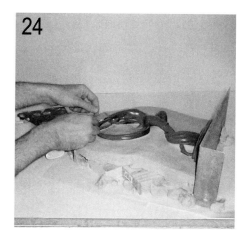

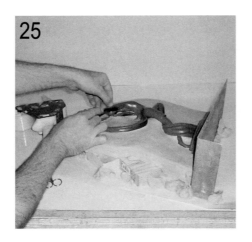

Fix The Shim

Use a detail tool to press the tape firmly onto the model. Use only enough tape to attach it to the statue. Then use a razor knife to trim off excess tape.

NOTE: The silicone will capture the texture of the tape just as it would the texture of the sculpture. Make the shim as clean as possible.

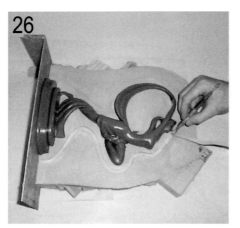

Cut A Zipper Key

Use a small loop tool to cut a zipper key around the entire perimeter of the model, leaving a ¼ inch space around the model. A zipper key must also be cut inside the larger window.

NOTE: The zipper key (also known as the linear grove key) method is the same as shown in Chapter 5 when making the two-piece mold of the urethane fish. (See page 83, photograph 4.)

Cut Cross Keys

A cross key is made by cutting a short groove across the main zipper key. The cross keys improve mold registration.

NOTE: A cross key should be cut ½ inch long.

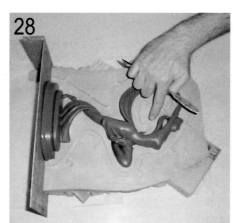

Clean The Zipper Key

When using a loop tool to cut a key, the clay will pull slightly upwards. Push the clay flat.

Apply The Parting Soap

Coat the model with thin layer of parting soap. Silicone will not stick to resin, but it will stick to fresh layer of spray paint. Since this model was spray painted for photographic clarity, it needs to be soaped.

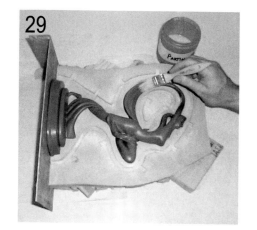

Remove Excess Parting Soap

Allow the soap to dry on the statue for ten minutes, then remove the excess soap with a dry paper towel.

NOTE: Parting soap is thick like melted Vaseline. It will leave brush marks on the surface if they are not buffed out with a dry paper towel. Brush marks will be captured by the silicone, creating the same texture on your finished castings.

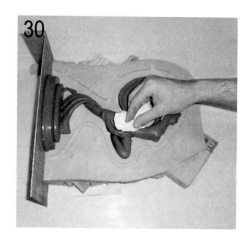

Section 2
Making the Silicone Liner

Needle a small batch of (regular setting) non-food grade silicone over the model.

NOTE: Liners are the silicone sections that fit into mother mold sections. This mold will have two silicone liners.

Use a brush to cover areas that did not get covered with the pour. Make sure to cover the entire surface of the statue and the clay dividing wall.

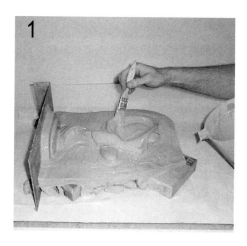

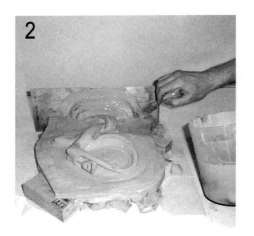

Build The Lip

Apply a small lip of silicone at least 1 inch wide, around the base of the statue. (See the casting on page 169, photo 6.)

NOTE: This is why the clink board was put on the bottom of the statue.

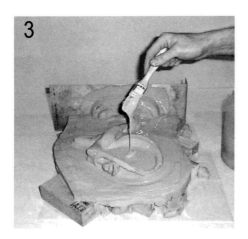

Make use of the excess silicone by pouring it into the interior of the oval window. Fill the zipper key grooves as well.

NOTE: The brush was used to scoop out the last bit of silicone from the mixing pale. The photograph was taken while the brush was draining into the oval window.

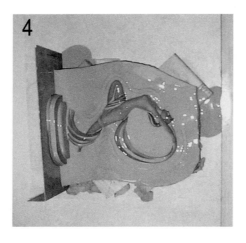

A top view of the first application of silicone. Notice that I did not apply silicone over every bit of the clay surface. It is important to only cover an area that extends ½ inch beyond the key line. Silicone that flowed beyond that point is going to be trimmed away.

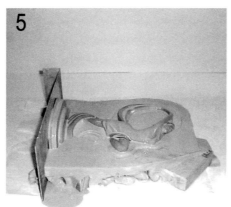

Allow the first layer of silicone to cure. It is expected that some silicone will drip over the sides of the dividing wall. Do not disturb the mold, just let the silicone drip.

NOTE: If the clay dividing wall had not been this level, much more silicone would have run off the mold.

Trim Off The Excess Cured Silicone

Use a razor knife to cut off the outer perimeter of silicone. Use the zipper key line as a reference point and trim ½ inch outside its perimeter. The goal is to leave a half inch boarder of exposed clay on the dividing wall. The exposed clay will be used to build the plaster mother mold. (See page 151, photograph 1.)

NOTE: An easy way to cut silicone is to pull the silicone (outwards) away from the knife while cutting. Do not pull hard, it may lift the silicone up off the clay.

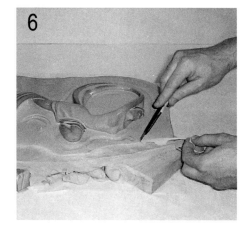

Apply Thickened Silicone To The Mold

Using a spade **tool**, thickened silicone is first applied to the FLAT surfaces of the clay dividing wall. There are many ways to apply thickened silicone. However, I have found that covering all of the flat surfaces first is the easiest.

This silicone blanket should not be more than ¼ inch thick. Making a thicker blanket than that will reduce the flexibility of the mold. A mold that does not flex easily, will crack the sugar casting when you demold it.

NOTE: The thickened silicone has been tinted for photographic clarity.

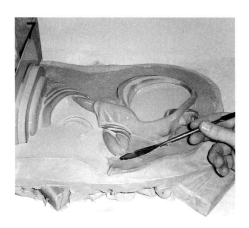

Top view of the mold.

The dividing wall has been covered with thickened silicone. Notice that the clay perimeter (trimmed in photograph 6) is left uncovered.

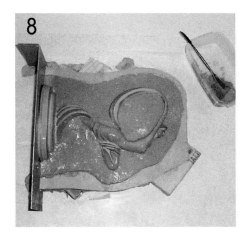

Next, cover the vertical edges of the figure with more thickened silicone.

NOTE: The work board has been rotated so that I can PULL the thickened silicone against the statue as it is applied. This will prevent air pockets from being trapped beneath the silicone.

It is important that each dab of silicone blends into the previous one. There must be pressure applied to the spade knife when pulling the silicone against the statue. Do not let the knife float lightly across the model. The silicone must be pressed onto the statue.

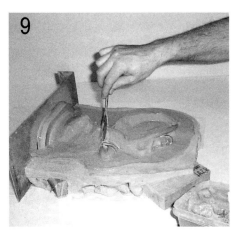

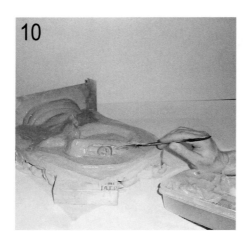

Apply Silicone Over The Windows

Special attention is given to the windows. Gently push silicone into the windows, being careful not to put to much pressure against the fragile tape shim.

NOTE: Be certain not to let any air pockets get trapped in the window area.

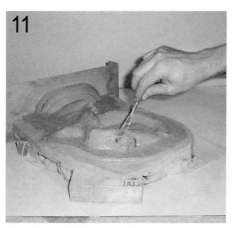

Draft The Silicone Liner

Fill the windows and then apply extra silicone over them to make the surface smooth. The surface should look like a ramp raising upwards towards the center of the model. (See page 149, photograph 16.)

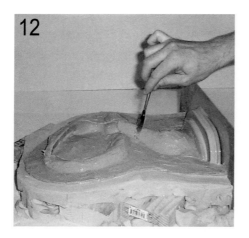

Next, rotate the mold on the work board so that the opposite side is facing forward. Repositioning the model allows me to PULL the silicone against the statue and is also a much more comfortable working posture.

NOTE: Always reposition the mold so that the silicone is pulled against the model. Having wax paper beneath the mold makes it easy to spin the mold around.

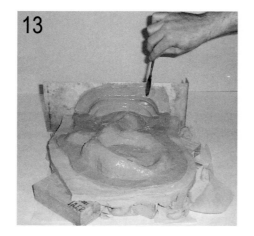

Apply The Silicone Lip

The mold is rotated again so that silicone can be pulled against the clink board. Build a 1 inch wide lip around the base of the sculpture.

NOTE: Having a lip around the pouring area of a mold is absolutely critical. It is difficult to explain the significance at this point. (See page 169, photograph 6 for more information.)

Apply Silicone To The Base Of The Figure, (Below The Lip)

Only one batch of silicone was needed to make the entire silicone liner. A thickened batch of silicone (with regular catalyst) will be workable for about one hour from the start of mixing. From experience, I know that I can work fast enough to apply a 1½ pound batch of silicone before it begins to cure.

NOTE: Silicone will bond to itself perfectly. If the silicone batch had been too small, more could be added directly on top of the first batch.

HELPFUL HINT: Unused silicone from a batch can be put in the freezer to slow the curing and will be usable for another day or two.

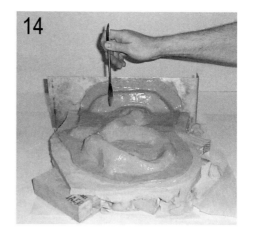

Shape The Perimeter Of The Liner

This is important. The silicone will get tacky in about 40 minutes. This is the perfect time to use the spade tool to compress the outer edge of the liner. The edge of the liner should look as if there is a small step on top of the clay wall. This step will be a significant registration point for the mother mold and the liner.

NOTE: While the silicone is tacky, smooth out the surface of the liner. Clean the spade tool and gently pull it over every bumpy surface of the liner. Keep the spade clean, or it will drag the material instead of smoothing it. Make the surface as smooth as possible.

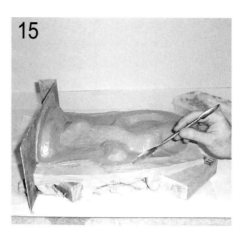

Check The Draft Of The Liner

A ruler is being used to visually exaggerate the angle (draft) that has been deliberately created (built up) along the raised sides of the statue. This draft is a critical design component in the mold.

Eventually, a plaster mother mold will fit directly over the silicone liner. The plaster mother mold must be able to slip easily off of the liner. (See pages 156–157, photographs 18 and 23.)

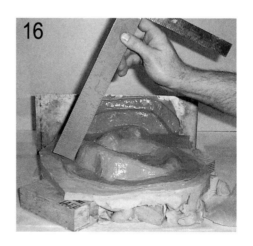

Attach Silicone Rubber Registration Keys

While the silicone liner is still tacky, small chunks of silicone are set into the surface of the liner. These silicone chunks are actually strips of cured silicone that have been cut into cubes. (See the ruler, blade and silicone to the left that were used to cut them.) The rubber keys will bond to the tacky silicone. The rubber keys will provide registration between the silicone blanket and the plaster mother mold.

NOTE: The keys should not be more than ¼ inch thick.

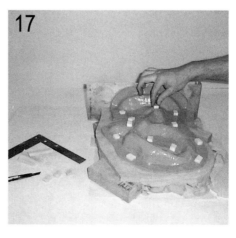

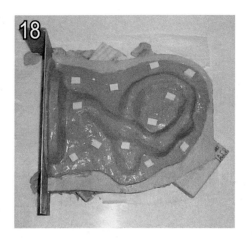

Rubber Mold Key Placement

The keys are only applied to flat (horizontal) surfaces. Putting keys on vertical surfaces will prevent the mother mold from sliding off the silicone liner.

Allow silicone to cure 24 hours.

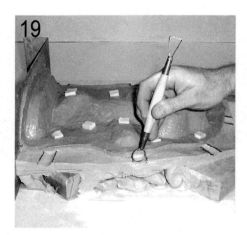

Cut Registration Keys In The Clay Dividing Wall

Use the round end of a trimming tool to cut the keys. These keys will become the registration keys that align the two plaster mother mold sections.

NOTE: Only the tip of the trimming tool is used to cut the keys. DO NOT CUT THE KEYS TOO DEEP.

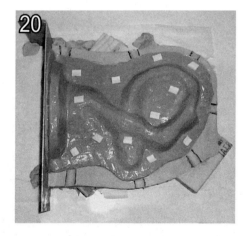

A view of the completed silicone liner. Next, a mother mold will be built over the liner.

NOTE: Registration keys have been cut in the clay dividing wall every three inches.

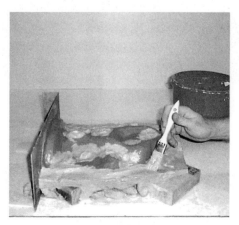

Section 3
Making the First
Mother Mold Section

Creamy plaster is brushed over the clay dividing wall and rubber mold keys. Creamy plaster will flow in and around the mold keys better than thick plaster. In order for the mold keys to work well, the plaster must cover the keys accurately.

After applying the creamy plaster, allow the same batch to thicken (just wait a few minutes). At this point the plaster will feel like soft butter. Continue by putting the plaster along the flat surfaces. At this point the plaster is still too soft to hold its own shape. The dividing wall provides a flat surface for the plaster to settle onto.

NOTE: It is a mistake to try and cover the high points of the statue while the plaster is still creamy. Creamy plaster will just drip down the sides of the high points, so wait a few more minutes for it to thicken.

To work with plaster successfully, you need to understand the various stages it goes through while it sets. (See appendix for more information.)

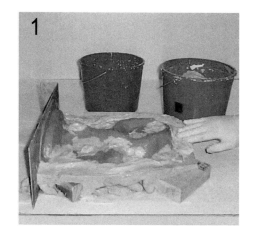

A few minutes later... The plaster has become quite thick.

Once the plaster has become paste-like it can be applied over the high points. Work fast. In only a few minutes the plaster will become too thick to work.

NOTE: A handful of chopped glass strand was added to the plaster mix (when it was creamy). These strands add extra strength to the plaster permitting the plaster to be much thinner and lightweight.

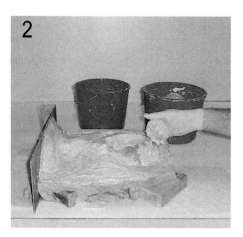

Smooth The Plaster Surface

Use a wet brush (or sponge) to smooth the plaster surface. Glass strands become will be very sharp if they are not blended into the plaster at this time (before the plaster sets).

NOTE: The entire plaster mother mold section was applied in less than 15 minutes.

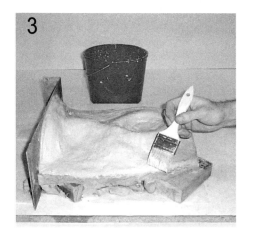

Top view of the mother mold. Let the plaster set for at least one hour.

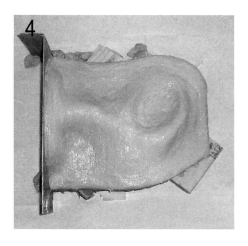

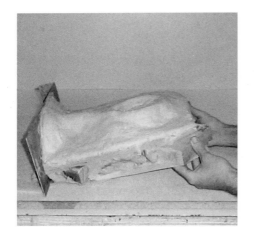

Section 4
Making the Second Half of the Mother Mold

Allow the plaster to set. Flip the entire mold over.

NOTE: This is where the use of wax paper beneath the model proves critical. If there had not been any paper, the clay would have been stuck to the work board. Prying a mold off the table is not a good use of your time.

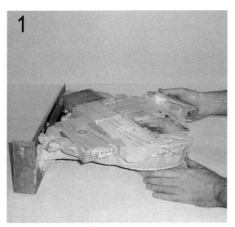

The mold is now seen upside down. This mess is the bottom of the clay dividing wall. Notice how much space the wood blocks filled in.

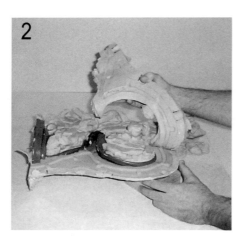

Remove The Clay Dividing Wall

Removed debris from the clay so that it can be saved for reuse.

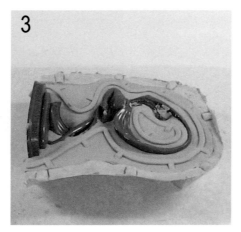

Halfway Done

Notice how every negative impression, key and groove that was cut into the clay is now 100% silicone.

NOTE: The half round cut outs (outer-most perimeter of the plaster mother mold) are now plaster registration keys. (Remember page 150, picture 19.)

Super Clean The Silicone Liner

EVERY BIT of clay should be removed from the mold. The pick **tool** (shown in the photograph) is the perfect tool for scraping clay away from the edges of the statue. Make the surface of the silicone liner as clean as possible; the cleaner the surface, the tighter fitting the mold will be.

NOTE: Remember to remove the tape that was used to make the shim near the head.

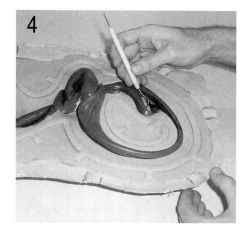

Soap The Figurine And The Surface Of The Mother Mold

IMPORTANT: Parting soap must be applied to the exposed surface of the mother mold section. This includes the entire plaster perimeter, including mold keys that are visible surrounding the silicone liner.

Apply two layers of parting soap on the plaster face. The second mother mold section will stick to the first if parting soap is not used to separate them.

NOTE: Do not put soap on the silicone. (See next step.)

Coat The Silicone With Vaseline

UNBELIEVABLY IMPORTANT: The silicone blanket MUST be coated with a thin layer of Vaseline. Use a heat gun to melt the Vaseline.

NOTE: Vaseline is used instead of parting soap because parting soap will not stick to the silicone.

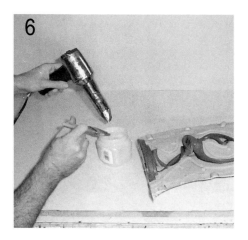

Brush Vaseline on to and in EVERY visible silicone surface. The next layer of silicone will stick to any area that is not coated with Vaseline.

NOTE: Remember to brush Vaseline in the small window area near the head.

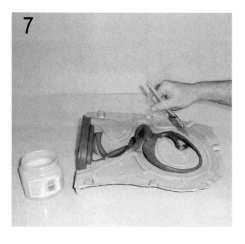

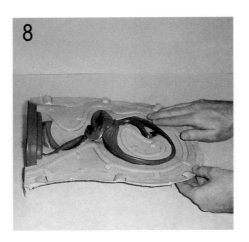

Blend In The Vaseline

Rubbing the Vaseline on the liner with your hands is the best way to verify that there is a sufficient coating of Vaseline. It is important to make sure that **ALL** of the silicone is coated. If it is not, the next layer of silicone will stick to it.

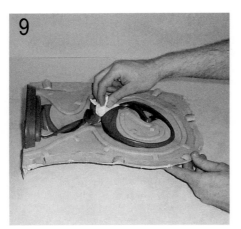

Clean The Model

Wipe off any Vaseline fingerprints or smears.

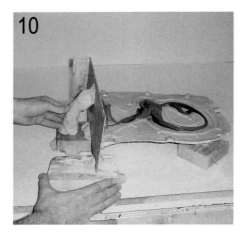

Reposition The Clink Board At The Base Of The Figurine

Notice that the clink board is resting on wood blocks. This was needed to make the clink board two inches taller than the base of the model. Use clay to hold it in position.

Needle The First Layer Of The Second Silicone Liner

Repeat the same steps that were shown earlier and needle the silicone over the model.

NOTE: The bottom half of the mold has been propped up with blocks of wood and clay to help the mold remain stable on the work board. Elevate the front of the mold so that the dividing wall is parallel with the table top.

Allow the silicone to cure 24 hours.

Clean Up The First Layer Of Silicone

Trim the first layer of silicone to mirror the edge of silicone beneath it. Both silicone liners need to have the same profile.

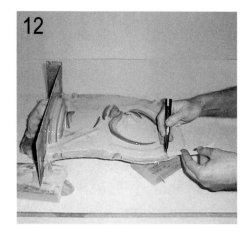

Apply The Thickened Silicone

The thickened silicone is applied on the flat surfaces, the exact same way as shown before. Remember to draft the silicone along the vertical edges, then attach the silicone keys. (See page 148–150, photographs 11–20.)

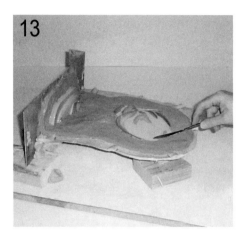

Soap The Plaster Dividing Wall

For a clean separation between the second mother mold section and the first, the dividing wall needs to be soaped one more time.

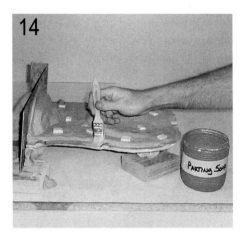

Add The Second Mother Mold Section

Apply a creamy layer of plaster over the registration keys and along the plaster dividing wall. Follow the same steps as before. (See page 151, photographs 1–3.)

Finish applying the plaster.

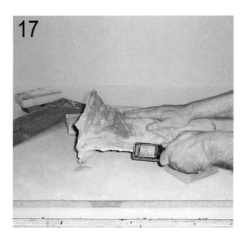

Shape The Mother Mold

Once the plaster has set, remove the clink board and shave the edges of the mother mold with SurForm™.

NOTE: Shaving the edges removes plaster that has dripped onto the first mother mold section. If the parting line is not shaved clean, it will be difficult to split the mold.

Split The Mold

Use a **mud knife** to split open the mold, but be careful not to cut through any of the plaster registration keys.

NOTE: Splitting a small mold like this should be easy to do. Place the mud knife in several different locations along the dividing wall. Do not try to split the mold from just one corner or else the mother mold will chip or break. If a mold is stuck together, chances are that there was not enough parting soap between the two mother mold sections. Use some force to split the mold.

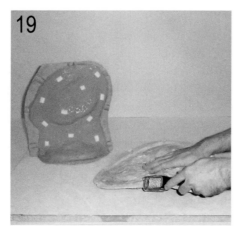

Use the SurForm™ to shave off all of the sharp edges around the perimeter. Do not shave any areas inside of the mother mold.

Seal The Mother Mold For Longevity

HELPFUL HINT: Apply mold soap liberally to the interior of the mother mold. At some point during casting, chocolate or sugar will get inside the interior of the mother mold. If there is a good layer of parting soap, the chocolate or sugar will not stick to the plaster and clean up will be easy.

If you do not soap the inside of the mother mold, a single leak can affect the registration of the mold.

NOTE: If the interior of the mother mold is not sealed, the plaster will absorb the oils from the silicone liner causing it to dry out over time.

Remove the silicone liner by gently peeling the two silicone liners apart.

Splice The Mold

This is a bit tricky to explain. Look back at the introduction photograph to this chapter and notice that one foot protrudes away from the body. In order to cover the foot, a lot of extra silicone had to be used to surround it. Extra thick silicone reduces the molds flexibility. This is just the opposite of what is needed. Remember, the foot will be a delicate part in sugar and must be able to be pulled out of the silicone liner without any stress.

Splicing the mold (cutting a pressure relieving slice) through the silicone that is covering the foot, will help the sugar casting to release from the silicone without breaking.

The second mother mold section is removed.

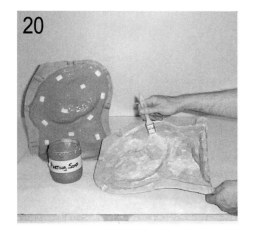

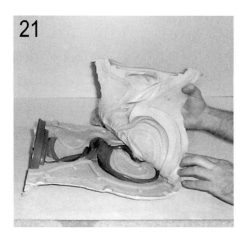

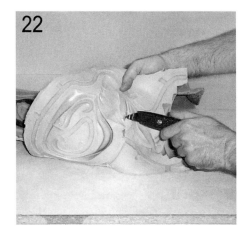

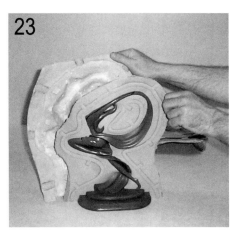

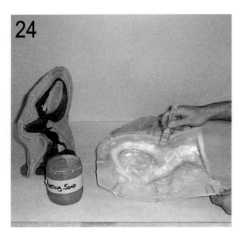

Soap the interior of the other side of the mother mold.

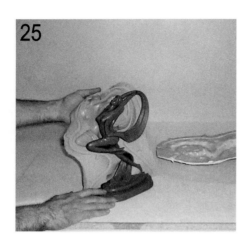

Remove the second silicone liner from the statue.

View of the finished brush applied silicone mold.

Section 5
Creating a Support Frame

The figurine mold can be set upside-down in a box or a
milk crate during casting. This is an acceptable method for
limited castings, but is clumsy for production. The following
illustrations will show how a plastic pipe frame is built onto
the mother mold so that it will be self-supporting and level
during casting.

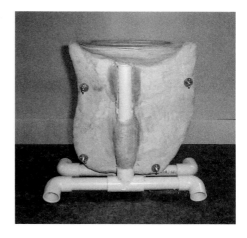

Drill Bolt Holes Into The Mother Mold

Remove the silicone liner and drill three or four ¼ inch holes
through one side of the mother mold. Always drill from
the *inside* of the mother mold to the *outside* and never drill
through an area that the silicone liner comes into contact
with. Drill only on the outer most edge of the mother mold.

NOTE: Drilling from the *outside* of the mold to the *inside* will
cause the mother mold to chip.

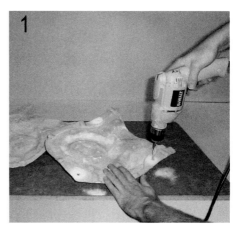

Drill The Second Side Of The Mother Mold

Clean off the debris from the first drilling and place the
empty mother mold section (that has already been drilled)
on top of the second mother mold section. Use the first drill
holes as a guide to drill through the second section

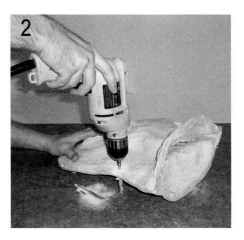

Clean off the mother mold.

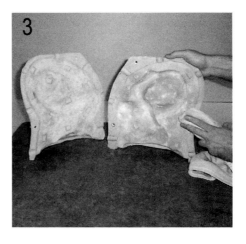

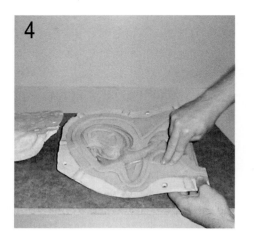

Re-**seat** The Silicone Liner

Put Vaseline in every registration key inside the plaster mother mold as this will help the rubber keys on the silicone liner fit into their matching key in the plaster. Press the liner into its mother mold, making sure that all of the rubber registration keys slip into the recessed keys in the mother mold.

NOTE: Check the fit by pressing down on all areas of the liner. A properly seated liner will not bulge (when pushed on) in the mother mold. It should feel like a solid surface is behind the liner.

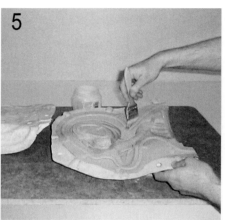

Grease The Zipper Key

Apply Vaseline on the zipper key. The Vaseline will help the two silicone liners fit together with minimal friction. Do this every time before strapping the mold together.

NOTE: Be careful not to get any Vaseline on the detail (statue) surface of the silicone liner.

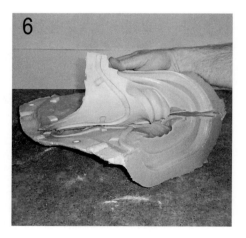

Seat The Mold

The second liner is carefully placed on top of the first. Press the two sections together along the perimeter of the silicone. You will feel the zipper key slide into place.

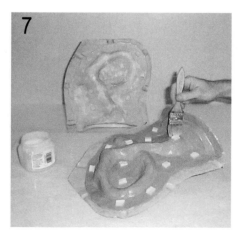

Put a liberal amount of Vaseline on the rubber keys.

NOT SHOWN: Put Vaseline in the recessed keys of the mother mold (seen in the background).

The second mother mold section is put on the mold.

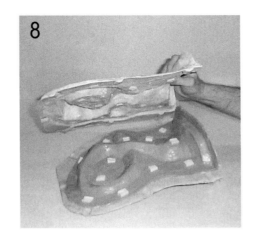

Bolt The Mold Together

Put a washer on both sides of the bolt. Use wing nuts so that the bolts can be tightened by hand. Do not tighten them too much as this can crack the mother mold, especially if the bolt hole is really close to the edge of the mold.

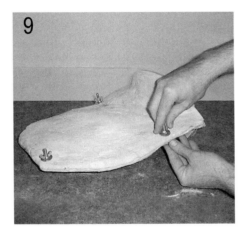

Cut The Plastic Pipe

Two sections of plastic pipe are cut slightly shorter than the overall height of the mold. Each pipe is wrapped in wax paper and is taped to the pipe.

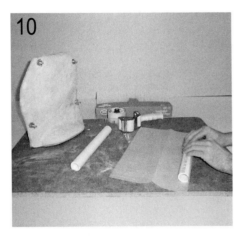

Attach The Pipe

The pipe is then strapped onto the side of the mold. Position the pipe in the middle of each side of the mother mold, pulling the pipes up so that the ends are equal with the top of the mold.

NOTE: The pipes will not sit flat against the mother mold. This will be remedied in the next step.

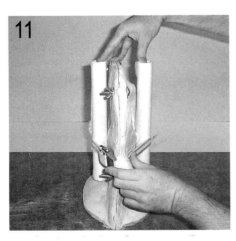

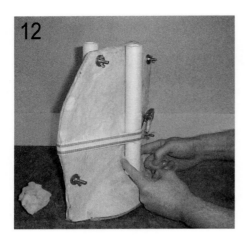

Center The Pipe

Use clay to shim the pipe so that it runs vertically up the side of the mother mold.

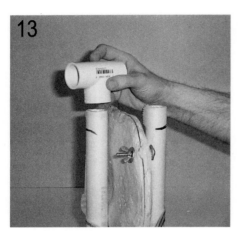

Fit a plastic T onto the top of the pipe and mark (with a pen) where the bottom of it ends, then remove the T.

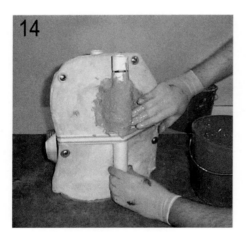

Put plaster over the pipe and connect it to the mother mold.

NOTE: Plaster does not always bond to itself well. To make plaster stick to itself it may be necessary to scratch up the surface of the mother mold. Spray the outside of the mother mold with water. Wet plaster sticks best to wet plaster and the rough surface will help the next layer of plaster bond to itself.

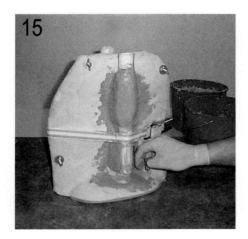

Put plaster behind the pipe, covering the clay shim with plaster. Fill in the area behind the pipe as much as possible, but be careful not to cover the pipe above the mark for the T fitting.

Smooth out the plaster with a wet brush or sponge.

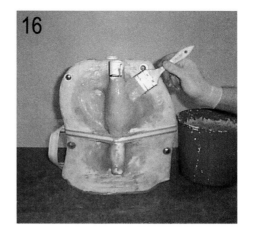

Let the plaster set. The pipe is not perfectly vertical… that is OK.

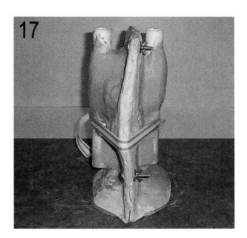

The straps are removed and the plastic T is fitted onto the pipe. Do not glue the T on, as it is meant to be removable.

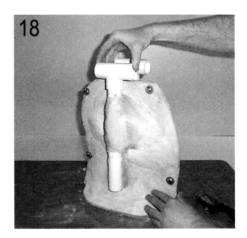

Two stubs of pipe are fitted into the T. They should be long enough to extend a few inches wider than the mold. Do not glue them.

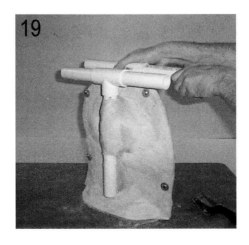

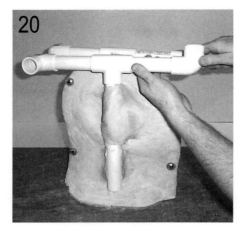

Plastic elbows are put at each end of the pipe stubs. Do not glue them either as they should be able to rotate slightly with force.

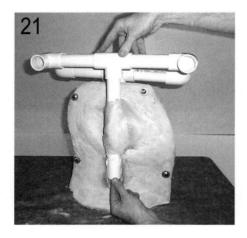

The pipe is slid off of the mother mold. This is easy to do because it was wrapped with wax paper.

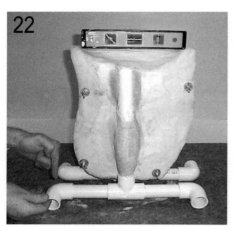

Take off the wax paper and put the pipes back into their sleeves. Position the pipes by twisting the elbows at the bottom of the mold and make the mold level (in one direction).

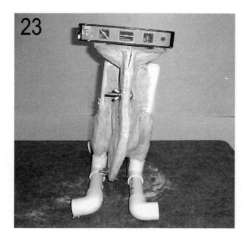

The mold is level in one direction but not the other. (See next step.)

One piece of pipe is slid upwards in the sleeve to raise the mold. Use a level to check for proper position. The pipe is held in place by hand while drilling a small hole through the plaster and the pipe. Do not drill through the mother mold, only the first wall of the pipe.

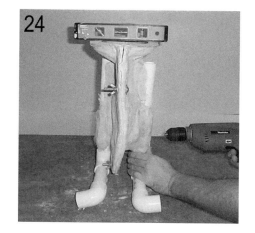

A drywall screw is twisted into the drill hole, leaving the other pipe undisturbed. The drywall screw is a set screw that holds the pipe in place.

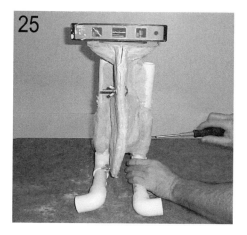

Both pipes can be removed at any time allowing for easy mold storage or reuse of plastic components.

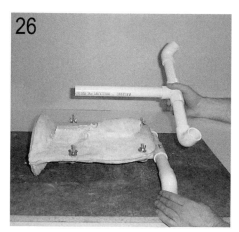

View of the finished mold. With support frame to hold it level.

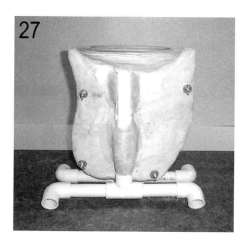

The figure is positioned upright to peel off the second liner. Chef Pfeiffer holds the base of the sculpture while pulling the liner in a downward motion. Keeping the statue upright while removing the second liner is the best way to support the casting. Pulling the liner downward transfers any pressure towards the base of the sculpture where it has the most strength.

NOTE: Remember, when Chef Pfeiffer removed the first liner, the sculpture had extra stability because it was resting in the second half of the mother mold. While de-molding the second liner, there is nothing to support the casting except its own structure.

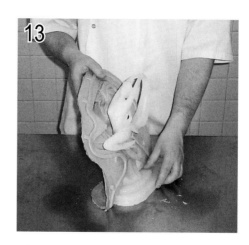

A view of the cast Isomalt sculpture.

NOT SHOWN: The casting seam lines were scraped off the casting with a razor knife. If the seam lines are not removed, they will become highly visible when the statue is airbrushed.

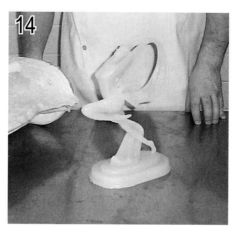

The finished casting can be decorated by airbrushing.

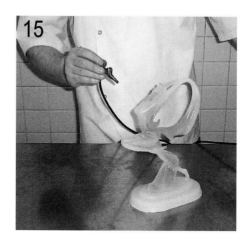

An endless variety of airbrushed patterns can be applied to the surface. However, Chef Pfeiffer preferred to keep the appearance clean and simple.

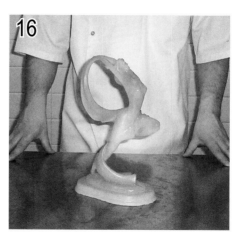

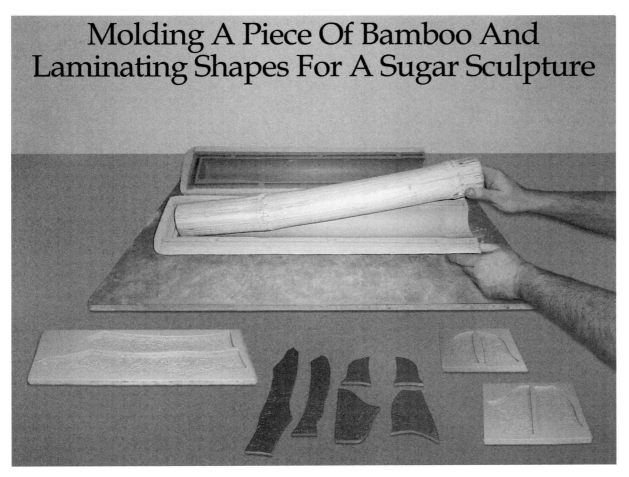

In this chapter, Chef Ewald Notter introduces a very useful technique that integrates a balance between both mold making and sugar handling. The mold making required for this sculpture began with a very specific design plan by Chef Notter. He chose to use a bamboo section and six laminated shapes to create an oriental style display. The design will allow him to assemble the laminated shapes into small oriental figurines. The bamboo mold will be used to cast a screen-like background behind the figures. The processes used to create the display piece could be adapted to create unlimited variations.

This process combines two mold making techniques. The first technique will show how to make a two-piece silicone mold of the bamboo section. The second section will show how the laminated cut-outs were created.

PLEASE NOTE: The instructional text accompanying the photographs in the upcoming chapters will become more and more abbreviated. This is because many of the steps shown have already been explained in previous chapters.

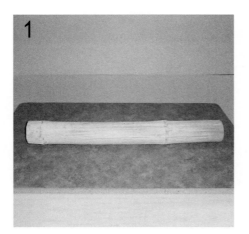

The model is a 25-inch long section of bamboo.

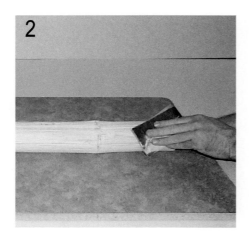

Prepare the model by sanding the surface with a fine grade sandpaper.

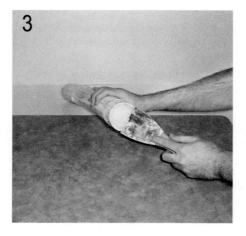

Fill both of the open ends with oil clay and flatten the clay flush with the bamboo.

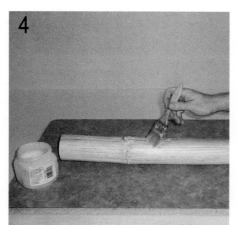

Coat The Model With Vaseline

NOTE: As shown before, a heat gun was used to melt the Vaseline.

The end cap is removed.

Section 2

Making a
Two-Piece
Plaster Mother
Mold for the
Bamboo Liner

A 1½ inch wide piece of pine is attached to the end of the mold to replace the end cap.

The wooden surfaces are coated with Vaseline a second time.

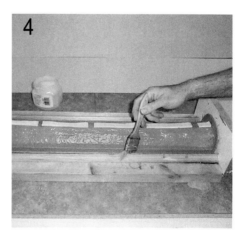

The mother mold is applied as described in previous chapters. A creamy layer of plaster should be brushed along the edges of the silicone blanket and over the rubber keys.

Finish the mother mold by applying plaster and chopped glass strands. Use the same technique as shown earlier in the book.

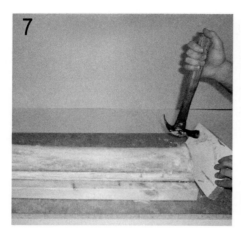

Next, the dividing wall will be disassembled.

After the mother mold has set, remove the end cap at the top of the mold and save it for reuse.

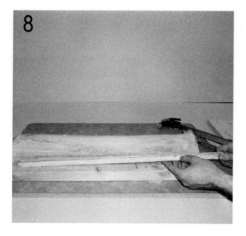

Remove the corner moulding.

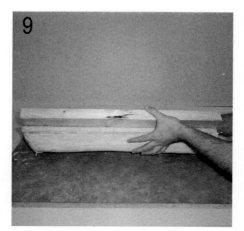

Flip the mold over.

Remove the pine dividing wall.

DO NOT REMOVE THE BAMBOO.

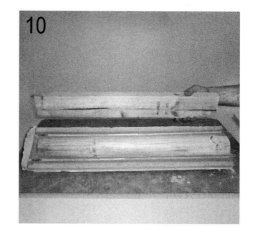

Section 2

Making a
Two-Piece
Plaster Mother
Mold for the
Bamboo Liner

Carefully pry the balsa wood strip keys out of the silicone liner with a screw driver.

Shave down the sharp edges on the mother mold.

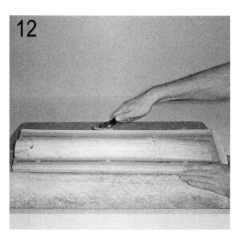

Prepare To Make The Second Silicone Liner

Coat all exposed silicone surfaces with Vaseline. It is critical to brush Vaseline inside the strip key groove.

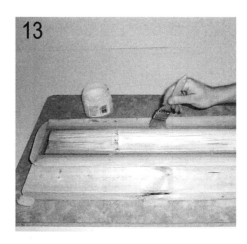

Reposition the end cap at the top of the bamboo and secure the wood in place with clay.

NOTE: Use a fettling knife to apply a small coil of clay into the gap between the bamboo and the end cap.

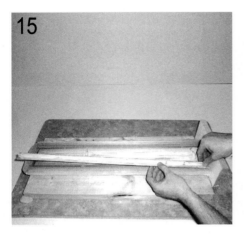

Reposition the two strips of corner molding so that each one sits directly on top of the first mother mold section.

NOTE: This step is exactly the same as seen on page 176, photograph 11. The main difference is that the corner molding is being attached to the mother mold, not to the pine dividing wall.

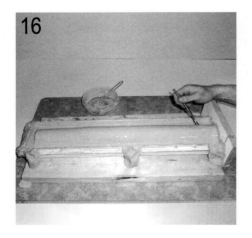

Apply the first layer of fast-setting silicone. The next 11 steps repeat the techniques used to make the first mother mold section.

NOTE: Columns of clay instead of brad nails are holding the wood moulding in place.

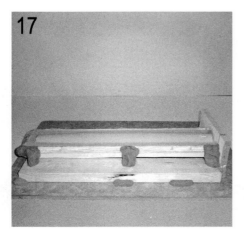

Allow the silicone to cure.

NOTE: Wood has been positioned under the mold so that the round mother mold cannot roll on the table. (See page 184, photograph 22.)

Apply a second layer of thickened silicone only over the raised bamboo surface.

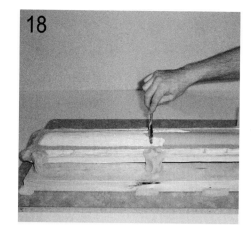

Section 2

Making a
Two-Piece
Plaster Mother
Mold for the
Bamboo Liner

Apply the silicone rubber mold keys remembering to apply the 1 inch silicone lip at the top of the mold.

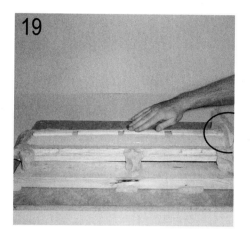

Allow the silicone to cure, then remove the corner molding and save it for reuse.

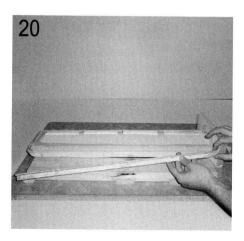

Trim the silicone flash by cutting off any silicone that seeped beneath the wooden corner molding.

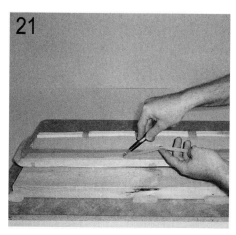

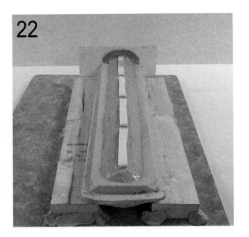

22

The orientation view of the completed silicone liner. Notice the pine wood under the mold. It is not a dividing wall. It is used to stabilize the mold so that it does not roll on the table.

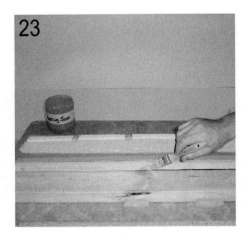

23

Soap the thin plaster wall of the mother mold section.

24

Apply the plaster mother mold section and follow the same steps that were shown earlier.

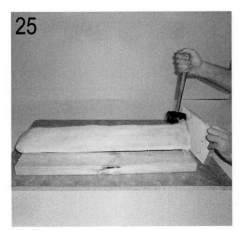

25

Allow the plaster to set, then remove the end cap.

Shave the seam line with a SurForm™. This will help reveal the exact parting line. Knowing the exact location of the parting line will make it easier to split the mold.

HELPFUL HINT: When making a two-piece mother mold, pigment one section with red iron oxide to help you identify the parting line.

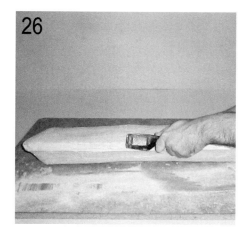

Section 2

Making a
Two-Piece
Plaster Mother
Mold for the
Bamboo Liner

Split the mold.

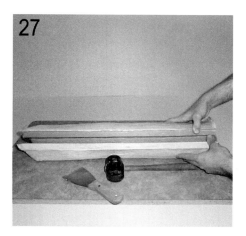

Remove the top section of the mother mold to expose the silicone liner.

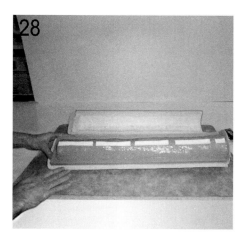

Remove the silicone liner.

NOTE: The result of using the balsa wood strip key is easy to see in this picture as the key line completely encircles the bamboo model.

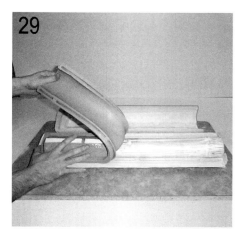

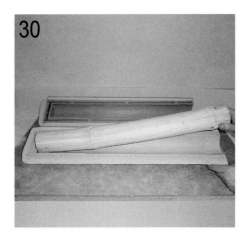

Remove the bamboo.

Remove the second silicone liner.

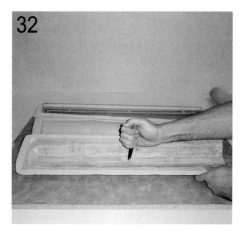

Carve out the center mold keys. Some of the recessed keys in the plaster mother mold must be slightly widened so that the rubber keys fit into them more easily.

NOTE: Rubber mold keys are cut by hand and are therefore, often irregular in shape. Some keys end up fitting too tightly in the mother mold. This is common, so shaving some of the plaster out of the mother mold will not harm the registration. A rubber registration key should securely, yet easily fit into the mother mold.

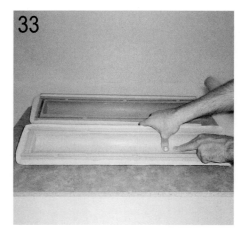

Reassemble The Mold

The rubber keys are pressed into the recessed keys in the mother mold on both separate mold halves.

NOTE: It is important to discover the best way to reassemble a particular mold. The bamboo mold fits together best when each liner has been put into its own mother mold section before placing both halves together.

Section 3
Assembling the Figurines

Chef Notter will demonstrate how he assembles the figurines.

Chef Notter twists the longest Isomalt section to form the body of the figurine.

NOTE: The Isomalt castings were placed in an oven (on a Silpat® mat) at 71° C/160° F to make them flexible again.

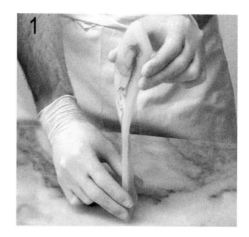

He positions the arched base so that the body of the figurine can be attached to it.

NOTE: The arched base was shaped in photograph 13 on the previous page.

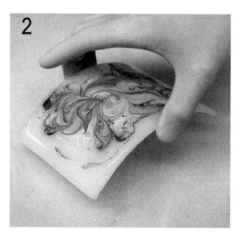

Chef Notter uses an alcohol burner to melt the bottom edge of the Isomalt body.

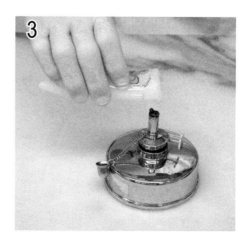

Chef Notter has attached the body to the base and is now attaching the arms onto the body. He is holding the arm in position until the bond cools.

NOTE: The ends of the arms were melted with the alcohol lamp so that they could be glued onto the body. (The arms are reshaped and attached to the body in the same way that Chef Pfeiffer shaped and attached the fins to the fish in Chapter 9.)

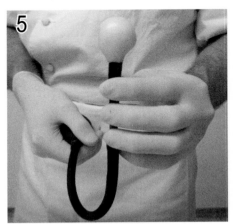

Chef Notter uses a small pump to blow a small sugar sphere. The ball will be used as the head of the figurine.

The Chef uses the alcohol burner to melt the base of the head.

He attaches the head onto the body of the figurine.

Chef Notter finishes the head of the figurine by pulling a small amount of black sugar for the hair and painting features onto the face.

NOTE: He has also pulled a small piece of sugar to create a belt around the waist of the figurine.

Chef Notter positions the entire figurine and base on top of a small pool of hot Isomalt. The hot Isomalt has been poured onto a Silpat® mat and can be released from the mat after the sugar cools.

He has completed both figurines and is preparing to position them on a larger base. A large pool of Isomalt sugar has been poured over a sheet of wrinkled tin foil, the resulting effect creates an attractive watery look.

Placed above the "water", the figures stand elegantly on their small arched (bridge) bases.

Chef Notter prepares to finish the showpiece by creating a bamboo screen behind the figures. Each section of bamboo has been cut with a hot knife to create varying heights. To mount the bamboo to the display, Chef Notter places one end of the bamboo into a hot pool of Isomalt on the Silpat® mat. He uses the hot Isomalt as a glue to attach the bamboo atop the hardened pool of sugar.

A view of the beautiful finished showpiece.

NOTE: Additional information on working with sugar, including the blowing and pulling techniques seen in photograph 5 and 8 can be found in Chef Notter's book, *That's Sugar*. (See the supplier list for Chef Notter's contact information.)

Making a Variety of Molds for An M.O.F. Competition

Competing for the prestigious M.O.F. (Meilleur Ouvrier de France) title, Chef Sebastien Canonne uses a variety of molds to cast several components for his buffet display. Chef Canonne's buffet design required that innovative mold making techniques be developed. (In particular, the apple mold which is designed so that it does not create a seam line in the final casting.) To help identify the various molds pictured above, corresponding letters (on the molds) have been matched with the itemized list below.

> A. Soft silicone molds made from dried gourds for casting tallow.
> B. Two-piece molds made from plastic lids for press-molding cookies.
> C. Soft silicone mold of a toy snake for casting hot sugar.
> D. Two-piece "plug" mold of a real apple for casting hot sugar.
> E. Molds of three acrylic spheres for casting translucent hot sugar.

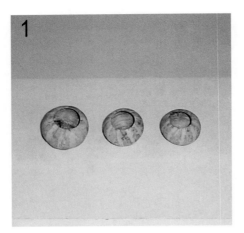

The gourds were part of a dried flower arrangement from a craft store.

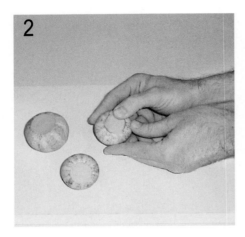

Fill the gourds with clay.

NOTE: It is important to fill the gourds so that they do not float when silicone is poured over them.

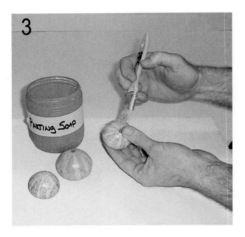

Soap the gourds.

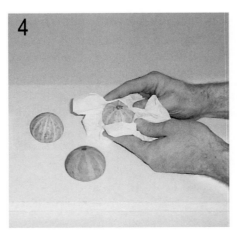

Buff off the excess parting soap.

The head of the snake is nailed onto the work board. A small nail is held in place with pliers then hammered through the snake and into the work board.

NOTE: The hot glue was not strong enough to hold the head down. (The toy snake was originally made with an upwards bend in its neck and would not sit flat on the table.)

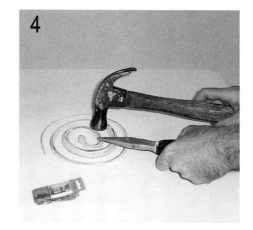

Small coils of clay are used to fill in gaps under the belly of the snake.

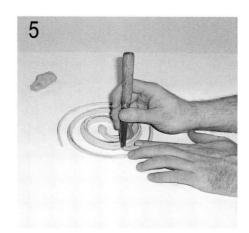

A mold box is assembled around the snake.

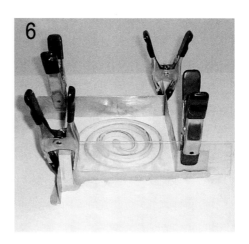

A batch of fast-setting, non-food grade silicone (20% thinner, 10% fast catalyst) is needled over the snake. The intention is to pour a small amount of silicone over the snake so that it will cure quickly and hold the snake securely to the work board.

NOTE: If regular (24 hours) catalyst had been used, the silicone would be liquid for a very long time. In that time, it is possible that the natural shape of the snake could flex off the work board allowing silicone to flash beneath the entire snake.

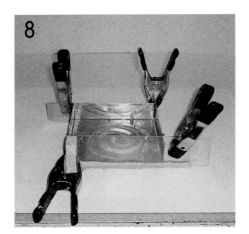

Allow the thin layer fast-setting silicone to cure.

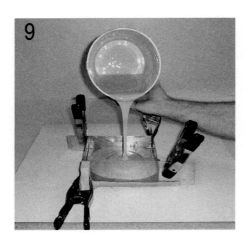

A second batch of silicone with regular catalyst is poured into the box. This batch has 20% thinner added to make the mold as soft as possible.

NOTE: The silicone is only poured ⅛ inch above the top of the snake. If the mold is too thick above the snake, it will not flex well. If the mold does not flex well, it will crack the sugar casting when the chef tries to de-mold it.

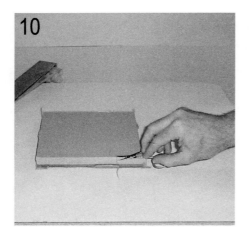

After the silicone cures, the mold box is removed and the mold is cleaned up.

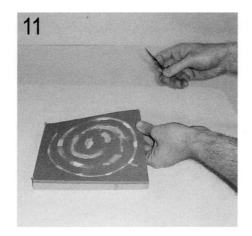

The mold is flipped over. Notice how much silicone flashed beneath the snake.

Carefully trim the flash that is "locking" the snake into the mold.

Remove the snake and trim away the flash from all sides of the snake body.

NOTE: Use caution when trimming a soft silicone mold as soft silicone does not cut easily. When a mold is very soft, the silicone stretches with the pressure of the scissors making it easy to cut gouges into the mold. A gouge cannot be repaired and the flaw will show up in every sugar casting.

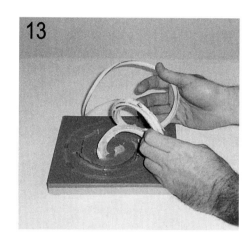

Top view of the completed mold.

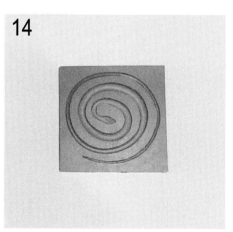

Section 4
Making a Plaster Model of an Apple

Shown here is the original apple, the mold and the plaster apple.

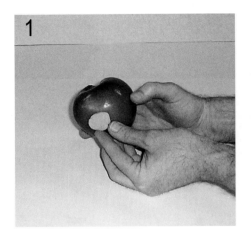

A ball of clay is put on the back of the apple. The clay will adhere the apple onto the work board.

It is important to understand basic logic of the clay placement. The position of the clay is exactly where the liquid plaster will be poured into the finished mold. Always design a mold with the understanding that the silicone mold should be filled (cast) from the least visible point. (In this case, the side opposite the bite mark will be the least visible area.) The reason for this is that the **pouring gate** (clay area) will require the most clean up after the casting is removed from the mold. When it is possible, design the mold so that the pouring gate is on a smooth surface. Smooth surfaces are easier to reconstruct on the final casting.

Press the apple onto the work board. The clay to hold the apple in position.

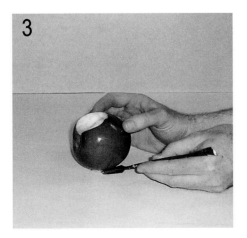

Use a detail tool to remove excess clay from the bottom of the apple.

A mold box is assembled around the apple (leaving about a ¼ inch space between the apple and the box). A batch of non-food grade silicone (with regrind) is poured into the box.

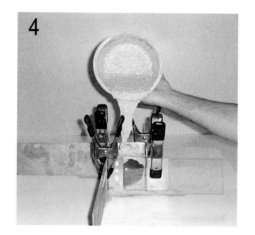

The silicone is allowed to cure and the mold is cleaned up.

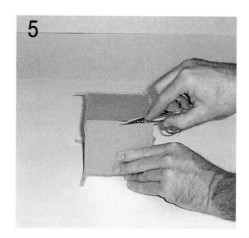

A **groove knife** is used to cut the mold open.

DO NOT CUT THE MOLD IN TWO HALVES. It is only necessary to cut the mold *halfway* down on both sides.

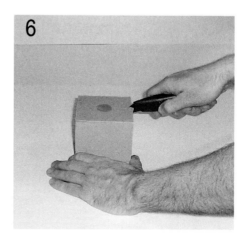

The apple is removed from the mold.

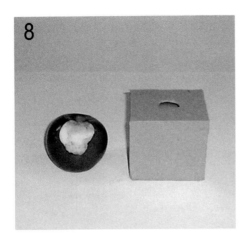

A view of the finished mold and the original model.

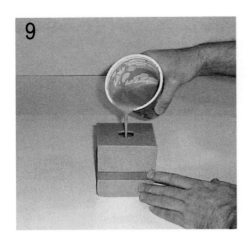

Next, a plaster model is poured.

First, the silicone mold is banded together with a large rubber band. Then fill the mold half way with plaster.

NOTE: Do not use bands that squeeze the mold so tightly that it distorts the mold. Packing tape could also be used in place of rubber bands.

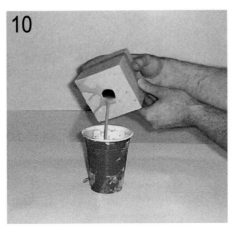

Rotate the mold while draining it. This will force plaster to coat the entire interior surface of the mold. This is called **slush casting** and helps to prevent air bubbles from being trapped on the surface of the casting.

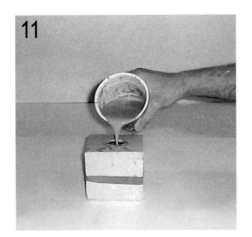

Refill the silicone mold with the same batch of plaster. Slushing can be repeated 2 or 3 times. However, slushing a mold with watery plaster will have virtually no effect. Wait until the plaster attains a thick creamy consistency.

Jog the mold by tapping all four sides of the mold. This will create a slight vibration in the mold that will help air bubbles rise up towards the open pouring gate.

Use a mud knife to scrape the plaster flush with the top of the mold.

Allow the plaster to set for a few hours, then remove the casting.

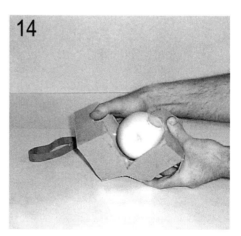

Use a SurForm™ to shave down the raised plaster "knot" around the pouring gate. A SurForm™ removes plaster quickly, but can leave heavy cut marks. It will be necessary to use wet-dry sandpaper to smooth out the cut marks.

NOTE: It is now easy to see why a pouring gate placed on the smooth surface of a model is easy to clean up.

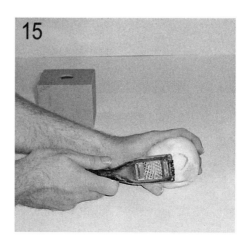

Buff the plaster apple. The cotton buffing wheel will create a dull shine on the Hydrocal casting.

NOTE: Dense plasters such as Hydrocal buff well. Softer materials like **Number 1 Molding plaster** do not.

A view of the apple, mold and finished plaster model.

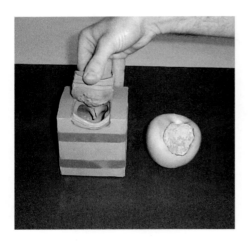

Section 5
Making a Two-Piece Plug Mold

A **plug mold** is a type of mold that is used when it is necessary to hide all traces of seam lines and pouring holes in the finished casting. Removing a seam lines by sanding and buffing is easy to do on a plaster model, but is impossible to do on a sugar casting.

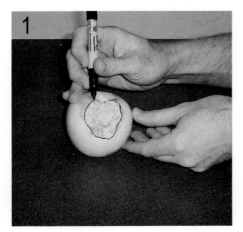

A line is drawn around the exact perimeter of the bite mark.

NOTE: The perimeter of the bite mark will become the **pouring gate** for the plug mold.

Stabilize the apple on the work board with clay. The apple is positioned so that the bite side is facing up on the work board.

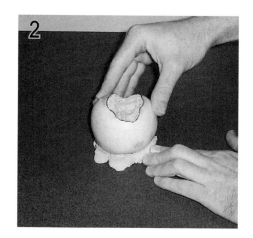

Section 5

Making a
Two-Piece
Plug Mold of
the Plaster
Apple

Coils of clay are used to make a dividing wall around the bite mark.

NOTE: The clay must make a watertight seal around the bite mark.

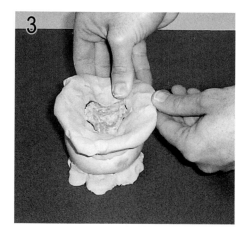

The dividing wall is tapered inwards like a funnel (towards the bite mark). A sculpting tool is used to clean up the seam line around the bite mark.

NOTE: Take the extra time to make a perfect dividing wall.

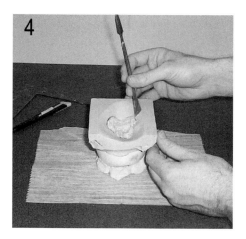

A coil of clay is gently pressed onto the clay dividing wall. The coil should completely surround the bite mark.

NOTE: The coil will become the registration key for the two silicone mold sections. (See page 217, photograph 11 and page 220, photograph 23.)

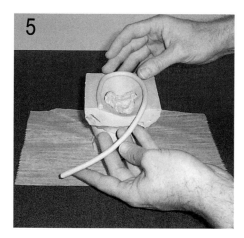

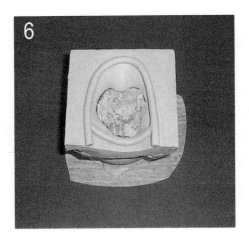

A view of the completed dividing wall and registration key (coil). Notice the small coil of clay along the bottom of the bite mark.

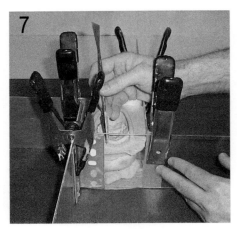

A mold box is assembled tightly around the clay dividing wall. Next, a detail tool is used to blend the edge of the clay dividing wall against the clink boards. A tight seal is critical, because if the clay seal is not water tight, silicone will leak down around the bottom of the apple.

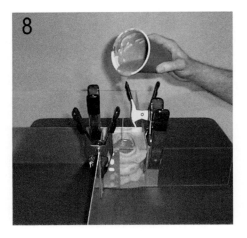

A small amount of food grade silicone is poured over the bite mark. The silicone is only filled up to the top of the clay coil.

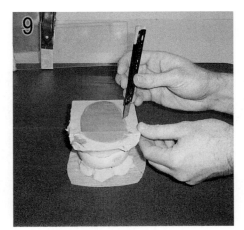

The silicone is allowed to cure and the excess silicone that flashed over the top of the coil is trimmed off.

The clay dividing wall is carefully removed. The thin edge of the silicone around the registration key is trimmed with small scissors.

NOTE: DO NOT LOOSEN THE SILICONE PLUG FROM THE APPLE. IT MUST STAY ATTACHED TO THE BITE MARK.

Section 5

Making a
Two-Piece
Plug Mold of
the Plaster
Apple

Close-up view of the apple and silicone plug.

NOTE: The groove along the perimeter of the silicone plug was created by the clay coil on page 216, in photograph 6.

The apple is flipped over so that it is resting on the plug.

NOTE: Vaseline was put under the plug so that the model is secured onto the work board.

The entire surface area of the silicone plug is coated with a thin layer of Vaseline.

NOTE: Make sure that Vaseline is brushed into the entire registration groove.

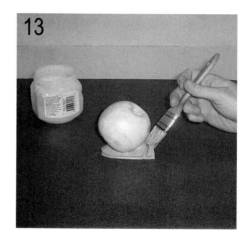

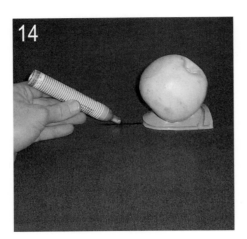

An **orientation line** is drawn on the work board.

NOTE: This line will indicate where the mold can be cut open.

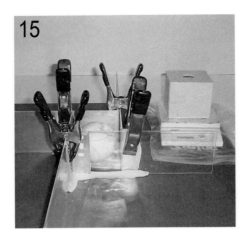

A mold box is assembled around the apple allowing a ¼ inch space between the apple and the clink boards.

NOTE: Weigh the first apple mold so that the appropriate amount of silicone can be made. (The weight of the first mold will provide a useful estimate.)

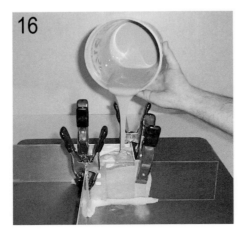

The mold box is filled with food grade silicone.

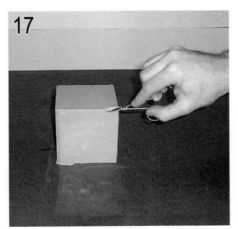

The silicone is allowed to cure and the mold is cleaned up.

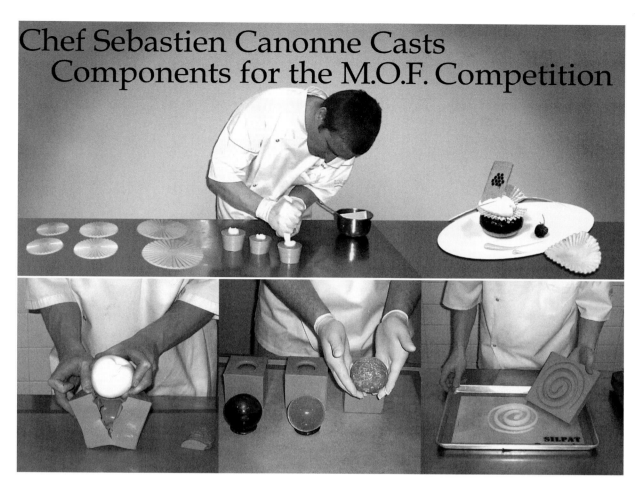

This chapter will illustrate several techniques that Chef Sebastien Canonne developed for the M.O.F. (Meilleur Ouvrier de France) Competition. Designing a mold for use in a timed competition requires that many aspects be considered ahead of time. Working cleanly and quickly is a serious consideration in the M.O.F. Competition. Each mold must be designed so that it casts easily and without any special handling.

To compensate for the risk of a casting not turning out perfectly, several duplicate molds were made of each design. As Chef Canonne explains, "If I need three spheres to support a base, I will use four sphere molds just to make sure that I do not loose any time if one casting fails." To familiarize himself with each mold, Chef Canonne made dozens of practice runs with the molds so that he knew exactly what to expect from each mold design. The test runs were critical in establishing the ideal casting temperatures for each mold. In addition to temperature control, the test castings provided extra models on which to practice coloration and air brush techniques.

If you are a chef planning on using molds for a timed competition, do not make the mistake of assuming that just because you have a mold nothing can go wrong. Allow yourself plenty of time in advance to experiment with the molds.

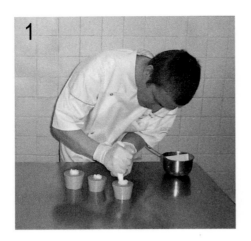

Chef Canonne has prepared a small batch of tallow.

The soft tallow has been put into a piping bag so that it can be easily piped inside of the mold. He is careful to pipe in a small circular motion from the bottom of the mold to the top. Filling the molds in a spiral pattern prevents air pockets from being trapped in the casting.

The excess tallow is removed with an off-set spatula.

The molds are allowed to chill for several hours before they are de-molded.

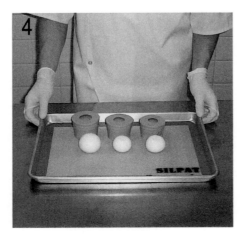

The finished tallow gourds.

Section 2
Using a Cookie Press Mold

Chef Canonne is shown preparing to make decorative cookies for a plated desert. He spreads cigarette cookie batter into a stencil sheet. The stencil is placed on top of a Silpat® mat.

NOTE: Cigarette cookie batter consists of equal parts egg white, butter, confectionery sugar and cake flour mixed to a paste.

The cookie batter is spread into the stencil. Make sure to scrape the batter flat with the surface of the stencil as only a very small amount of cookie batter should remain in the stencil.

NOTE: See supplier list for custom stencil information.

The stencil can be removed right away.

NOTE: At this time, he has placed the silicone cookie press molds in an oven. It is important to preheat the molds so that they will be warm when he is ready to press the cookies.

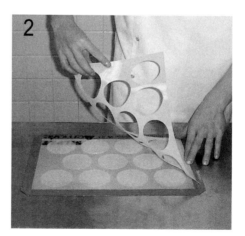

The cookies are baked at 163° C/325° F for approximately five minutes (to a light golden brown color). Working very quickly, Chef Canonne places the hot cookie on the silicone mold.

Chef Canonne applies firm, hard pressure to the cookie mold.

NOTE: The press mold must be warm. A cold mold will chill the cookie and cause it to crack when it is pressed.

When pressing a lot of cookies, work in front of an oven and keep the pan in the oven so that the cookies stay warm and flexible. Remove the cookies from the oven one at a time for pressing because as long as the cookies are warm, they will remain flexible.

The press mold is opened. The pressing motion should take less than a second.

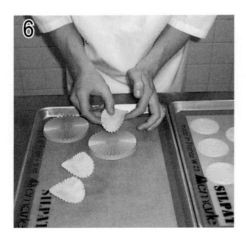

While the cookie is still warm and pliable, Chef Canonne shapes the cookie to give it a more dynamic look. The cookies are very thin and will cool quickly so they must be shaped immediately or else they will crack.

NOTE: The press molding process should be done as quickly as you can. This entire pressing process was completed in three seconds.

Chef Canonne presents the fluted cookie in this beatiful dessert plate.

Section 3
Casting the Hot Sugar Snake

Chef Canonne prepares a batch of white Isomalt.

NOTE: A small amount of titanium dioxide is added to the hot Isomalt. After the titanium dioxide has been mixed into the batch, yellow colorant is added to the sugar and brought to a quick boil. The mixture is then allowed to cool to 125° C/257° F.

Chef Canonne pours the hot Isomalt into a paper cone.

NOTE: The paper cone was made with several layers of parchment paper. It is important that the cone be strong enough not to break under the heat or under the pressure of your hand. Always wear latex gloves when working with hot sugar. The Chef is wearing a large high heat glove as an added safety precaution during the pour.

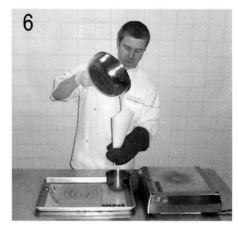

Chef Canonne cuts the tip of the paper cone.

He pipes the hot sugar into the snake mold. The mold should be filled from the tail to the head in one continuous pour.

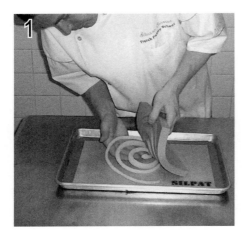

The Isomalt is allowed to cool for about 20 minutes. Chef Canonne then removes the snake from the mold tail first by flexing the mold against the baking pan.

A view of the finished snake.

NOTE: The snake can be reshaped by placing it under a heat lamp (a 250 watt light bulb) until it becomes malleable. Once reshaped, use a fan to cool the snake to maintain its new shape.

Section 4
Casting the Sugar Apple

Chef Canonne illustrates how to use the silicone plug mold. The unique design of the plug mold provides him with a seamless casting.

The apple mold has been taped together with clear packing tape. Chef Canonne pours white Isomalt into the mold through the open area where the bite mark is.

NOTE: Titanium dioxide is often added to Isomalt in order to make a very white casting. A bright white casting is easier to airbrush.

The Isomalt is allowed to cool inside of the mold for ten minutes before it is drained back into the pitcher. It is important to time (10 minutes) how long the Isomalt remains in the mold. If the Isomalt is drained too soon, the wall thickness of the casting will be too thin.

NOTE: Chef Canonne is rotating the mold as he drains it. The rotation ensures that Isomalt comes out of the mold evenly on each side to create an even wall thickness. (Spraying **cold spray** inside the casting is a great way to cool the sugar quickly.)

While the Isomalt is cooling, yet still flexible, Chef Canonne folds in any excess drippings. In order for the plug mold design to work well, the area around the bite mark must be completely free of sugar.

Chef Canonne tilts the mold to show the clean edge around the bite mark.

NOTE: The protrusion at the top of the mold can only be covered by patching a small piece of Isomalt into the mold by hand.

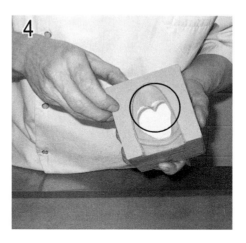

Chef Canonne pours two small patches of Isomalt onto the Silpat® mat. (At this point the Isomalt in the pitcher has cooled considerably.)

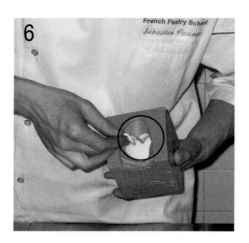

Chef Canonne inserts the small patch over the raised protrusion in the mold.

NOTE: The protrusion in the mold is actually the indentation from the stem of the real apple.

The Isomalt is re-melted in the microwave safe pitcher and Chef Canonne refills 30% of the mold with Isomalt.

The specially fitted silicone plug is placed into the bite mark. Chef Canonne rotates the mold slowly by resting it on each corner for one minute. After the mold has been rotated on all sides, it is allowed to cool for about twenty minutes.

NOTE: This process is time consuming. It is best to do this while you have another project going on. (Keep the mold nearby with a set egg timer.)

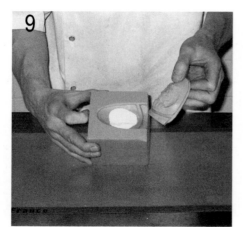

Chef Canonne removes the plug and allows the Isomalt to cool for one hour.

NOTE: The mold can be placed in a freezer to accelerate cooling. However, the possibility of creating condensation is increased. Condensation is the enemy of sugar sculpture as it makes everything sticky and will cause sugar to lose its shine.

The finished Isomalt apple is de-molded.

NOTE: The slice down the front of the mold does not leave a seam line because the mold was cut with the special groove knife. Molds cut with a groove knife retain seamless registration.

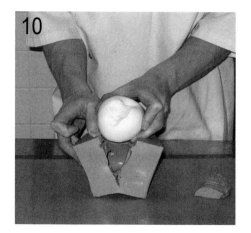

The silicone plug mold, white Isomalt apple, and finished airbrushed apple are shown.

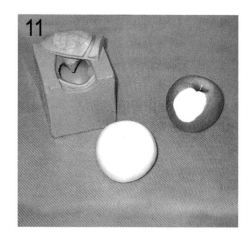

Section 5
Casting Sugar Spheres

Chef John Kraus demonstrates how to cast a variety of colored sugar spheres. The uses for colorful sugar spheres are endless. These spheres can be used to support a base or as decorate elements for a showpiece.

NOTE: See the true colors of these spheres in the color gallery at the back of the book.

Chef Kraus has prepared the sphere molds by taping them together with clear packing tape. (Banding a mold with rubber bands can distort the shape of the mold.)

The Isomalt was first heated to 165° C/329° F then allowed to cool to 109° C/228° F before being poured into the mold. (The Chef melted clear Isomalt in a heavy duty, microwave safe pitcher.)

NOTE: Pouring Isomalt at low temperatures reduces the amount of air bubbles in the casting. If a silicone mold is filled with very hot Isomalt, the insulating qualities of the mold will allow the Isomalt to continue cooking in the mold, creating bubbles.

The spheres are cast solid by filling the mold to the top in one continuous pour. Chef Kraus uses a pastry triangle to cut off the flow from the pitcher when the mold is full. The sphere mold is then set aside to cool for several hours.

NOTE: When filling a small mold, pour from a heavy duty pitcher. Do not use a thin walled plastic pitcher as the Isomalt will melt through it.

Chef Kraus prepares to demonstrate a second casting technique. He has prepared two different colors of Isomalt in two separate pitchers. When both pitchers are carefully poured into the mold at the same time, the two colors swirl together to make a beautiful, semi-translucent marbled look.

NOTE: As mentioned before, the Isomalt was heated to 165° C/329° F and then allowed to cool to 109° C/228° F before it was poured into the mold.

Chef Kraus demonstrates another method for marbling by adding a small amount of dark color directly into a pitcher of clear Isomalt.

He swirls the color in the pitcher to get the effect started, then pours its contents into the mold. The turbulence created inside the mold when the Isomalt is poured will create a convincing marbled look.

NOTE: Chef Kraus has the option of setting the mold aside to cool and being satisfied with the casting, or he can elaborate by adding another step. (The next photograph will show how he elaborates on this casting.)

After the mold has cooled for about ten minutes, Chef Kraus drains the contents back into the pitcher, keeping the mold inverted until it is completely drained. Only a thin layer of Isomalt should remain in the mold.

Chef Kraus allows the mold to cool (a second time) for 10 more minutes.

Next, Chef Kraus refills the mold with gold colored Isomalt and sets it aside to cool completely.

NOTE: A small amount of gold metallic powder was added to the Isomalt. The gold dust creates a glitter-like effect inside the sphere.

Chef Kraus de-molds the multi-colored sphere.

NOTE: Please see the color gallery at the back of the book for the effect in color.

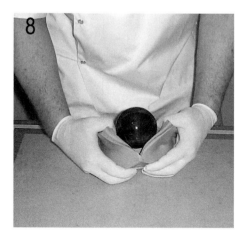

As a third casting technique, Chef Kraus will demonstrate how to make a sphere that appears to be shattered. The mold is filled with amber colored Isomalt. He then allows the casting to completely cool.

NOTE: Chef Kraus puts the mold in to the freezer for about five hours.

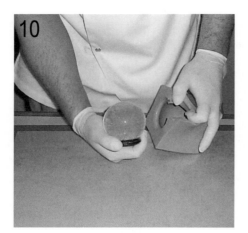

The amber sphere is removed from the mold.

Chef Kraus displays the sphere that was cracked by heating it in the microwave oven.

NOT SHOWN: Chef Kraus put the sugar sphere in a microwave oven for thirty seconds, watching closly until it cracks. Make sure to put a plastic container over the sphere in case it blows apart. (The sphere was put in the microwave without the mold.)

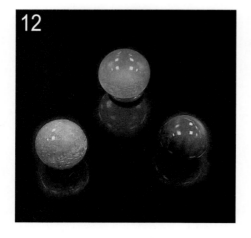

The finished sugar spheres.

The cracked amber microwave sphere is on the left. The clear Isomalt sphere is in the center and the multi-colored, marbled sphere is on the right.

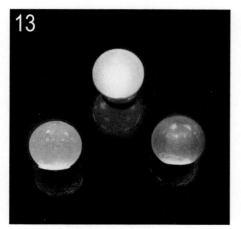

Another beautiful effect can be created by illuminating the spheres from below.

The paper "shell" is removed. Notice the clay post at the back of the jaw that allowed adjustments to be made to the position of the plaster jaw.

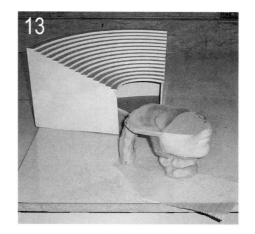

The position of the jaw is made permanent by filling in the back side with plaster.

The paper stairs are glued onto the plaster jaw. Notice that the front flaps of the poster board have been folded in towards the chin.

NOTE: The poster board has been spray painted for photographic clarity.

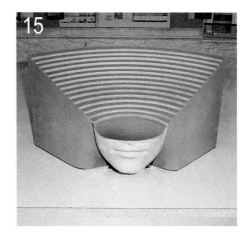

The model is turned upside down. A neck is sculpted in clay beneath the jaw.

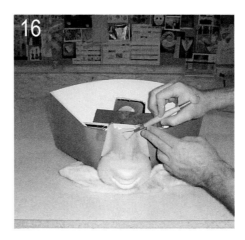

Make Window Templates

A stencil with three windows is drawn onto poster board.

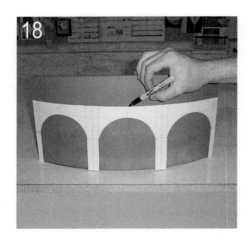

The stencil is outlined onto the back of the model.

A single arch is outlined onto the left and right side of the model.

The windows are cut out.

View of the working model with all five windows cut out.

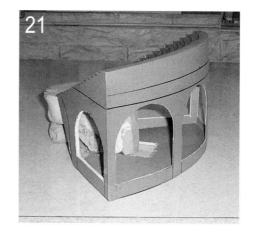

Make Recessed Window Inserts

Five custom window inserts are made out of foam core. Each insert ½ inch deep.

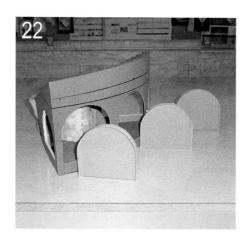

The inserts are hot glued into the windows.

A dremel tool is used to widen the window so that the inserts will fit inside.

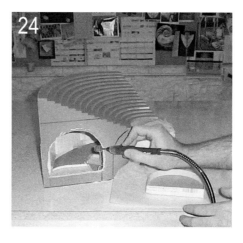

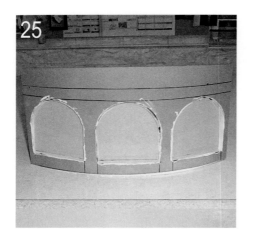

View of the inserts glued onto the model.

NOTE: It was not necessary to be precise when enlarging the window cut outs with the dremel tool.

Spaces around the windows are filled with a plaster paste.

A stippled texture is applied to the paper model.

NOTE: Plaster was mixed with craft glue to make the plaster stick to the poster board. This can be done by mixing a small amount of plaster in a cup and adding a tablespoon of craft glue directly into the plaster mix. Stir it and apply when it thickens.

Paper columns are glued in between the windows.

Thin strips of balsa wood are cut and fitted to create a small frame along the back of the model. In the final casting, this frame will contain a row of small gears.

Back view of the completed working model.

Front view of the completed working model.

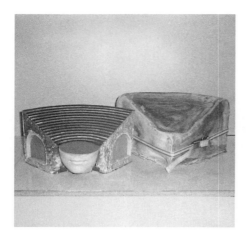

Section 2
Making a Silicone Mold of the Working Model

This section will illustrate how a silicone mold can be used to create a *new* plaster model from the working model. It is important to understand that the silicone mold (in the following sequence) is not intended for casting chocolate. This mold will be used for a special plaster casting process to divide the model into five interlocking (plaster) sections.

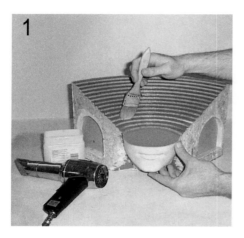

Vaseline The Model

The entire model is coated in melted Vaseline. Extra Vaseline is applied to the white edge of the foam stairs to help prevent the silicone from bonding to the "cell" structure of the cut foam edges.

NOTE: Many of the following steps in this chapter have been abbreviated since detailed instruction has already been given in earlier chapters.

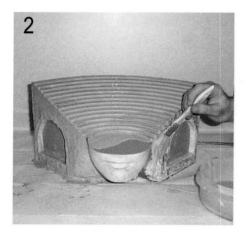

The first layer of fast-setting silicone is brushed on the model.

NOTE: The fast-setting silicone included 10% silicone thinner and 6% fast catalyst. The lower percentage of fast catalyst allowed the silicone more time to flow into the detail of the working model.

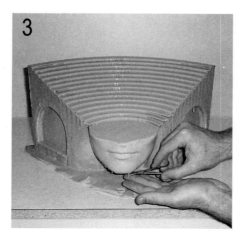

After the first layer of silicone has cured, the small drips beneath the chin are cut off.

NOTE: The large amount of silicone that has pooled around the base of the model will help create a lip for the mold. (See page 245, photograph 6, for more detail.)

The mold is frosted with a batch of thickened silicone.

Silicone registration keys are cut from pre-made slabs of silicone.

NOTE: 4 inch long, ¼ inch wide strips of silicone are being cut. Enough strips are being cut to encircle the entire perimeter of the mold lip.

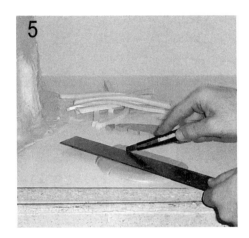

To attach the strip keys, fast-setting silicone is brushed onto the silicone strips so that they will bond to the lip of the mold.

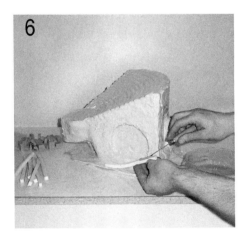

Reinforce The Silicone Liner

A small batch of fast-setting silicone is mixed and applied to all of the sharp edges of the model. Extra silicone is needed along these edges because the first layers tend to sag off the sharp edges.

NOTE: Thickened silicone was used to build a **draft** under each window arch. Drafting the silicone under the windows will help the plaster mother mold release easily from the silicone blanket.

Allow the silicone to cure.

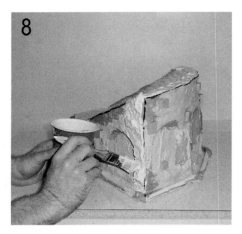

Make A Plaster Foundation For The Clay Dividing Wall

Before beginning to make the mother mold, the silicone liner must be divided into separate sections. The liner is divided into four sections by black marker lines. The *back arch* is the first section that will be made.

Attaching a clay dividing wall directly onto silicone will not work as oil clay will not stick to silicone. Therefore, a **plaster foundation** must be applied to the area where the dividing wall is needed. Once the plaster foundation has set, the clay dividing wall can be attached to the plaster.

NOTE: The plaster is only applied BEHIND the dividing line (black ink). The plaster foundation should be at least two inches wide.

Attach The Clay Dividing Wall

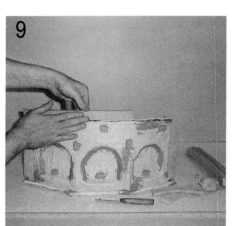

The clay dividing wall is carefully blended onto the plaster foundation.

NOTE: Heat the clay strips before applying them to the plaster foundation. Soft clay will stick better to the plaster foundation.

NOT SHOWN: Behind the clay dividing wall, extra coils of clay have been built up to help stabilize and reinforce the clay strips.

Make Registration Keys

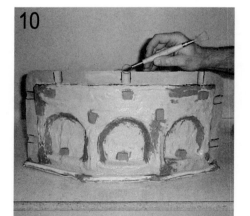

Half-round registration keys are cut into the clay wall. The keys will register the plaster mother mold sections together.

NOTE: The first mother mold section is only intended to stabilize the *back arch* section of the mold. Additional mother mold sections will stabilize the sides and top of the mold.

The plaster mother mold is applied.

Once the plaster has set, the clay dividing wall and plaster foundation are completely removed.

NOTE: Do NOT separate the newly created mother mold section from the silicone.

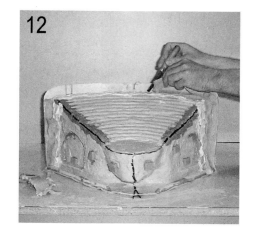

Parting soap is applied to the front of the plaster mother mold section.

NOTE: The location of the upcoming mother mold sections can be seen by looking at the ink lines that have been drawn onto the silicone blanket.

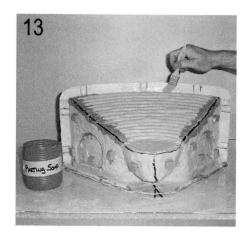

Make The Second Mother Mold Section

A plaster foundation for the oil clay dividing wall is applied behind the ink dividing line.

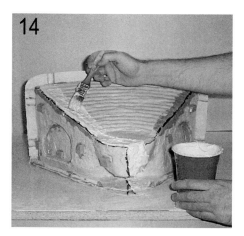

The clay dividing wall is assembled on top of the plaster foundation and parting soap is applied to the clay surface.

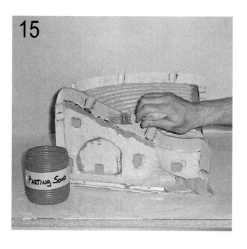

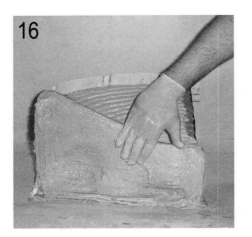

The second plaster mother mold section is applied.

NOTE: Gloves are not necessary when working with plaster. (I use them because the plaster dries out my skin.)

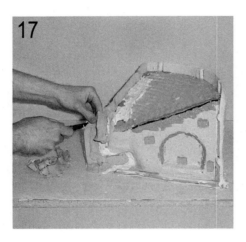

Once the plaster has set, the clay dividing wall and plaster foundation are completely removed.

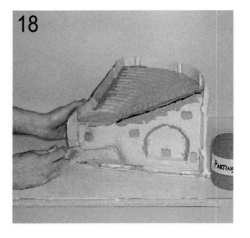

Parting soap is applied to the surface of the second mother mold section.

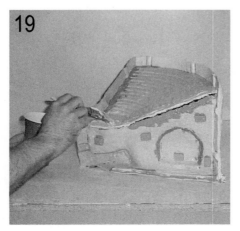

The mother mold process is repeated by laying a plaster foundation behind the ink dividing line.

The clay dividing wall is assembled on top of the plaster foundation and parting soap is applied to the clay dividing wall.

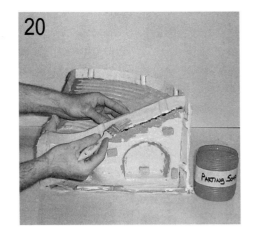

The third plaster mother mold section is applied.

Once the plaster has set, the clay dividing wall and plaster foundation are completely removed.

Parting soap is applied to the third mother mold section.

NOTE: The mold is strapped (or taped) tightly together. This is a useful thing to do because the mother mold sections are designed to *fall* away from the silicone blanket. At this point, the mother mold could separate slightly if it is not banded together. If the three mother mold sections separate before the fourth mother mold section is built, the entire mother mold will never register tightly together.

The fourth and final mother mold section is applied.

NOTE: It was not necessary to build a clay dividing wall for the final mother mold section as the plaster walls of the previous mold sections provide the division.

The plaster is allowed to set and the edges along the parting lines are shaved down. This is a helpful thing to do, because it is common for plaster to drip over the edges while making the mother mold. If too much plaster drips over the sections, it can cement them together.

The mother mold is easily split apart. First remove the sides, then the back, and lastly the top section.

After the mother mold has been disassembled, the silicone liner (blanket) can be removed from the model.

NOTE: Since this mold is only going to be used once, it is acceptable to cut the liner along the edges of the back arch to ease removal.

This is a good picture to illustrate why a mother mold is needed. Without it, the silicone liner would fold up on itself like a towel. The mother mold provides an exterior support case for the liner.

NOTE: The interior surface of the mold is cleaned out. Any paper or plaster debris is removed.

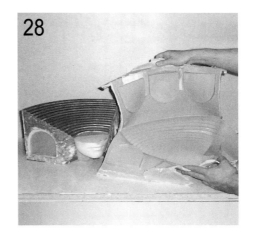

A view of the paper model and completed mold.

NOT SHOWN: The plaster mother mold was assembled and strapped together. Next, the silicone liner was repositioned inside the mother mold. (See photo 1 below.)

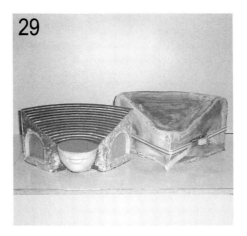

Section 3
Casting a Multi-Piece Plaster Model

This section will illustrate how a silicone mold can be used to cast a multiple piece plaster model. A plaster model is needed so that each component (jaw, stairs, sides, back arch and base) can be remolded and cast in individual pieces. In order for this sculpture to be cast hollow in chocolate, the sculpture must be assembled in numerous sections. (The first paper model could not be separated into such sections.)

Seat The Mold

The silicone liner is repositioned into the mother mold. This is where the rubber registration keys play a critical role. The rubber keys prevent the liner from falling in on itself inside the mother mold. With the keys, the silicone liner fits into place easily. Without the keys, the liner would not grip on to the interior wall surface of the mother mold.

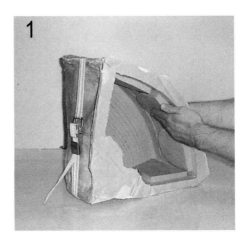

Casting The Stair Section

The mold is positioned so that the stairs are at the bottom. A small batch of No. 1 Molding Plaster is then poured into the mold. (Only enough plaster was poured to cover the stairs one inch deep.)

NOTE: All sections of the model are cast in No. 1 Molding Plaster.

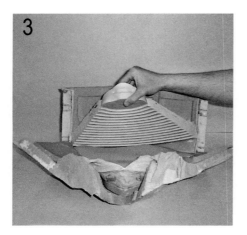

After the plaster sets, the stairs are removed from the mold.

Cleaning Up The Plaster Casting

The rough front edge of the stairs is shaved smooth with a trimming tool. This is necessary because the foam texture from the original paper model was duplicated in the silicone mold.

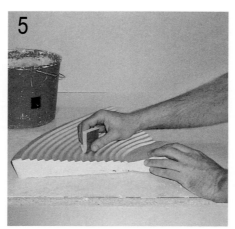

The stairs are sanded smooth with a wet sanding sponge.

The jaw section is cut off and discarded.

NOTE: The jaw will be cast as a separate section.

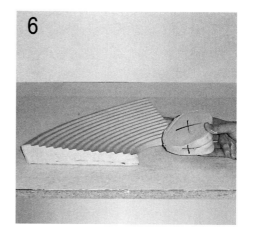

The back of the stairs is shaved and sanded smooth.

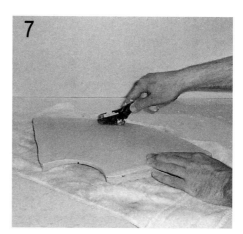

Parting soap is applied to every surface (front, back and side) of the stairs.

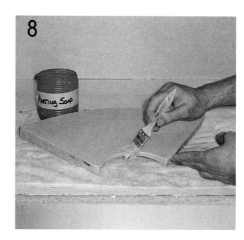

The stairs are refitted into the silicone liner.

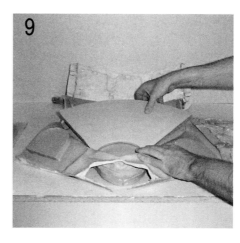

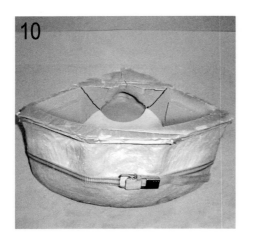

The mold has been reassembled and strapped together.

This photograph shows the interior of the mold where the plaster stairs have been reinserted. The hollow cavity in front of the stairs is the face (jaw) area. A marker has been used to draw the outline of the next plaster casting.

Making The Plaster Jaw

Plaster is poured and shaped into the face area of the mold. Since the face section is being poured against the back of the stairs they will fit perfectly together when they are removed from the mold.

The goal is to pour five plaster sections that will fit perfectly together, yet not bond together. This is why it was important to apply parting soap in between each plaster section.

NOTE: The jaw section being cast will duplicate the one seen on page 238, photograph 9.

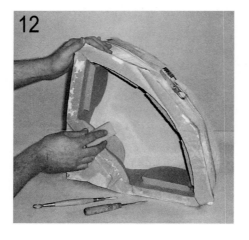

Smooth The Plaster Jaw

The outside edges of the plaster jaw are sanded smooth with a wet sanding sponge. A smooth surface is important when making plaster sections that fit together.

NOTE: Each section that is being made in plaster will eventually be re-molded and cast in chocolate. The final chocolate sculpture will be several separate sections that are assembled together. (See page 258, photograph 26.)

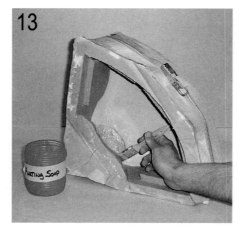

Parting soap is applied to the back of the plaster jaw.

NOTE: The mold was not disassembled. The plaster jaw was left in place so that it registers perfectly with the plaster stairs. (The only reason the plaster stairs were removed was to cut the face section off them.)

Making The Support Frame For The Base Mold

Two pieces of plastic pipe are cut slightly longer than the mother mold. Each pipe has two long bolts extending through it. The bolts will provide a point of attachment between the mother mold and the frame.

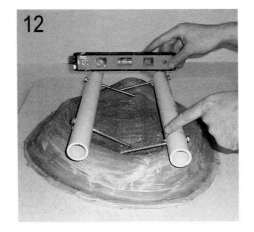

Level The Frame

Use bits of clay to shim the pipe level. This is a very important step. If the frame is not level, the mold will not sit level on the table. (See page 264, photograph 18.)

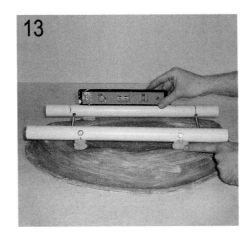

Attach The Frame

Plaster is applied over the bolts. Do not remove the clay shims, plaster right over them.

NOTE: Do not apply plaster on top of the pipe. The pipe surface must remain smooth.

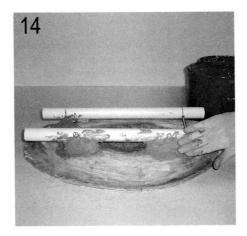

Clean The Frame

A wet sponge is used to wipe off the excess plaster.

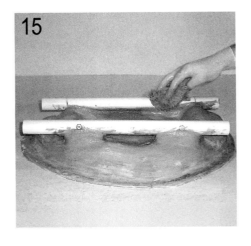

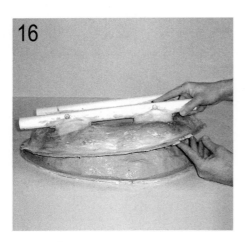

The Mother Mold Is Removed

Due to the draft of the silicone blanket and coating of Vaseline, the mother mold lifts off easily.

NOT SHOWN: The sharp edges of the plaster mother mold are shaved down.

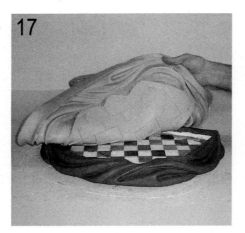

The silicone blanket is peeled off the base.

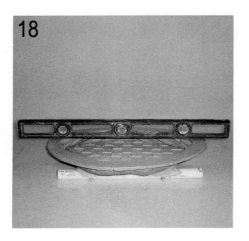

View Of The Completed Base Mold

NOTE: The support frame makes the mold sit level on the table.

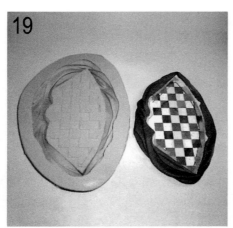

View of the silicone mold and the model.

Section 4-B
Making the Tile Insert Mold

Section 4

Making
Individual
Silicone Molds
for Chocolate
Casting

Several wood squares are secured to a work board with Vaseline. A metal square and wood spacers are used to position the tiles in a tight grid.

NOTE: The wood tiles will float if they are not secured onto the work board.

A mold box is assembled around the tiles and a batch of soft (with 20% thinner) non-food grade silicone is poured over the tiles.

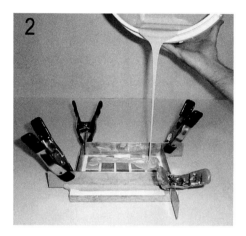

After the silicone is allowed to cure, the mold is flexed to release the tiles.

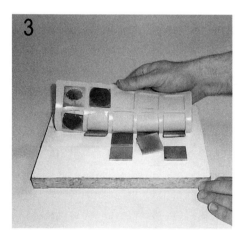

A view of the finished tile mold.

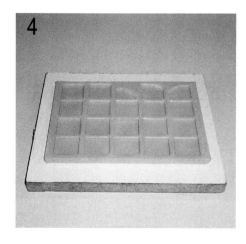

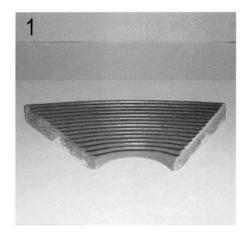

Section 4-C
Making the Stair Mold

The stairs have been painted for photographic clarity.

NOTE: The stairs have been coated with parting soap.

A mold box is assembled and a batch of silicone with regrind is poured over the stairs.

NOTE: Wood slats have been fitted into the mold box in order to reduce the amount of material needed to cover the stairs.

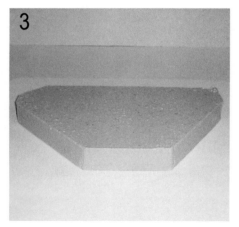

The silicone has cured and the mold box has been removed.

NOTE: Do **NOT** remove the model from the mold.

Making The Mother Mold

A new mold box is assembled around the silicone mold. Wood slats have been positioned in the mold box to reduce the amount of plaster needed to cover the silicone mold.

The plaster mother mold is poured.

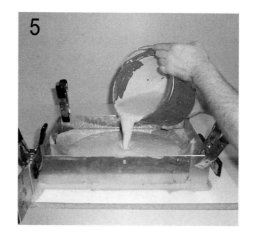

Section 4

Making
Individual
Silicone Molds
for Chocolate
Casting

When cured, the entire mold is flipped over and the silicone liner is removed from the mother mold.

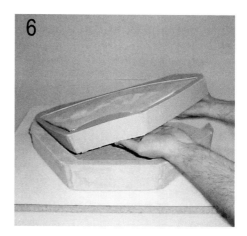

The plaster stairs are removed from the silicone liner.

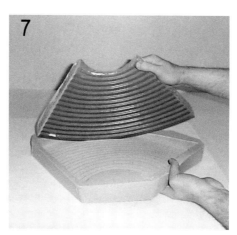

View of the finished stair mold and model.

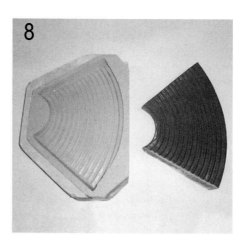

Section 4-D
Molding The Side Walls

The two plaster side walls are secured onto the work board with Vaseline.

NOTE: The models have been painted for photographic clarity.

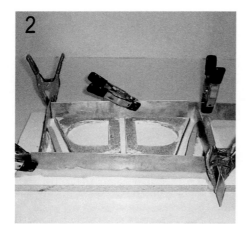

A mold box is assembled around the models.

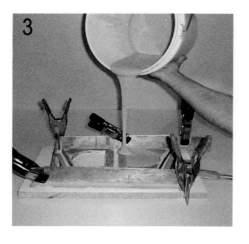

A batch of soft silicone (with 20% thinner) is poured over the models.

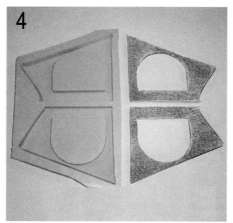

View of finished mold and models.

Section 4-E
Molding the Jaw Section

Section 4

Making
Individual
Silicone Molds
for Chocolate
Casting

The model is secured to the work board with Vaseline.

NOTE: The flat surface above the jaw is the ideal area to position onto the board. This area will become pouring gate that the chocolate will be poured into. (See page 290, photograph 1.)

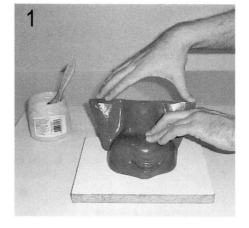

Coat the model with parting soap.

The first layer of silicone is applied.

NOTE: The following steps have been abbreviated to reduce repetition. Please review the earlier chapters for more complete explanations.

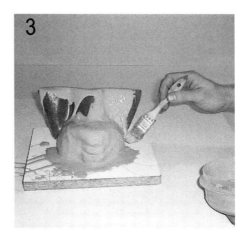

A second layer of thickened silicone was applied over the model.

NOTE: While the second layer of silicone is still tacky, wide strip keys are attached to both sides of the model. The strip keys have a dual purpose. The first is for registration, the second is to allow enough thickness for a groove knife to be used when cutting open the mold. (See page 272, photograph 15.)

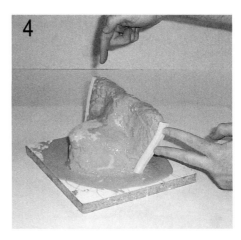

Glaze The Mold

A layer of fast-setting silicone is brushed over the silicone surface. This is called **glazing**. This layer of silicone (glaze) will help bond the strip keys to the mold.

Glazing will smooth out any bumps or irregularities on the surface of the silicone blanket. A smooth (glazed) surface will be easy to release from the mold.

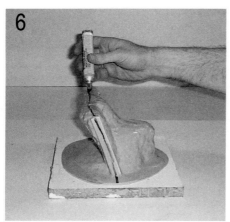

Make The Mother Mold

After the silicone has completely cured, a dividing line is drawn down the center ridge of the silicone liner.

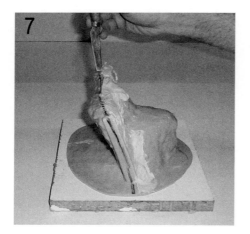

Make The Plaster Foundation

A plaster foundation is applied to the silicone blanket. The foundation (as introduced on page 246, photograph 8) is necessary so that the clay dividing wall can stick on top of the silicone liner.

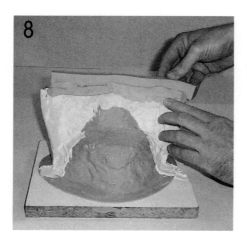

Build a clay dividing wall

The clay dividing wall is built on top of the plaster foundation.

NOTE: This photograph shows the back side of the dividing wall. Notice how extra clay is used to hold the dividing wall in place.

The mold has been rotated to face the working surface towards the camera.

NOTE: As shown previously, the registration keys are cut into the clay and the dividing wall is coated with parting soap.

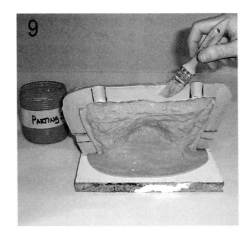

The first mother mold section is made.

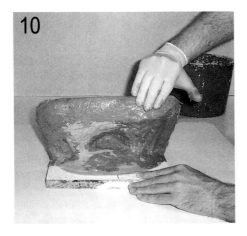

After the plaster sets, the clay dividing wall and plaster foundation are removed.

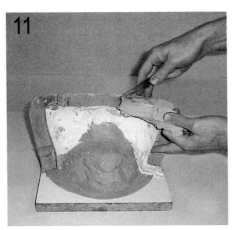

Make The Second Mother Mold Section

The first plaster mother mold section is coated with parting soap.

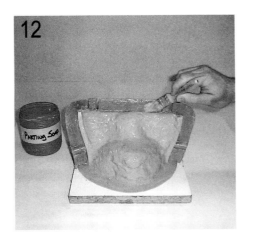

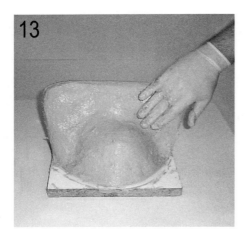

The second mother mold section is applied.

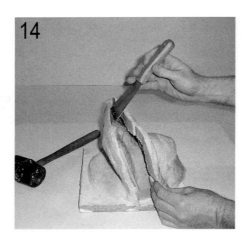

Split The Mother Mold

After the plaster has set, the mold is separated.

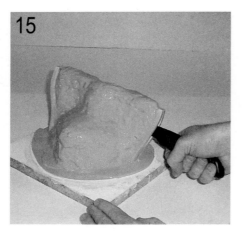

A groove knife is used to cut the silicone mold.

NOTE: The thick strip keys provide enough depth to allow the groove knife to cut a channel in the rubber.

A groove knife is useless when there is not a thick enough area of rubber to cut through. There must be enough depth for the groove in the blade to slice through the silicone. Without the extra thick strip keys, there would have not been enough rubber to cut through.

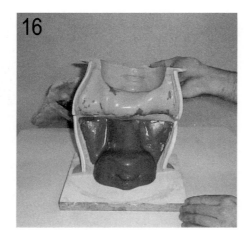

The silicone blanket is removed from the model.

NOTE: A small amount of spray paint stuck to the silicone. A clean out cast of fast-setting urethane resin will remove it.

Make A Support Frame For The Jaw Mold

The mold is reassembled without the silicone model inside. A coil of clay is used to level the mold and a second coil of clay is used to lift the lower left side of the mold.

NOT SHOWN: Bolts have been drilled into both sides of the mother mold.

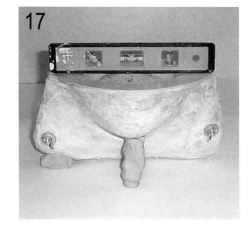

A piece of plastic pipe is cut to fit beneath the mold.

NOTE: Measure the clay coil to indicate where to cut the pipe.

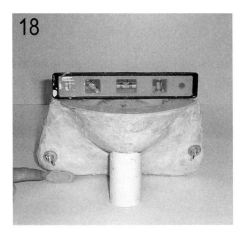

Plaster is applied around the pipe and beneath the low corner (left) of the mother mold in order to attach the frame.

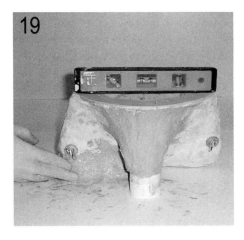

View of the finished mold and model.

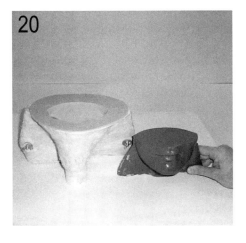

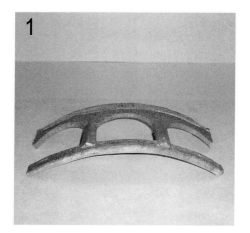

Section 4-F
Molding the Back Arch

View of the back arch section.

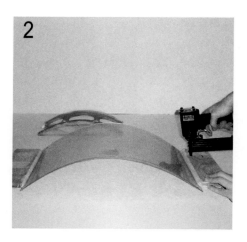

Make A Plexiglas Dividing Wall

A piece of $1/8$ inch Plexiglas is flexed (to closely match the angle of the back arch) and pinned between two blocks of wood. The Plexiglas arch will create the dividing wall for the mold.

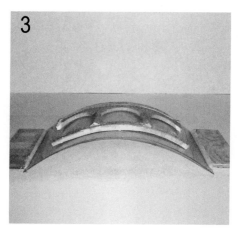

The plaster arch is centered on the Plexiglas.

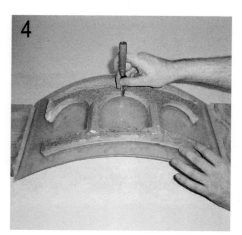

Any gaps beneath the plaster arch are filled with clay.

The arch is coated with parting soap.

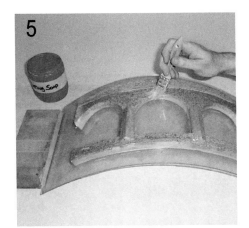

Section 4

Making
Individual
Silicone Molds
for Chocolate
Casting

A ¾ inch tall clay wall is attached along the bottom of the arch. The clay wall will provide a surface to create a silicone lip in the mold.

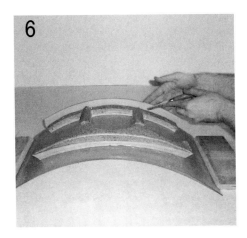

The first layer of silicone is applied.

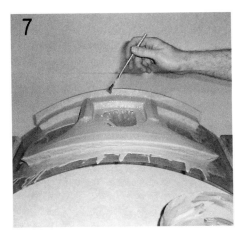

An ⅛ inch layer of thickened silicone is applied.

Extra silicone must be added along the edges to create a draft as the draft will allow the mother mold to release easily.

NOTE: The clay wall at the bottom of the arch has been covered with silicone.

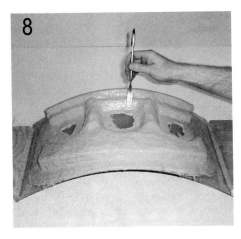

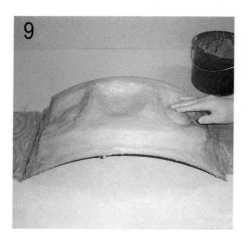

The first mother mold section is applied.

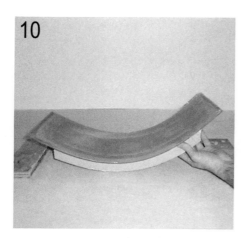

The mold is turned over with the Plexiglas still attached to the model.

NOT SHOWN: The Plexiglas is carefully removed from the arch.

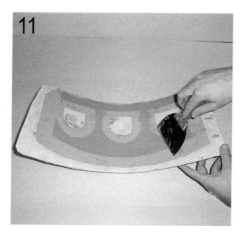

A small amount of plaster paste is filled into the back of the arch to create a smooth surface.

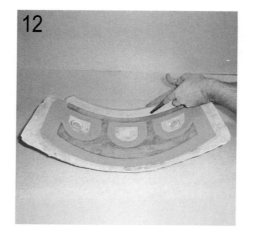

A second strip of clay is built up along the bottom of the arch. The clay strip is positioned directly on top of the previous clay strip. This will create the lip in the second half of the mold.

Attach The Silicone Registration Keys

Silicone strip keys are attached around the center arches and perimeter of the silicone blanket. The keys will make the two silicone liners register together.

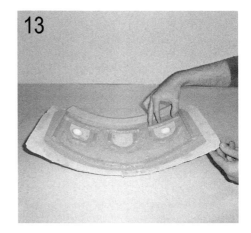

Section 4

Making
Individual
Silicone Molds
for Chocolate
Casting

The entire silicone surface is lightly coated with Vaseline.

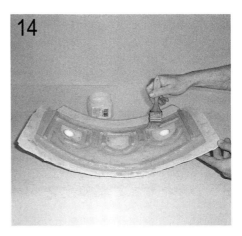

The second silicone liner is applied.

NOT SHOWN: The two white circles in the middle of the silicone liner are registration keys. They are helpful, but not critical to the mold design.

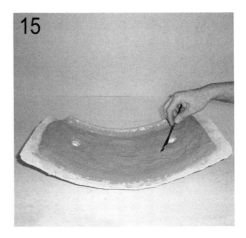

The second mother mold section is applied.

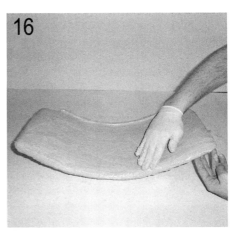

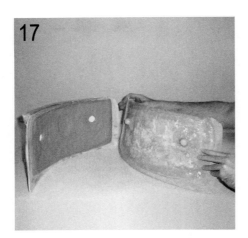

The mold is split open.

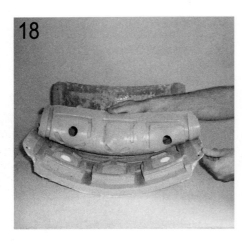

The silicone liner is peeled off the plaster arch.

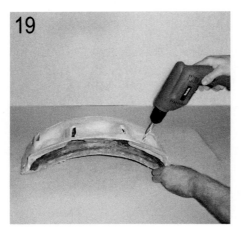

Drill bolt holes through the mother mold.

NOTE: Open slats can be seen in the top of mother mold. These openings are called **pokes** and will be explained in the next section.

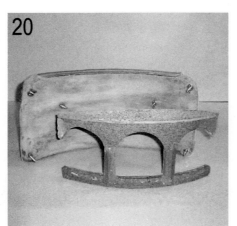

View of the completed mold and the plaster model.

Section 4-G
Molding the Columns

The following technique shows a new way to make a one-piece silicone mold and one-piece plaster mother mold. The difference with this mold is the large holes drilled through the back of the mother mold. These holes are called **pokes** and allow one to push the silicone liner out of the mother mold without damaging the casting. (See page 285, photograph 27.)

NOTE: Plastic columns like these can be purchased in the cake decorating section of a craft store. The hollow columns are filled with clay.

Without a taller set of clink boards, the columns are too tall to be molded upright.

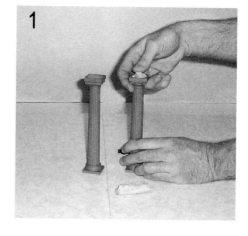

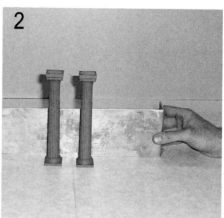

The columns are mounted horizontally onto the work board with a few drops of fast-setting glue.

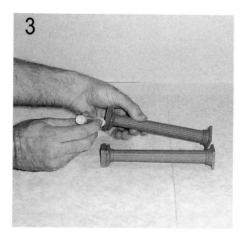

A mold box is assembled around the columns.

The mold box is touching the bottom of the columns. Any surface that touches a clink board will remain open in the finished mold. The opening will become the pouring gate where the chocolate is poured into the mold.

NOTE: It is very important that the clink boards have been assembled so that the sides are nearly vertical on the work board. If the clink boards are tilted inwards (or outwards), the silicone mold will have slanted sides. This will make it difficult to release from the mother mold. (See page 282, photograph 14.)

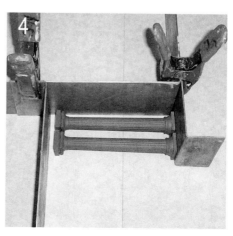

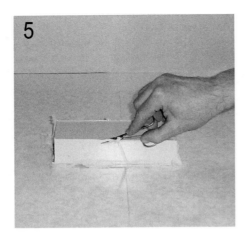

5

The silicone has been poured, allowed to cure and then cleaned up.

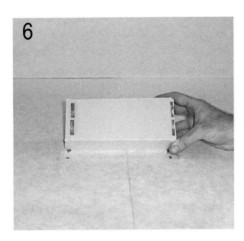

6

The mold is separated from the work board and flipped over. Notice the four gray points where the columns were glued to the work board. These points must be covered with silicone in order for the mold to work.

7

Another mold box is assembled around the mold, making sure the gray points face up.

NOTE: Do not put any Vaseline on the surface of the mold. The next layer of silicone is meant to bond to the first.

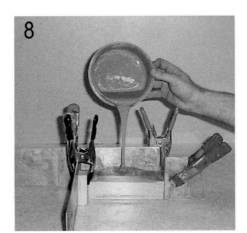

8

A second batch of fast-setting silicone is poured over the mold. It is only necessary to pour a thickness of ¼ inch.

NOTE: The second layer of silicone has been pigmented for photographic clarity.

Chef Sebastien Canonne Casts and Chef Jacquy Pfeiffer Assembles A Chocolate Sculpture

This chapter is divided into two sections. The first section illustrates Chef Canonne filling molds (made in the previous chapter) with chocolate. For our purposes, dark chocolate was selected. It is important to note that casting sculpture from molds does not mean that all of the casts must be the same. One of the chief benefits of using molds is being able to experiment with coloring and surface treatment. A completely new look can be achieved by simply casting different colors of chocolate or a different material, such as sugar or water (ice).

The second section shows Chef Pfeiffer assembling the chocolate sculpture. The short length of Section 2 is a testament to the molds practical design. The ease in which this sculpture is assembled is due to the many hours invested in pre-planning and mold construction. The net result of the long hours is clearly realized by viewing the finished sculpture that Chef Pfeiffer was able to assemble in 10 minutes.

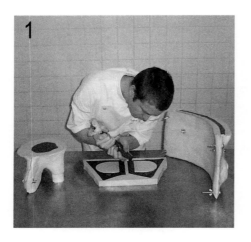

Chef Canonne pipes **coating chocolate** into a few of the molds. There are two types of chocolate that are good for this type of work. The first is a non-tempering chocolate called *pâte à glacer* (made by Barry-Callebaut). *Pâte à glacer* is unique because its very liquid constancy makes it ideal for casting highly detailed molds. Just warm it up to the desired consistency and use it as a casting medium.

NOTE: The molds shown in this photograph from left to right are, the jaw, side wall and back arch.

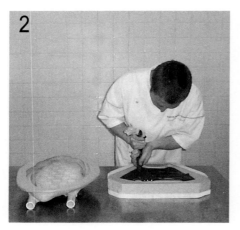

Chef Canonne fills the stair mold using a disposable plastic piping bag without a tip. Eliminating the tip on the bag allows him to pinch the bag at the end of the pour, quickly stopping the flow of chocolate.

NOTE: Coating chocolate (like *pâte à glacer*) contains vegetable oil and does not require tempering. Almost every large chocolate distributor (such as Albert Uster Imports) sells a non-tempering coating chocolate that can used for casting in molds.

Chef Canonne fills the drapery base. When pouring large quantities of chocolate, it is more efficient to pour from a plastic pitcher. Filling a large mold with a piping bag requires that the bag be filled too many times.

NOTE: The most traditional approach to casting chocolate is to pour tempered (heated to 31° C/89° F) couverture chocolate, which can be purchased through any large chocolate distributor. Tempered couverture should be used if the casting is intended to be eaten. *Pâte à glacer* and other coating chocolates are not typically recognized for their flavor.

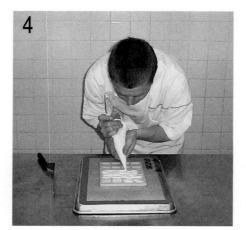

Chef Canonne uses a piping bag to cover the tile insert mold with white coating chocolate. For small intricate pieces, it is easier to overfill the mold and then remove the excess material in the next step.

NOTE: The tile insert mold creates the individual squares that will be inserted into the checkered floor.

Chef Pfeiffer holds the side wall in place while the chocolate cools.

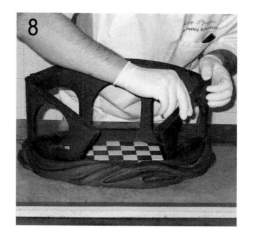

He prepares to attach the jaw onto the base. Before attaching the jaw, he melts the top surface of the jaw on a warm baking pan to ensure that it is smooth and straight.

He slides the melted surface on a piece of paper in order to remove the excess chocolate from the top of the jaw. The result will be a flat, even surface on the jaw.

Chef Pfeiffer prepares to attach the jaw onto the showpiece. A bead of chocolate is piped onto the base and both of the side walls.

Chef Pfeiffer attaches the jaw.

He then prepares to attach the marbled columns. A small amount of chocolate is applied to the base of the column so that it will adhere to the interior floor of the sculpture.

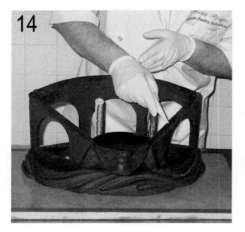

He prepares to attach the stairs by piping a bead of chocolate along the top perimeter of the entire showpiece.

Chef Pfeiffer carefully positions the stairs onto the top of the sculpture.

Chef Pfeiffer cleans the seam lines by smoothing them with a cotton pad.

He fills any open seams with a small piping cone filled with dark coating chocolate.

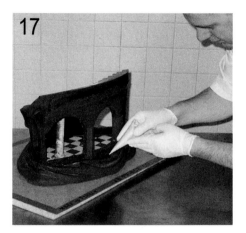

Chef Pfeiffer uses the cotton pad to smooth out any excess chocolate from the patching.

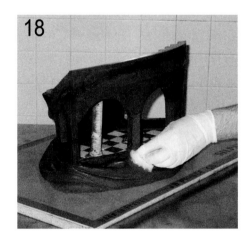

The gears are removed from the mold.

Chef Pfeiffer uses a small amount of chocolate to attach the gears to the back of the arch.

NOTE: The arrangement of the gears was determined and laid out on the work table before assembly.

Chef Pfeiffer attaches the final gears.

The sculpture is sprayed with food grade lacquer. The lacquer gives the showpiece a shiny appearance. It also provides a good surface for the metallic dust to adhere to.

He holds a small cap full of non-toxic metallic dust in his hand. With a gentle blowing motion, he blows gold dust onto the sculpture.

Proper mold design allowed Chef Pfeiffer to assemble this sculpture in less than ten minutes.

Front view of completed chocolate sculpture.

Rear view of the completed sculpture.

Detail rear view of completed sculpture.

Extreme Casting; Taking Chocolate Sculpture In A New Direction

There is a small story behind this chapter. When Chef Gerhard visited my studio for the first time, he saw my sculpture, *A Bird in the Hand*, and thought it would look fantastic in sugar or chocolate. I was interested in the prospect, but I realized that new, more feasible molds would have to be made to accommodate casting in chocolate.

The sculpture was made by assembling several different objects. The roof top was molded from a paper birdhouse. The feet were duplicated from an antique lamp. The corner columns were molded from dowel rods and the flat base plate of the birdcage was molded from a wood pattern. Lastly, the hands were cast from my own.

After a circus of mold making, Chef Gerhard worked with the molds and charted out a plan for casting and assembly. Our main concern was structural stability. It was a tall order to expect the four corner columns and the small feet to support both the weight of the roof and the solid chocolate hands suspended from the center. To accommodate these unusual structural needs, we cast aluminum rods in the center of each corner column.

On the day of the photo shoot, Chef Gerhard assembled the sculpture from the bottom up. The feet were attached to the base plate, then the columns, top base plate, cage wire, roof top and, finally, the hands. This was a delicate casting project as the combined weight of the top plate, roof and cast hands was about 10 pounds. That weight might not seem like a lot, but if you consider that the hands can swing freely like a pendulum whenever the sculpture is moved and the feet are small, the stability issues become magnified.

This chapter has come a long way from molding the cloisonné bell. We hope that you have been inspired by what these chefs have created and will try your own hand at mold making.

Chef Gerhard brushes coating chocolate into the roof mold. Brushing the chocolate into the mold ensures that all of the detail will be captured and that no air bubbles will appear in the casting. Several layers of chocolate were brushed into the mold to build up a wall thickness of 1/8 inch.

NOTE: The roof mold was not filled with solid chocolate because it would be too heavy for the structure of the birdcage.

After the final layer of chocolate is brushed into the mold, a piece of parchment is placed over the surface.

NOT SHOWN: A work board is placed over the parchment paper. The weight of the work board helps prevent the chocolate from warping as it cools.

Allow the chocolate to cool for several hours.

The mold and work board are flipped over in one quick turn.

The plaster mother mold is now removed.

NOTE: The silicone liner is visible beneath the mother mold.

The silicone liner is carefully removed from the chocolate casting.

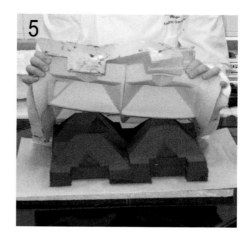

A view of the roof mold and completed chocolate casting.

Chef Gerhard fills the column mold with chocolate.

NOTE: Fitted aluminum rods were inserted into the mold prior to pouring the chocolate. The rods will be encapsulated in chocolate and provide additional strength to the sculpture. Without the rods, the sculpture could not support itself.

The chocolate columns are de-molded after cooling for about 45 minutes.

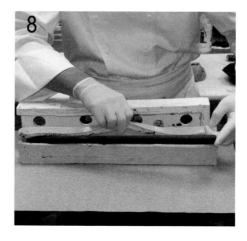

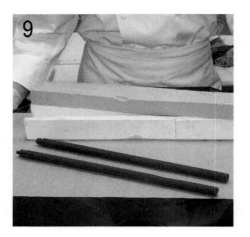

Finished view of two columns. Notice the aluminum rods protruding from the end of the column.

NOTE: The mold was cast twice to make the four columns.

Chef Gerhard prepares to cast the top plate of the birdcage. A brush is used to force chocolate into the fine detail along the outer perimeter of the top plate.

NOTE: Because the top plate will be used to support the roof of the birdcage, it will be attached to the underside of the roof.

The mold is completely filled with chocolate.

NOT SHOWN: A sheet of parchment paper and a work board were placed on the back of the mold to prevent warping while the chocolate cooled.

Once the chocolate has cooled, the silicone mold is removed from the casting.

A view of the chocolate top plate and silicone mold.

NOTE: This process was performed two times. The first to create the chocolate top-plate, which will support the roof, and the second to make the base-plate, which will support the bottom of the birdcage.

Chef Gerhard presses the back of the chocolate casting against a warm baking tray. The warm tray melts the back of the casting, creating a very flat surface.

He carefully drills out casted indentations to create holes that will support the wire rods of the birdcage. By drilling completely through the *top* plate, the wires can be inserted from the top.

NOTE: Holes are not drilled in the *bottom* plate.

Chef Gerhard is piping chocolate around a piece of Plexiglas. The Plexiglas is on the back side of the top plate and will not be visible after assembly.

NOTE: The Plexiglas has a hole drilled through its center. The Plexiglas will help disburse and support the weight of the hands that will be suspended in the center of the cage.

Chef Gerhard brushes chocolate into the detail of the leg mold. After the detail layer has been brushed into the mold, the mold is assembled and filled with solid chocolate. The legs must be cast solid so that they can support the weight of the sculpture.

The finished chocolate legs are removed from the mold.

Chef Gerhard brushed white chocolate into the detail surface of the hand mold.

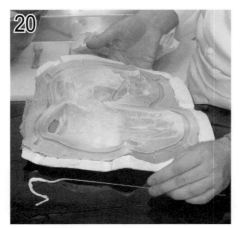

A pre-measured wire has been cut and bent to fit inside the hand mold. The end of the wire has been dipped in white chocolate. If the wire is not coated with chocolate, its copper color may show through on the finished piece if it comes into contact with the surface of the mold.

NOTE: The end of the wire has been bent so that it will not shift when it is encapsulated in the chocolate hands. If the wire remained straight, it would easily to slide out of the center of the chocolate hands.

The wire is placed in a specially fitted channel in the mold. Chef Gerhard is careful not to let the wire touch the surface of the mold as the wire must float freely inside of the mold in order for chocolate to flow completely around it.

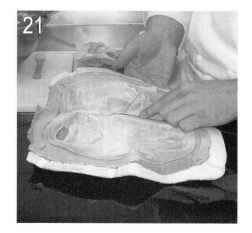

The mold is strapped together and placed in a milk crate for support while Chef Gerhard pipes white chocolate into it.

The mold is rotated and drained while the chocolate is still liquid. Slush casting the mold ensures that chocolate will flow into every detail. It also prevents air from getting trapped in the casting.

The mold is completely refilled with chocolate and allowed to cool overnight.

NOTE: The hands are several inches thick and need a long time to cool.

Once the chocolate has cooled, Chef Gerhard removes the silicone liner from the chocolate hands.

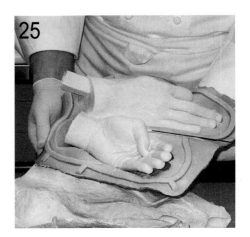

Chef Gerhard removes the second half of the silicone liner.

Notice the copper wire extending from the center of the hands. This is the wire that will suspend the hands in the birdcage.

He removes the seam lines and patches any casting flaws.

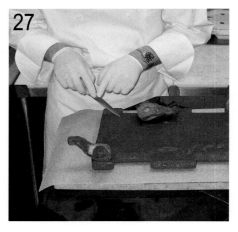

Chef Gerhard scores the surface of the base plate and the surface of the support legs. It is important to score both surfaces prior to gluing them together with chocolate.

Melted chocolate is smeared over the scored surfaces.

Chef Gerhard carefully attaches each support leg.

A small piping cone is used to apply extra chocolate around the base of each leg. The extra chocolate will provide additional strength for the legs.

Chef Gerhard positions the support columns into the base plate of the birdcage. He is careful to position them so that each one stands perfectly vertical. A small amount of melted chocolate is applied to the top of each column.

NOTE: The support columns are placed in pre-drilled holes in each corner of the base plate.

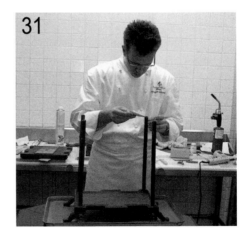

The top plate is carefully set into position on top of the support columns.

NOTE: The support columns fit into pre-drilled holes in each corner of the top plate.

Chef Gerhard reinforces the support columns by piping extra chocolate around the base of each column.

Cold spray is used to chill the chocolate around the base of each column. The cold temperature of the spray accelerates the crystallization of the chocolate.

NOT SHOWN: A support hook has been attached through the center of the top plate. The Plexiglas support on the surface of the top plate is still visible at this time.

He inserts pre-cut wire rods through the holes in the top plate. Several wire rods were not inserted along the back of the cage. The resulting open space will allow him to hang the hands inside the cage at a later point.

NOTE: The holes were drilled through the top plate on page 305, photograph 15.

Chef Gerhard patches the edge of the roof top.

NOTE: A cotton pad was used to smooth and blend the finished surface.

He pipes a large bead of chocolate along the top plate. There must be enough chocolate on the top plate for the roof to adhere securely.

The hollow roof is carefully set onto the top plate.

The seam line between the roof and the top plate is filled with melted chocolate.

Chef Gerhard sprays liquid chocolate over the entire sculpture. The chocolate spray unifies the coloration of the piece.

A good formula for spraying chocolate is:

300 g cocoa paste
300 g cocoa butter
300 g dark couverture chocolate

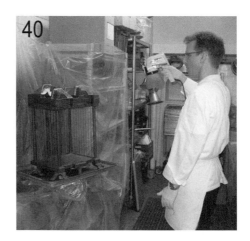

Chef Gerhard inserts the white chocolate hands through the open side in back of the birdcage. The hands are suspended from the hook that extends through the top plate and Plexiglas beneath the roof.

The opening in the back of the birdcage is closed by inserting the remaining wire rods. The rods are pushed up through the holes in the top plate and then pulled back down onto the base plate.

Chef Gerhard blows non-toxic metallic dust on the finished sculpture. The gold dust creates a beautiful antique look and highlights the details of the sculpture.

The finished view of the sculpture, *A Bird in the Hand*, illuminated for display.

APPENDIX

How to Mix:
Food Grade Silicone

This is a recommended formula for all models as excellent detail and good mold quality are achieved. *Always wear rubber gloves, apron and safety glasses when mixing silicone.*

Three components are used to make this batch. The **base** (usually white) is in the 5-gallon pail. The **catalyst** (varies in color) is in the 1-gallon container in front. The **silicone thinner** is in the small pint container on the work board. A clean plastic mixing pail is placed on a digital scale. Make sure that the pail is new or has only been used to mix food grade silicone. Zero out the scale.

NOTE: The digital scale has been enclosed in a Ziplock® bag in order to protect it from spills.

A sufficient amount of base is ladled into the mixing pail. For this sequence, 100 grams were put into the pail. Measuring an exact amount of base is not critical. It is the ratio of the catalyst that is important.

NOTE: Some types of food grade base that are too thick to pour must be ladled out of the pail.

Seven percent (7 grams) food grade thinner is added to the base. The thinner is thoroughly mixed into the base. The formula is forgiving. If you are slightly off on your measurements, the batch will still work.

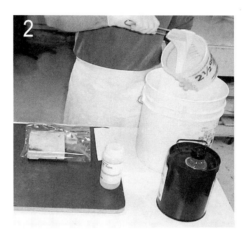

NOTE: The silicone thinner is a clear liquid and is difficult to visually see when it has been mixed into the white base. Allow the thinner time (30 minutes or more) to be absorbed into the base. If you do not want to wait each time, premix a large amount (several pounds) of base and thinner and keep it ready in a separate container. (If the thinner is premixed into the base, it will only be necessary to add the catalyst.)

Ten percent catalyst (10 grams) is added to the base-thinner mix. Pour slowly. It is important that the catalyst be accurately measured. (However, the batch will still cure if the measurement is not exact.) The manufacturer provides an exact amount of catalyst to activate the base. If you repeatedly use too much catalyst, you will not have enough to activate the rest of your base.

NOTE: For quicker cleanup, the mixing spatula has been set on a piece of wax paper.

A metal handled spatula is used to thoroughly mix the catalyst into the base. The spatula should be new or one that has ONLY been used to mix food grade silicone. The silicone is very thick to mix so be sure to use a spatula that has a strong handle. Mix the pigmented catalyst until the base becomes one solid color (the color of the catalyst).

NOTE: Make sure to repeatedly scrape the silicone off the walls of the mixing pail. This will ensure that all of the base is properly catalyzed. Any base that remains uncatalyzed (white) will not cure. Mixing in a clear mixing pail will help you see if there is any uncatalyzed material stuck to the sides of the pail.

NEVER POWER MIX SILICONE IN A CONTAINER WITHOUT A HANDLE. The blade will grab the side of the bucket and send it flying.

NOTE: The mixing blade shown in the photograph is inexpensive and can be bought at a hardware store. If you use this type of blade, make sure not to scrape the sides of the plastic pail with the blade. If the blade is brand new, the sharp blades can cut off small bits of plastic and mix them into the batch. To avoid this, do not wipe the silicone off the blade after using it. Eventually, layers of silicone will cover the blade and reduce the cutting effect it has on the bucket. A special helical shaped blade can be bought if desired. (See page 317, photograph 2.) I use both types in my studio.

Use a strong plastic pitcher with a handle if you are going to power mix silicone.

NOTE: Remember to use a spatula to scrape material off the inside of the mixing pail. The drill will mix the batch well, but it will not draw everything off the walls.

Review of Formula:
Mixing food grade silicone. Formula for molding a highly detailed model.
Always wear rubber gloves, apron and safety glasses when mixing silicone.

100 grams food grade silicone base
   7 grams (7%) food grade silicone thinner, mix together
  10 grams catalyst (10% of silicone base weight), mix together
Remember to needle the silicone over the model. Platinum cured food grade silicone molds work well with heat. However, never heat a food grade mold above 300° C/572° F as the mold can give off toxic formaldehyde.

NOTE: Most food grade silicones have a high durometer (not very flexible). A higher percentage of thinner can be added to the batch to make it softer.

The regrind is power mixed into the base mix.

NOTE: Power mixing is the only way to do this. It is important that the regrind is thoroughly mixed into the base mix.

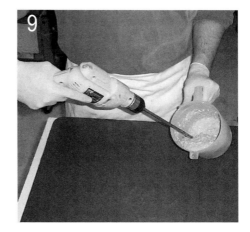

The regrind is ready to be poured into a mold box.

NOTE: This formula will make a batch of silicone that is clumpy like oatmeal and must be scraped out of the mixing bucket with a spatula. Thick silicone does not always level itself out. After filling the mold box with silicone, it may be necessary to level the batch out with a mud knife. (As seen in Chapter 7, Molding the Palm Frond.)

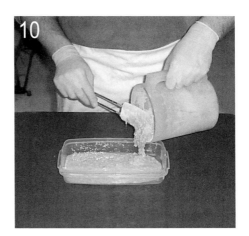

Review of formula:
Using recycled (regrind) silicone. Formula for molding a detailed model.

Always wear rubber gloves, apron and safety glasses when mixing silicone.

200 g non-food grade silicone base
  30 g (15%) silicone thinner, mix together
  20 g (10% of silicone base weight) of regular 24 hour catalyst, mix together
  75 g (approximately 30% total weight of 250 g) batch, power mix regrind into batch

Use a drill to mix the regrind into the batch. Power mixing will add air into the mix, but the extra thinner will compensate for that by lowering the overall viscosity. The lower viscosity makes it easier for air bubbles to rise upwards to the top of the mold.

How to Mix:
FAST-Setting, NON-Food Grade Silicone

This is an acceptable formula for molding objects with medium detail. The mold can be used in about five hours, but if there is no hurry, use the regular setting formula.

Always wear rubber gloves, apron and safety glasses when mixing silicone.

100 grams of base are poured into a plastic mixing dish.

NOTE: Remember to label the detergent bottle so that people know that new contents have been poured into it.

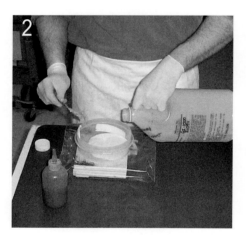

Add 10 grams (10%) of thinner to the base. The formula is forgiving. If you are slightly off on your measurements, the batch will still work.

NOTE: The thinner was purchased in a five pound quantity. The large bottles are easier to work with.

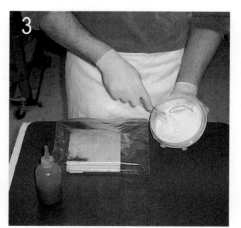

Thoroughly mix the base and the thinner together.

NOTE: The plastic mixing dish fits easily into my hand, making it easy to hold and rotate. Purchase a size that fits your hand.

Add 7 grams (7%) of fast catalyst to the base.

NOTE: The catalyst can be added to the batch right away. It is not necessary to wait for the thinner to be absorbed into the base.

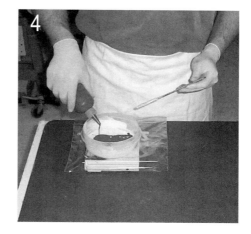

Mix the pigmented catalyst into the base until the batch is uniform in color (same as the catalyst). This should take two or three minutes. Do not mix too long as the fast catalyst will gel the silicone quickly.

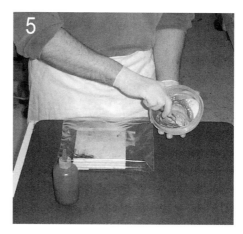

Pour the silicone into a mold box. When pouring the silicone over a model, remember to needle the silicone into the mold box to reduce air bubbles.

NOTE: This batch is being poured into a rectangular plastic container. The cured layer of silicone will be cut into strips and used as rubber registration keys.

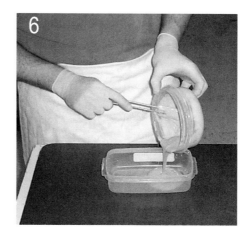

Stop pouring when the silicone no longer flows from the mixing dish. Do not scrape the remaining silicone into the mold box without remixing. Stop, and use the spatula to scrape the sides of the dish and remix the remaining silicone. Now it is safe to *nag* the pail. Scrape all of the material from the mixing dish into the mold box.

NOTE: Scraping silicone off the container walls without remixing is an easy way to pull un-catalyzed silicone into your mold.

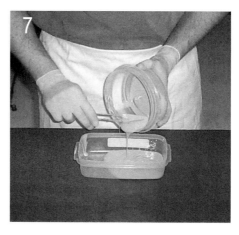

Review of Formula:

Mixing fast-setting silicone. Formula for molding a model with medium detail, such as a piece of fruit.
Always wear rubber gloves, apron and safety glasses when mixing silicone.

100 g non-food grade silicone base
  10 g (10%) silicone thinner, mix together
    7 g (7% of silicone base weight) fast catalyst, mix together

Remember to needle the silicone over the model. Mold will reach initial cure in a few hours, and should be ready to use in about five hours.

How to Mix SUPER FAST-Setting Silicone.
Suitable for molding a model with low detail, such as a geometric shape.
Always wear rubber gloves, apron and safety glasses when mixing silicone.

Follow the same mixing instructions as stated above. Alter percentages as seen below.

100 g non-food grade silicone base
  15 g **(15%)** silicone thinner, mix together
    13 g (13% of silicone base weight) fast catalyst, mix together

Work fast, you must pour this mix in less than five minutes. This formula is way beyond what a supplier will recommend. It is likely that mold quality will be compromised. Please note that the modified formula can make silicone become adhesive. Make sure to soap the model properly to prevent any adhesion. The silicone will gel in about 15 minutes and can be used in a few hours. Since bubbles are likely to be in the mold, I only use this formula when I need a rough prototype in a hurry.

How to Thicken Non-Food Grade Silicone

This is the best way to change a liquid silicone into a semi-paste. Thickened silicone is used to make frosted molds. A frosted (also known as brush applied) mold is one in which the silicone is applied to the surface of a model when it has a paste-like consistency. The following demonstration was done with Smooth-On's Mold Max™ 30 silicone. This particular silicone accepts a special liquid additive that changes the liquid silicone into a semi-paste.

NOTE: If a supplier tries to sell you a silicone that can only be thickened with Cabosil, refuse it. Cabosil is a very fine powder (fumed silica) that is added to materials in order to make them thicker, but is hazardous to use. **Use only silicones that can be thickened with a liquid additive**.

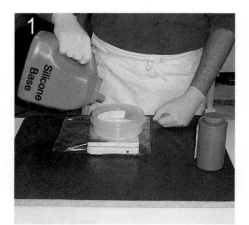

100 grams of Mold Max™ 30 silicone base are weighed out.

10 grams (10%) catalyst is added to the base.

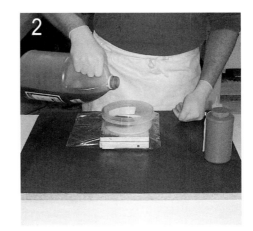

The base and catalyst are thoroughly mixed together.

1 gram (1%) of Smooth-On's Thi-Vex™ additive is mixed into the batch.

NOTE: 2% Thi-Vex™ can be added to make the batch thicker if desired. Thi-Vex™ is sold in small bottles that are difficult to measure in small amounts from, so transfer the material into a spouted container for easier handling.

The Thi-Vex™ is thoroughly mixed into the batch.

It will be visually apparent when the silicone begins to thicken. Do not add more Thi-Vex™ at this time, as the batch will continue to thicken for a few minutes after mixing.

NOTE: Thi-Vex™ will slightly accelerate the cure of the silicone. Make sure not to mix a larger batch than you can safely apply within 20 minutes working time.

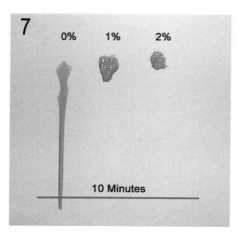

This photograph charts the flow of three different viscosities of silicone over a 10 minute time period. The first (left) column shows how far a teaspoon of liquid silicone (with regular catalyst) will flow on a vertical surface in 10 minutes. The second column shows how silicone with 1% Thi-Vex™ flowed in 10 minutes. The third column shows how silicone with 2% Thi-Vex™ flowed in 10 minutes.

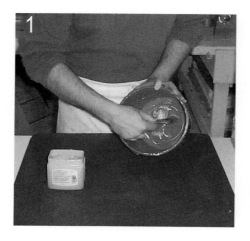

Mixing Hydrocal

There are hundreds of different plasters available. Each one has been formulated to be mixed with a specific water ratio that yields the optimum strength properties for that particular type of gypsum.

The readers of this book probably will not have reason to get overly technical when it comes to mixing plaster. Therefore, I have taken liberties to standardize the formulas.

Brush a light coat of Vaseline into your plastic, 2-gallon mixing bucket (available at hardware stores). This will make the bucket easier to clean out after mixing.

Measure out one quart (two pounds) of warm water in a separate bucket. Always keep your water bucket and your "dry" plaster bucket separate.

NOTE: When mixing plaster, always measure out the water first. (Hot water will make the plaster set faster, cold will retard the setting.)

Put on a dust mask and weigh out six pounds of Hydrocal in a SEPARATE bucket. (A children's beach toy scoop is perfect for getting dry plaster out of the bag.) It is always best to weigh out the materials. Do not try to mix the plaster by eye. Plaster that is mixed this way will probably not achieve its maximum strength.

NOTE: Control dust by making a filtered box fan. Do this by taping a filter on the back of a common (24"x 24") household fan. The box fan will only be as good as the filter you tape onto the back of it. Use only the highest quality filter available (HEPA). Spend the extra money on this or do not do it at all. A cheap filter will not catch the dust and allow it to get blown through the fan and increase the problem.

Sift the plaster into the water bucket, dispersing it evenly, one large handful at a time. Do not pile it up in the center. It should not take more than two minutes to get the dry plaster into the water bucket.

NOTE: When mixing plaster, always add the dry plaster to the water. Do not add water to dry plaster as it will not mix well.

This is very important. Let the plaster soak undisturbed for five minutes before mixing.

NOTE: Mixing the batch before the dry plaster has had a chance to absorb the water will make it lumpy and full of air bubbles.

Turn off the fan and gently mix the plaster for about three minutes. Make sure to break up any lumps in the mix.

NOTE: Wear rubber gloves or put Vaseline on your hands before putting them in wet plaster as mixing plaster without a barrier will dry out your skin. Never let plaster set on your skin, it will stick.

Keep a bucket of water nearby for rinsing your hands. Do not rinse your hands in the sink. Plaster will ruin your pipes.

Add a teaspoon of plaster accelerator. (Refer to appendix: Making Plaster Accelerator.)

Hydrocal is a very slow setting material. It is designed to be power mixed with a drill and mixing blade. (Rapid agitation is a natural accelerator for plasters.) Because most people will not have this equipment, an accelerator can be used to speed up the setting process. Without the accelerator, it will take about an hour for the plaster to set. Hydrocal is very dense and will settle to the bottom of the bucket (or mold) if it remains liquid for more than 15 minutes. If the Hydrocal settles to the bottom, the water will rise to the top, making for a very weak mix.

Mix the accelerator into the plaster.

The plaster will begin to thicken in a few minutes (faster if a lot of accelerator is used). The plaster is ready to pour when it turns into a thin creamy consistency. To check readiness, dip your hand into the batch. If plaster coats the glove like cream instead of like milk (glove still shows through), it is ready to pour.

NOTE: When testing the plaster, mix longer if it looks like your finger was dipped in milk.

A second way to tell when the plaster is ready to pour is when the plaster "tracks" on the inside of the bucket when tipped. Only a thin skin of plaster should "hang" on the wall. If a lot of plaster is sticking to the sides, it is about to set and is too thick to pour.

NOTE: Practice mixing plaster before pouring the actual master molds.

Pour the Hydrocal into the mold slowly as pouring plaster into a mold too fast will create turbulence, increasing the amount of air bubbles in the casting.

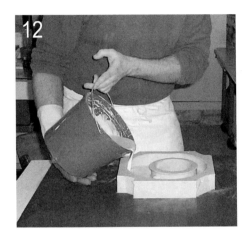

Pour off excess plaster directly into the trash. Rotate the bucket in a full circle so that plaster coats the entire interior of the bucket. Let the coated plaster set in the bucket. Do not wipe it out. Leave it alone.

NOTE: Do not rinse the bucket in the sink. NEVER POUR PLASTER DOWN A DRAIN as plaster will set under water and ruin your pipes.

When the plaster has set, it can be easily removed from the bucket by flexing the sides.

NOTE: The Vaseline coating (which was applied before mixing) makes the plaster crack off the walls more easily. Always mix plaster in a flexible bucket so that the plaster can be cracked out after use.

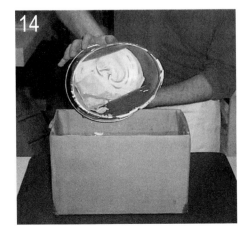

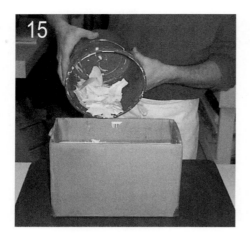

The dry chunks are disposed of in the trash. This is the best method for throwing out excess plaster.

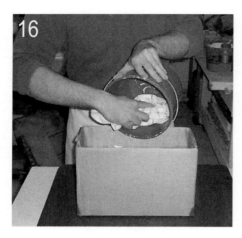

Wipe out the bucket with a towel. Do not use any tools to scrape plaster out of a bucket as the tools will scratch the bucket and create a "tooth" for more plaster to hold onto in the next mix.

Hydrocal Formula for Pouring a Master Mold

1 pound (or ½ quart) of warm water
3 pounds dry Hydrocal.

Add Hydrocal to water by sifting it gently with your hands. It should not take more than two minutes to put the Hydrocal into the water.
Allow plaster to soak for five minutes. Mix plaster for three minutes or until smooth with no lumps. Add a teaspoon of accelerator. Mix plaster until it becomes creamy.

The batch size can be increased proportionately by multiplying the material weight. Do not add more than a tablespoon of accelerator to the batch as it will make the batch set too fast.

Finding the Right Gypsum

Look online for a local gypsum supplier. Large gypsum suppliers such as United States Gypsum or Industrial Gypsum (Georgia Pacific) will list distributors and provide technical data sheets on all of their products. Each company has their own brand names for comparable products. There are many brand names of gypsum cements that do not contain the name Hydrocal (a USG brand name) that are suitable for master molds. If you are not sure which is which, ask them to provide you with an equivalent material for FGR 95 or White Hydrocal (material used for the book). If FGR 95 is not available in your area, use White Hydrocal.

Do not pay to have this material shipped as it is too heavy and expensive. It can be picked up at a local building material supply yard.

Making Plaster Accelerator

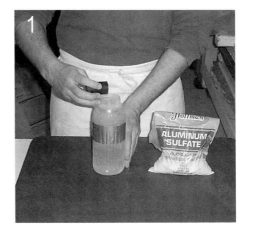

Put ½ quart of hot water into a plastic "sip" bottle and add two tablespoons (I use a 35 mm. plastic film canister) of aluminum sulfate into the water. Shake the mix together and let it sit overnight. (Make a batch of accelerator before you need it.)

NOTE: Aluminum SULFATE (not phosphate) is a white granulated soil additive. It is sold in 5-pound bags and should be available at garden supply centers (local or on the web), but call ahead before you go as not everyone carries it. The brand name on my bag is *Hoffman*.

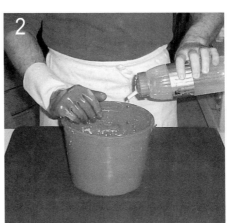

Add accelerator to a batch of liquid plaster that has already been mixed. A teaspoon should be enough.

Mix the accelerator into the batch. If it does not seem to do anything within five minutes, add more.

A batch of plaster can be made to turn thick very quickly by adding about a tablespoon of accelerator. This is the thickness that is needed for hand applying mother molds (as seen in Chapter 10). Work quickly. Plaster will set quickly from this point on. You have about five minutes.

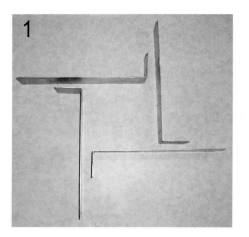

Clink Boards

Clink Boards are without a doubt the most valuable mold making accessories you can own. A mold maker should have numerous sets of clink boards always on hand. Here are some common set ups of clink boards.

This is the standard clink board arrangement. The bent corner is always facing away from the center of the mold box. A flat surface always meets a bent surface.

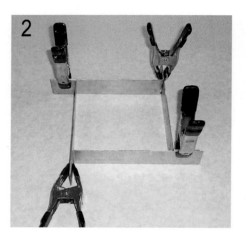

This photograph shows clink boards at maximum extension.

NOTE: Front left clamp is placed flat for photographic clarity.

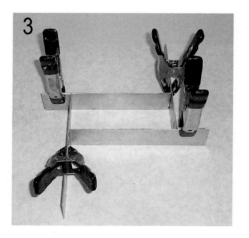

Clink boards can be quickly adjusted by removing the clamps and sliding the boards inward.

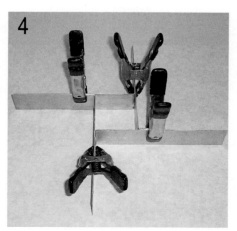

The clink boards can be adjusted to make small mold box.

The mold box can be extended by adding additional clink boards.

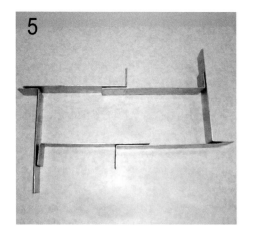

A clamping arrangement for an extended mold box.

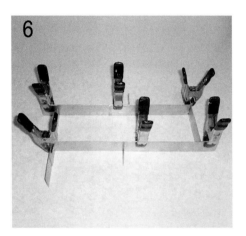

The width of clink boards can be doubled temporarily by taping two boards together, applying packing tape to both sides of the boards. (Two clink boards that have been taped together can be seen standing in the background.)

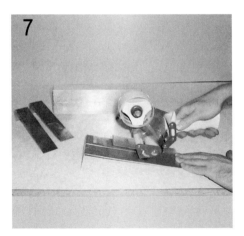

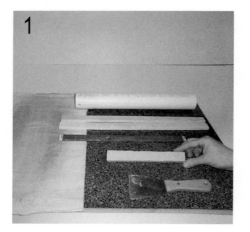

How to Make Clay Strips for Dividing Walls

Clay strips can be made quickly by rolling out soft clay between two slats of wood. Supplies needed are, two sheets of canvas, a mud knife, a weighted rolling pin, two wood slats, and oil based clay.

Oil based clay is temperature sensitive, so do not even bother trying to roll out cold clay. Use a space heater to soften the clay before handling, as soft clay will roll out easily.

NOTE: A heat lamp could be clamped onto the clay storage tote for the same effect. Another quick way to soften clay is to put a few pounds into a microwave oven for a minute or two. **BE VERY CAREFUL** when removing (over cooked) hot clay from a microwave as you can get badly burned.

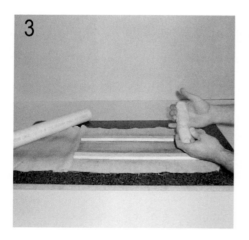

One piece of canvas is laid on the table. (Canvas will prevent the clay from sticking to the table.) A large coil of soft clay is formed. Slightly flatten the coil by hand before rolling.

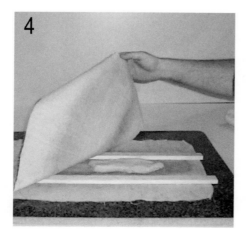

The flat coil of clay is set in between two strips of wood. The second piece of canvas is laid over the wood strips and the clay.

NOTE: The thickness of the wood slats will determine the thickness of the rolled clay strips.

The clay is rolled even. Make sure that the rolling pin is resting on the surface of both wood slats.

NOTE: Filling a large piece of plastic pipe with Hydrocal will make a terrific weighted rolling pin. A second type of weighted rolling pin can be made from a large piece of steel pipe. (Kitchen rolling pins are usually not durable or heavy enough to roll out clay.)

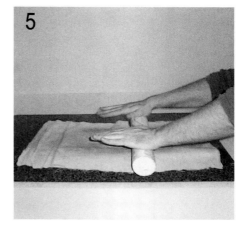

A wooden straight edge such as a louver from a wooden shutter will allow you to automatically cut even strips equal to the width of the louver. Make multiple passes with a mud knife to cut the clay.

NOTE: Do not use a real knife to cut the clay strips. It is dangerous and will either cut through you or the canvas.

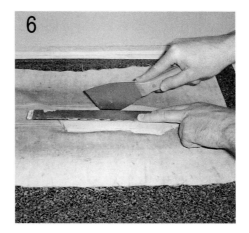

The uneven tips at the ends of the clay are trimmed off. Make extra clay strips so your next molds can be made without this interruption.

NOTE: Save all of the clay scraps for the next run, as they are already warm and partially flattened.

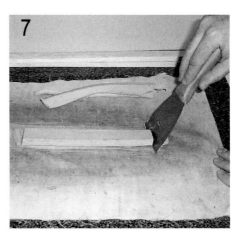

Everything is rolled up in the canvas for storage.

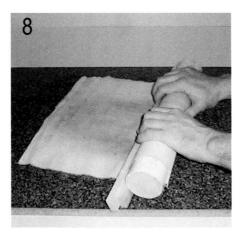

Using Banding Straps

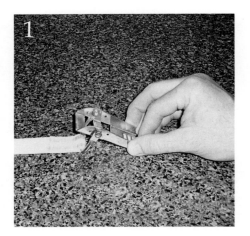

These straps are tricky to use. When you purchase them, they are wound in small bundles. Unwrap them and set them on the table as shown, making sure the "stirrup" is below the slotted buckle.

Hold the end of the strap, making sure that it is not twisted.

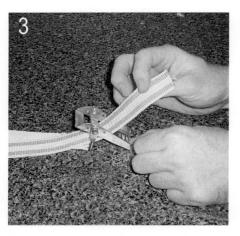

Feed the end of the strap through the "stirrup" and into the furthest slot in the buckle.

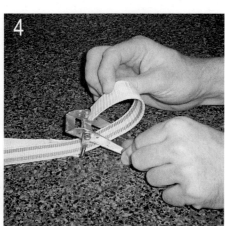

Return the strap through the front slot of the buckle.

Pull the strap through to adjust it to the approximate size of the object that needs to be banded.

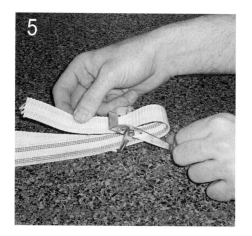

The strap is looped around a board. Do not pull the strap tight onto the board. Leave it slightly loose.

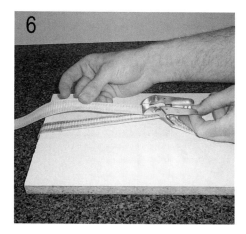

The buckle is flipped forward. This is a tension strap, and the buckle will pull the strap tight when it is pushed forward. The buckle will snap in place. Do not over tighten the strap, as moderate tension is all that you need. Make sure the buckle rests directly over the strap. If the buckle is angled over the strap, it can come loose. You will hear the buckle "snap" in place when it is properly secured.

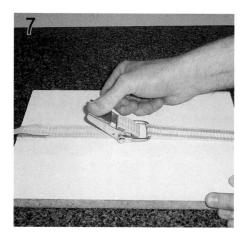

To remove the strap, hold your hand behind the buckle and pull on the open end of the strap. This will release the buckle.

NOTE: Be careful. If the strap is really tight, it can pop open very quickly when it is released and injure your fingers.

SUPPLIERS

**Chicago School of Mold Making
and Casting for the Arts**
* Clink boards, groove knives and more.
* Complete mold making tool kit
* Pre-made silicone molds
* Custom mold making services
* More products being added monthly
* Large web site: **www.ChicagoMoldSchool.com**
Join our e-mail list to learn about new mold
making books and traveling workshops.
(773) 955-1837   Joymold@earthlink.net

**Notter International School of
Confectionery Arts**
Sells soft silicone (used in Chapter 4), offers dozens
of interesting silicone molds for sale as well as his
own instructional books and videos.
Chef Notter teaches classes all around the world.
See his web site for more information.
www.NotterSchool.com or call **(301) 963-9077**

Albert Uster Imports
International Distribution. Everything a pastry
chef could need, including a large selection of
chocolate, Isomalt, tools, books and much more.
www.AUIswiss.com or **1-800-231-8154**
Great current events web link:
www.auiswiss.com/siteplan_home.cfm

Amoretti
Ultimate pastry ingredient manufacturing company.
www.Amoretti.com or **(818) 718-1239**

Ball Consulting
Chopped glass strands. **1-800-225-2673**

Barry-Callebaut
All things chocolate. World's largest chocolate
manufacturer with world wide distribution.
(Their Belgium factory produces 1 ton of chocolate
every 2 minutes!) **www.Barry-Callebaut.com**

Demarle, Inc.
Silpat® mats, flexible baking pans and lots of
culinary supplies.
www.Demarleusa.com

Dow Corning
Food grade silicones.
Go online to find a local distributor.
**www.DowCorning.com/content/moldmaking/
moldfood/default.asp**

Isomalt sugar
Distributed by Albert Uster Imports or contact
directly at: **www.isomalt.com**

Jiffy® Mixer
Good mixing blades that don't cut buckets.
www.jiffymixer.com

Chef Ewald Notter assembling the oriental centerpiece.

Laser Excel
Stencils **1-800-285-6544**
www.LaserExcel.com

Patisfrance
Gourmet Ingredients galore
www.patisfrance.com/patisfrance/

PCB Creation
Lots of everything, ingredients, chocolate, transfer
sheets and more.
www.pcb-creation.fr/indexuk.htmPerma-Flex

Perma-Flex Mold Company
Parting compound, PMC 30 liquid urethane rubber
(used to make flexible fish in Chapter 6). Premier
distributor of all Smooth-on products. This is one
of the most knowledgeable distributors that I have
found. **www.Perma-Flex.com** or **1-800-736-6653**

Plaster
United States Gypsum, White Hydrocal, FGR 95
www.GypsumSolutions.com
(Search under Art and Statuary)

Industrial Gypsum Supply, Division of Georgia
Pacific that sells many USG equivalent materials.
**www.gp.com/gypsum/industrial/artscrafts/
products.html**
Compare both companies for best price and
nearest distributor.

Smooth-On
Major distributor of non-food grade mold
making materials (silicone, urethane and resin).
They will recommend a distributor in your area.
www.Smooth-On.com or **1-800-762-0744**

Spring USA
Induction Stoves **1-800-535-8974**

GLOSSARY

Aluminum tape
A highly adhesive tape made of very thin aluminum that does not tear. It is backed with a strong glue and can be bought at a hardware store in the heating and cooling section. It is NOT the same as the cloth duct tape.

Air inhibition
Occurs with some platinum-based silicones (such as Dow Corning's Silastic L) after you have poured a mold. Any surface that is left exposed to the air does not completely cure, leaving the affected area tacky to the touch. To solve the problem put the mold in the oven at 65° C/150° F for several hours. Heat accelerates the cure of platinum-based silicones.

Blocking up a mold
When making a clay dividing wall, wood blocks are used as filler to reduce the amount of clay needed to build up to the parting line.

Cold spray
Cold air in a can. Available through culinary suppliers such as PCB Creations.

Choke
If you pour casting material into a mold too fast it will choke. This happens because the air inside the mold cannot escape fast enough to allow more casting material into the mold. Usually, molds with small pouring gates choke. A mold that has choked cannot continue to be filled. When it does choke, tap it on the table to release the air or drain the mold and fill it again more slowly.

Another reason that a mold can choke is that the casting material is too thick to flow through the mold, or it has cooled down too much and has chilled in place.

Chopped glass strands
Chopped glass is a fiber that is added to plaster to increase its strength. Chopped glass looks like short, white paint brush bristles that have been cut off the brush. It can be purchased ready to use from Ball Consulting.

Clean out cast
It is the first casting made from a new mold. The casting bonds with any excess residue and is not intended to be a usable casting. A clean out cast is a good way to "read the mold", looking for flaws in the design (mold errors). It will help you understand how the mold should be handled when casting. A clean out cast is also when fast-setting urethane resin is used to remove paint or other debris that are bonded to the molds surface.

Clink board
Clink boards are specially designed aluminum sections of a mold box. They are called clink boards because of the sound made when they knock together and because they make a clink (jail cell) around the model. Witty or not, they are a mandatory part of your mold making tool kit. (See Appendix page 330.) *They are included in the mold making tool kit (or sold separately) from The Chicago School of Mold Making.*

Coating chocolate
A non-tempering chocolate containing vegetable fats. It is very good for casting chocolate sculptures that are not intended to be eaten. Coating chocolate is not a desirable chocolate to consume. (Use couverture chocolate when castings are meant to be eaten.)

De-aired silicone
De-aired silicone is liquid silicone that has been put into a vacuum chamber and "de-aired" under a very strong (29 inches of Mercury) vacuum. The vacuum pump pulls all of the air out of the liquid silicone so that there will not be any bubbles in the mold. Silicone will work well without de-airing as long as you add 10% thinner and use a regular 24–hour catalyst. A vacuum chamber and pump is expensive, between $1000–$2500. (A vacuum cleaner is nowhere near strong enough to de-air silicone.)

Draft
Draft refers to a tapered angle on a mold or a model. Visualize the way an ice cube tray is tapered so that the cubes can pop out of the tray easily. If the ice cubes where perfect (flat walled) cubes instead of being tapered like a bell, they would not release easily from the tray. A silicone liner has the same type of relationship with the mother mold. A liner must have a surface that is smooth and tapered so that it can release easily from the mother mold.

Glossary

Durometer
The measurement of a materials hardness. A low durometer silicone is very soft and flexible. A high durometer silicone is just the opposite. (See Questions and Answers page 346.)

Fettling knife
A fettling knife is common in the ceramic industry. It is a small, narrow bladed knife used to remove the seam lines in ceramic castings. They can be customized to make a perfect mold knife by cutting the tip short and grinding it flat. A fettling knife is an essential part of your mold making tool kit. *They are included in the mold making tool kit (or sold separately) from The Chicago School of Mold Making.*

Flash
Flash is the term used to describe any small amount of mold making material that has seeped into an unwanted place. Flash typically occurs in the corners of mold boxes or under the model and can be easily removed by trimming with a small pair of scissors.

Flashed
A term used to quickly reheat a material, usually sugar, to make it malleable.

Food grade production mold
A food grade silicone mold that has been produced from a master mold.

Frosting
Slang term for applying thickened silicone over a model. More commonly known as brush applying.

Gang mold
A term used to describe a mold that has numerous cavities which allow several castings to be made at the same time. An ice cube tray is a gang mold.

Glaze
In mold making, the term glaze means to pour a thin coat of fast-setting silicone over the outer surface of a silicone liner. The glaze is meant to flow into all of the tiny crevices on the surface of the silicone liner. The result is a very smooth surface on the mold, which makes it easier for the mother mold to register properly. (It is important that glazing be done with fast-setting silicone. If regular setting silicone is used, it will remain liquid too long and simply run off the mold.)

Groove knife
A custom made knife that has a small bend in the blade. When the bent blade cuts through the silicone it leaves a groove. This groove creates a registration key along the entire length of the cut.

Cutting a mold with a razor knife will make a smooth, flat cut which will not register well because (smoothly cut) surfaces can slide against each other. The groove knife creates a ridge in the mold as it cuts. The ridge will not allow the two halves of silicone to slide past each other. A groove knife is an essential part of your mold making tool kit. *They are included in the mold making tool kit (or sold separately) from The Chicago School of Mold Making.*

Hydrocal
Hydrocal is a United States Gypsum brand name for a group of formulated gypsum cements. There are many different types of Hydrocal. Generically, Hydrocal is a very dense, very strong and very heavy type of plaster. Because of its low cost and easy workability, it is an ideal material for most master molds.

Jog the mold
Bumping or tapping the mold while it is full of plaster. Doing so will help the air bubbles in the plaster rise off the detail surface of the model. However, jogging a mold box that is full of silicone will not do anything because the material is too thick.

Induction stove
A very convenient stove that generates heat through high frequency magnetic energy. Costs range from $300-$500. Available through Spring USA.

Isomalt
A non-hydroscopic sugar developed for people with diabetes. It is available through large culinary suppliers like Albert Uster Imports.

Liner
Liner is the term used for the silicone section of a mold that fits into a mother mold. A liner seats into a mother mold. A liner is also called a blanket.

Lip
Look back at page 169, photograph 6. The lip is the extra width of silicone surrounding the bottom of the model. A wide silicone lip is a critical part of the mold design. The lip must *extend over* both mother mold sections. It creates a gasket over the mother mold and prevents casting material from leaking down between the outside of the liner and the inside of the mother mold. Without the lip, the soft silicone liner can sag away from the mother mold and create a gap. If there is a gap between the liner and the mother mold, sugar can leak between them. Casting material that leaks into the mother mold will alter the registration and be difficult to clean out of the mold. (Sugar will bond to the mother mold.)

Master mold

A master mold is a mold that makes a mold. Typically, a master mold is made of Hydrocal. The master mold is a self-contained mold box with the model attached inside. Using a master mold eliminates all of the set up time (preparing the model, building a mold box) normally needed to create a single mold. To use a master mold, just fill it with food grade silicone and let it cure.

If you need to make several production molds in a short time, it is worth it to make several master molds of the same object. The master mold is also a very good way to archive molds as silicone rubber does not last indefinitely. A rigid master mold can last for decades.

Mold box

Any container that is used to retain silicone during a pour. The best mold boxes are made of clink boards. Plexiglas strips, wood planks, Legos™ or plastic containers can also be used to make a mold box.

Mold cavity

A mold cavity is the negative impression that is filled with casting material. A multiple cavity (or gang mold) is a single mold that has several cavities. An ice cube tray has multiple cavities.

Mother mold

A mother mold is a rigid form that holds the flexible silicone liner in the correct position. Without a mother mold, the liner would collapse under its own weight. A mother mold is also referred to as a case, shell or jacket. It can be made of many different materials. A plaster mother mold is heavy, but it is easy to make and is non-toxic to work with.

Mother mold support frame

A mother mold frame is a plastic pipe (or wood) frame that is attached to the exterior of the mother mold. The frame is built in such a way that it supports the entire mold upright and level on the worktable.

MSDS

Material Safety Data Sheet. Practically every mold making material that you buy will come with an MSDS. If it does not, call the sales department, or look up the information on the companies web site. The MSDS contains valuable safety and handling information. Read them and keep them in your files.

Mud knife

Commonly used by drywall contractors for applying spackle or joint compound. Also known as a putty knife or triangular spatula. Used in mold making for splitting molds apart and other miscellaneous tasks. *They are included in the mold making tool kit from The Chicago School of Mold Making.*

Nagging the pail

Scrapping every last bit of mold making material out of the mixing container. When nagging the pale, be careful not to scrape unmixed material (off the container wall) into the mold box. The unmixed material will not cure.

Natches

Plastic natches are specially made (male and female) plastic mold keys. They are commonly used in the plaster mold making industry. *They are included in the mold making tool kit from The Chicago School of Mold Making.*

Needle / Needling

Needling is the term used to describe pouring silicone (into a mold box) in a very thin stream. Needling causes the air bubbles in the silicone to stretch out and burst before they enter the mold box. Needling is very important to do for reducing the chance of air bubbles being trapped on the detail surface of your mold.

Nitrogen air blanket

A product that is sold in pressurized spray cans. Each company gives it their own brand name such as DryPurge™ or Xtend-it™. It is sprayed into containers of unmixed urethane materials (before storing them) in order to prevent moisture contamination. (See Questions and Answers page 348.)

No. 1 Molding Plaster

An inexpensive plaster that is very good for making plaster mother molds. Available from United States Gypsum or Georgia Pacific.

Open face, or one-piece mold

A silicone mold that has been made by pouring silicone over a model, resulting in five closed sides and one open side (the face). Think of a covered box or cube, with four walls and a bottom. The open face would be the top where casting material is poured into the mold.

Oil base clay

Oil based clay is a non-drying, reusable clay. There are several brands available. I prefer Klean Klay (soft grade) for all mold making tasks. There are several different colors available. Select one color for use with Tin-based (non-food grade) silicone, and a second color for use with Platinum (food grade) silicone. The color difference will help you keep the two clays separate. Do not use any oil clay that has sulfur in it as it will inhibit the cure of silicone. *It is included in the mold making tool kit from The Chicago School of Mold Making.*

Orientation line

This is a line that is drawn on the work board (near the model) before pouring the silicone. When the mold box is removed, the ink line will be on the surface of the silicone. The line will indicate exactly where the groove knife should be positioned to cut the mold open. This is much easier than trying to remember where to cut the mold open when the model is not visible through the silicone.

Parting Soap

Parting soap is a release agent. There are numerous types of release agents on the market, but the one that was used throughout the book is named polyurethane parting compound. It is **NOT** food grade safe but, is the best release agent that I have worked with. For food grade needs, use Vaseline. (See page 336, Suppliers, available through Perma-Flex Mold Company.)

Parting line

A line that is drawn onto a model to distinguish how the mold will be divided into two or more sections. It is also referred to as the dividing line. The line is used as a reference point when building a clay dividing wall around the model. In effect, the parting line is where the dividing wall will be built.

Plaster foundation

Plaster foundations are necessary when building a clay dividing wall on top of a silicone liner. Because oil clay will not stick to silicone, it is necessary to apply a small amount of plaster onto the surface of a silicone liner to provide a temporary platform that the clay dividing wall can stick to.

Plug mold

A plug mold is a mold into which the casting material is poured through a specially designed pouring gate. The casting is made by slushing one layer after another of material into the mold and then draining it. The layers are allowed to cool or set between pours. A fitted plug is secured into the pouring gate and the mold is rotated so that the casting material covers the surface of the plug.

Once the casting material has set, the plug is removed and the casting is pulled out of the mold through the plug opening. The result is a casting that does not have any seam lines. (Using a plug mold can be seen in Chapter 15.)

Pokes

Pokes are holes that have been drilled through the plaster mother mold. They permit the user to push their fingers through the holes and so as to press the silicone section out of the mother mold.

Poured block mold

Term for a one-piece mold that is made by pouring liquid silicone over a model.

Pouring gate

A pouring gate is the opening in a silicone mold into which the casting material is poured. It is also referred to as the mouth or open face of the mold.

Pouring indication line

This is a line drawn inside of the mold box slightly above the top of the model before the silicone is poured. It is a good way to determine how thick the silicone mold will be. The line is used as a reference mark so that you know when to stop pouring the silicone. Without a line in the mold box, it is difficult to tell how thick the silicone is once the model has been covered.

Press Mold

A mold that is used by hand pressing a casting material against the texture of the mold.

Red iron oxide

An inexpensive, powdered mason stain used to pigment silicone in unique situations. Available from ceramic supply houses.

Re-grind

Re-grind is recycled silicone. Old silicone molds can be shredded (in a meat grinder) down to small gravel sized bits. Up to 30% re-grind can be added to virgin silicone (with 20% thinner). Using re-grind is a great way to reduce your material costs.

Resin

There are hundreds of different types of resin; acrylic resins, epoxy resins, polyester resins, urethane resins and more. Each resin has specific characteristics that are useful to the mold maker. Resins are sold in two component kits with a base and a catalyst that can be mixed in either weight or volume ratios.

ALWAYS READ THE MATERIAL SAFETY DATA SHEET THAT COMES WITH A RESIN KIT.

For the book, I selected a fast-setting urethane resin (Smooth-On's Smooth Cast™ 300). The selection was made because of its ease of mixing, water like viscosity, fair cost and the fast setting time. Take appropriate safety precautions when working with resin. Wear gloves, goggles, an apron, and always mix the resin outside or with proper forced air ventilation. Resins should be handled with care, as they contain many hazardous ingredients. Some resins have a terrible smell and others do not. Just because you cannot smell it does not mean that the vapors are not harmful.

Many people attempt to work with polyester resins because they can be purchased at hobby stores. I would never recommend working with polyesters. They are known carcinogens and are extremely hazardous. They remain legal because so many industries depend on them for their low costs. Don't mess with this stuff.

Sanding sponge
A sponge that has waterproof sandpaper glued to one side of it. Using a wet sanding sponge is the best way to smooth a plaster model. *They are included in the mold making tool kit from The Chicago School of Mold Making.*

Scrape level
To use a mud knife (or other flat tool) to smooth out the liquid surface of a casting before it hardens in a mold. When a mold is filled with plaster or other casting material, it is common for extra material to overflow the top of the mold. Leveling the mold is done to wipe off the excess material and make the casting flat. It is easier to remove excess material when it is a liquid than a solid.

Seat the mold
Seating the mold is the term used for placing a silicone liner into the mother mold. A mold must be properly seated in order for it to cast well. Registration keys in the mold help to assure proper alignment between the liner and the mother mold.

Shim
1. A small wedge, either wood or a mud knife, fit beneath a work board to level it.

2. A shim (also called a fence) is a very thin dividing wall that is placed into any "window" on a model. (A small shim/fence made of packing tape was used in Chapter 10 to divide a "window" that could not be separated with clay.)

Picture a small statue of a Super Hero standing tall with his/her feet apart and hands held firmly on his hips with elbows bent (the classic super hero pose). To mold such a figure, the dividing wall or fence must be built into the open spaces (windows) between his legs and bent arms.

If the statue were small, it could be laid flat on a table so that a clay dividing wall could be built up around it as in Chapter 10. However, a large (2' to 8') statue with the same pose is too heavy and too big to be laid on its side and divided with clay. It would take too much clay and too much time. The fastest way to divide a large mold like this is to cut pieces of thin aluminum and fit them in between the legs and arms like a windowpane in a frame. (The windowpane is the aluminum and the frame is the legs and arms.) The shims provide a dividing wall that can be removed after the first half of the mold has been built.

Silicone
The following information is meant only to provide a quick reference for some common silicone components. It is not intended to provide comprehensive data about silicone. If you are interested to know the molecular workings of silicone, go to www.ChemCases.com. They have a lot of information about the chemical make up of various silicone materials.

Silicone Base
The liquid rubber portion of RTV (room temperature vulcanization) silicone. The base will not cure without the addition of a catalyst.

Silicone Catalyst
The active ingredient added to the base in order to make it catalyze and cure. Some silicones have a variety of compatible catalysts that will work with the base. Different catalysts can be used to accelerate the curing time of the silicone.

Silicone / Thickened
In order to apply silicone to a vertical surface, it must be thixotropic (thick enough not to flow off the surface). Some liquid silicones (like the Mold Max™ 30 used in this book) can be made thicker by adding a small percentage of Thi-Vex™, a special liquid additive.

Not all liquid silicones are formulated to accept a thickening additive, so check with the supplier before making your purchase. They may advise you to buy a silicone that is already thixotropic. I recommend purchasing the liquid silicone because it can be used for both pouring and "frosting" molds. Two uses from the same batch.

Glossary

Silicone Thinner

Thinner is a clear liquid silicone fluid that can be added to silicone base in order to lower the durometer and viscosity of the original formulation. Adding 10% thinner to the silicone will help reduce the amount of air bubbles in the mold. This happens because the silicone is less viscous and easier for the air bubbles to rise up through the material. Thinner is also referred to as dilutant or silicone fluid. Not all thinners are food grade.

Silicone / Tin-based

Tin-based silicones are also known as condensation cure silicones. Most of them are not food grade. There is a wide variety of tin-based silicones on the market. Tin-based silicones are excellent for model making. I use tin-based silicone for casting competition or display pieces that are not intended to be eaten. They are less expensive then platinum-based silicones and are less heat resistant and less durable than platinum-based silicones.

Silicone / Platinum-based

Platinum-based silicone, also known as addition cured silicone. There are both food grade and non-food grade platinum based silicones. Do not assume that a silicone is food grade just because it is platinum-based. Food grade silicones are specially formulated products.

Platinum and tin-based silicones are not compatible. Any surface that has contacted tin-based silicone will inhibit the cure of a platinum-based silicone. Keep separate work boards, clink boards and clay for use with platinum silicones. (See Questions and Answers page 345–346.)

Silicone paste

See page 322 in the Appendix, "How to Thicken Non-Food Grade Silicone."

Silpat™ mats

Food safe silicone mats that will not stick to food. Safe for baking or freezing. Available through Demarle, Inc.

Single use mold

A mold that is only used to make one casting. They are made quickly and with less expensive materials. It might not seam realistic to make a mold just to cast one thing, but for certain model making purposes it is worth the cost. Typically, the reason to make a single use mold is to cast a particular object into a different material.

For example, you have a brass picture frame that needs more detail. Clay can be added to the areas that you want to change. Next, a single use mold is made of the modified frame. The mold is then used to cast a plaster copy so that the model can be sanded (blended) in the areas where the clay meets the metal.

If the frame were to remain in metal, the options for altering the surface are limited. But when it is in plaster, the model can be reworked using many methods (sanding, carving, buffing, etc.). The modified plaster frame is now clean and can be remolded. For models that need to be highly professional, a single use mold is always made to make a perfect model.

Slumping

The act of setting a silicone mold in or over a second shape such as a bowl to alter the original shape of the mold.

Slush casting

A casting method where the mold is filled half way, rotated and then drained. The process is repeated several times. Slush casting is an excellent way to make a hollow casting or just to ensure the elimination of air bubbles on the surface of the casting. (Slush casting an apple can be seen in Chapter 15.)

Snap Key

A small wooden plug that is placed on a dividing wall and encapsulated with silicone. Once the silicone cures, the wooden snap key is removed from the silicone liner. Snap keys are unique because they snap together, preventing two mold sections from pulling apart. See page 111, photograph 6. *They are included in the mold making tool kit from The Chicago School of Mold Making.*

Stencil

Specially cut plastic sheets. Custom stencil patterns can be ordered through Laser Excel. (See page 336, Suppliers.)

Stipple

Stippling is a textural effect usually created by brushing on paste-like material in an up and down, stabbing motion. It creates a heavy textured surface. When using Vaseline to adhere a flat mold or model to the work board, stippling is ideal because when the stippled surface is compressed a strong suction is created between the silicone surface and the work board.

SurForm™

A SurForm™ is the brand name for a small rasp used for smoothing wood. They are perfect for shaving down sharp edges of plaster mother molds and master molds. They can be bought at any hardware store.

Helpful hint: Wet plaster that sets on the rasp will rust the blade. Always clean the SurForm™ with a wire brush after each use. They are an essential part of your mold making tool kit. *It is included in the mold making tool kit from The Chicago School of Mold Making.*

Tack up

"Wait for the silicone to tack up." This simply means to wait for the layer of silicone to become partially cured, tacky to the touch. Layers of silicone adhere to themselves best if the under layer is still tacky.

Tools: detail, loop, pick, trimming

Extremely useful tools for a mold maker. Common in the ceramic industry. *They are included in the mold making tool kit from The Chicago School of Mold Making.*

Transfer sheet

Thin plastic sheets that have decorative images silk screened (with food safe colors) onto them. A transfer sheet is like food grade carbon paper. The image on the sheet will stick to chocolate (that has been poured over the sheet). When the chocolate has cooled, the plastic is peeled off to expose the image newly transferred onto the chocolate. They are easy and fast to work with. Hundreds of patterns are available through culinary supply houses.

Urethane rubber

There are too many types of urethane rubber to list. Each one has specific properties (durometer, etc.) Urethane rubber was a precursor to silicone rubber. The key difference is an RTV silicone will not stick to many things whereas urethane will bond to everything (except silicone). Urethanes were developed as adhesives and are tricky to work with. Urethanes contain more hazardous ingredients than silicone. Use urethane rubber only when you need to make a flexible model. Urethanes are nowhere near food safe. (See page 336, Suppliers, Perma-Flex Mold Company.)

Viscosity

Viscosity is the measurement of how easily a liquid flows. Water has a viscosity of one. The higher the viscosity number, the thicker the material.

Window

A term used to describe a hollow opening in a model. For example, the shape of the number 0 has a window in the center of it.

Work board

A work board is any non-porous or laminated surface you can build your mold on. Laminated press board shelving (from a hardware store) makes a good work board. *They are included in the mold making tool kit from The Chicago School of Mold Making.*

Working Model

The term working model is used to describe a preliminary model that has been assembled (from a combination of materials) to create a 3-dimensional sketch. It is not intended to be a finished model.

If you have technical questions about mold making e-mail us at Joymold@earthlink.net . We will do our best to give you a prompt answer.

I want to make a mold in my kitchen, what do you think?

Do not confuse the USE of a mold in a kitchen with the MAKING of a mold in a kitchen. The mold making processes shown in this book should be done in an environment separate from your kitchen, as there are too many chemicals that can get into unwanted places. Remember, food grade silicone is not food safe until it is mixed and cured. The catalyst from unmixed silicone contains toxic components that have not yet been molecularly locked up during curing. Keep all mold making materials away from kids or anyone who may be careless with them.

Always read the MSDS (manufacturers safety data sheet) for all materials that you work with. The data sheet will tell you the contents or ingredients of the material, its OSHA rating, and recommend specific handling precautions and other critical safety information. Often times a products MSDS can be looked up on the Internet or it can be requested from the supplier.

Mold making sounds hazardous. How can I be safe with the materials?

Mold making processes can be performed safely provided that you are aware of the hazards inherent in using toxic materials. In fact, many household or common hobby activities use materials that have equivalent health risks, such as painting or refinishing furniture, woodworking, gluing plastics and other craft materials, and oil-based painting. Educate yourself and research what is in every material you use. I am often surprised to discover how many of the solvents, cleaning materials, and surface preparation items available at a neighborhood hardware store bear labels that identify their contents as highly toxic. Just because you can buy it at the corner store doesn't mean that it is not carcinogenic.

If you are going to make molds, be clean and organized. If you are the impatient type or in a hurry, you should be advised to stay clear of mold making. This process can offer tremendous rewards, but it requires that you proceed with patience and clear thinking. Always take precautions and wear rubber gloves, safety glasses and an apron when mixing materials. Make sure you have good, clean air circulation. Treat yourself like royalty and do not take short cuts with safety.

What is the difference between Food Grade silicone and Non-Food Grade silicone?

Without getting into molecular chemistry, the two silicones differ primarily in the way they cure.

The non-food grade silicone that was used in this book is known as a tin base or "condensation cure" RTV (room temperature vulcanization) silicone rubber. The term "condensation cure" refers to the by-products (water and alcohol) that tin-based silicones give off when they are curing. For a chef, the biggest reason for using a tin-based silicone is its relatively low cost. Tin-based silicones can be used for casting food for display, competitions or other purposes that do not involve consuming the food that was casted from the mold. If you want to make something that is safe to eat, use a food grade silicone.

Most food grade silicone is a platinum-based or "addition cure" RTV silicone rubber. In general, platinum-based silicones are more durable, more temperature resistant and more expensive to manufacture because of the platinum content in the catalyst. Not all platinum-based silicones are food grade. Although the food grade and non-food grade platinum silicones have similar formulations, the food grade silicones have been manufactured in a clean environment with specially treated mixing equipment and food safe colorants in the catalyst.

Platinum-based and tin-based silicones are NOT compatible with each other.

This is cardinal rule for people who use both silicones in the same environment. Anything (tools, clink boards, mixing containers, work boards, models, clay) that has come into contact with a tin-based silicone cannot be used again when making a mold with platinum-based silicone.

Any trace of tin on a surface will prevent the platinum-based silicone from curing, so keep the two materials separate from each other. If you only have a few sets of clink boards and need to use them for both types of silicone, they must be cleaned with denatured alcohol whenever using the platinum-based silicone.

If you do not clean the tin from a surface, the platinum silicone will not cure against it and you will have a gummy mess and a worthless mold.

How can I realistically deal with the two non-compatible silicones?

1. Make a master mold and never use it for anything other than food grade silicone. This is the method of choice shown throughout the book. Pour only food grade silicone into a Hydrocal master mold. Make all your molds with the less expensive tin-based silicone and then make a Hydrocal master mold.

2. Always use platinum-based silicones.

I was told that silicone is a great mold material because it won't stick to anything. Is that true?

No. Different silicones stick to different materials. If you are not sure, try a small test cure on the model.

Tin-based silicone WILL stick to anything that has a high silica content. Ceramic objects have silica in them, as also do cement and glass. Always put parting soap or Vaseline as a parting compound on any surface that has silica in it.

Platinum-based silicone WILL NOT stick to silica-based models. If you want to capture the shine of glass or a glazed ceramic piece, you must use platinum silicone. You will not need any release agent when molding glass.

Both silicones will stick to porous objects like wood, fabric or tree bark. The silicone is not actually bonding to the material, it is just soaking into the texture and making a mechanical lock with its surface texture. Always saturate highly porous surfaces with melted Vaseline before trying to mold them.

How do I choose which silicone to buy?

This is tricky because you will find yourself at the mercy of large marketing machines and technical reps who want to sell you their material. Some silicones are better than others. The best way to select which to purchase, is to be very clear on your intended use.

If your needs are simple and you only need to make a few small molds for casting food, Ewald Notter sells a very good silicone. It is easy to mix and is sold in small quantities. You will be happy with your purchase.

If you are going to do a lot of mold making (for a display or competition) and do not need a silicone that is safe for food, then use a tin-based silicone. There are many available. For this book I made the molds with Smooth-On's Mold Max™ 30 because,

it is versatile and can be accelerated with a fast catalyst, thickened with a liquid additive, or diluted with a thinner to make it softer. There are other companies that sell similar materials. It is a matter of service, product consistency and cost. Smooth-On is one of the largest suppliers of mold making materials to the art and restoration industry. (See page 336, Suppliers for contact information.)

If you need to make numerous food grade production molds, you can use one of Dow Corning's food grade silicones. It is more expensive than non-food grade silicone and might take longer to get (depending on the distributor). Distributors can be located by contacting Dow Corning directly. (See page 336, Suppliers for contact info.) You may find that there are price differences between distributors, so shop around. For many distributors it is not a common product that they sell, so be persistent and do not wait for them to call YOU back. You are paying a lot of money for this material, so be adamant about service.

If you are working with other people who are making molds, split the cost and buy a larger kit (for instance: 45 lb. base and 4.5 lb. catalyst) to save some money.

What does "durometer" mean and why is it important for me to know?

All rubber, (silicone and urethane) is manufactured with a specific durometer. By definition, a durometer is the name of a tool in a laboratory that measures the hardness of rubber. Soft silicone has a low durometer number; rigid silicone has a high durometer. Most mold makers use rubber that ranges from what is called "Shore A 20" up to "Shore A 50."

"Shore A" indicates that the material is flexible and the number indicates the hardness. As a result, many suppliers name their products with the durometer in the name. For example, Mold Max™ 30 is a silicone with a durometer of "Shore A 30". It is critical to know which durometer to request when buying material. If you want to cast detailed chocolates, you will need a low durometer (Shore A 20 or Shore A-30 as Ewald Notter's material possesses). Conversely, if you want to press hot sugar into a mold, you will need a high durometer (such as Shore A 40 or higher).

For mental reference, "Shore A 10" rubber feels like a soft gel sole insert for a shoe, "Shore A 25" is like a baby bottle nipple, "Shore A 30" is like a rubber ducky and "Shore A 40" is like the tread of a running shoe. "Shore A 50" is like a mountain bike tire and "Shore A 60" is like a car tire.

Can I change the durometer of silicone?

Yes. Adding thinner to silicone will reduce the durometer. Most manufacturers will not recommend adding more than 10% thinner to a batch. They say more thinner will compromise the properties of the rubber. This is true for many mold applications; however, I regularly add up to 20% thinner to molds that I do not use for heavy production.

It is important to know that using an excessive amount of thinner can make the silicone become adhesive, sticking to surfaces that it would usually not. Silicone thinner is the same for both tin and platinum-based silicones. Remember, a special food grade thinner should be used when thinning food grade silicone.

Regarding food grade silicone, manufactures will not recommend more than 10% thinner to be added to a base. They say that higher amounts of thinner can leach out of the mold over time. I assume this is possible, as it is true with any silicone even though they do not point to the exact tests that demonstrated their position.

As a rule, wash your molds with a mild detergent before use, especially after a mold has been in storage for a long time.

What is the best way to add thinner to food grade silicone?

The base of food grade silicone is very thick and is difficult to pour out of some containers. This is a hassle when it comes to mixing because scooping material out of a bucket is messy. To reduce the mess and make the material easier to handle, transfer a several pounds of material into a clean bucket. Mix the thinner into the base mix and let it sit for a day. This does two things: first, it gives the thinner more time to be molecularly absorbed into the base mix, second, the batch that has been thinned can be poured easily out of the small bucket when you are ready to use it. (Adding thinner to the base ahead of time does not harm the material. Remember to keep the thinned base in a covered container.) For these reasons, I keep a bucket of base with silicone thinner already mixed into it. The catalyst can be added at any time.

What kind of clay should I use for mold making?

I recommend using Klean Klay, because it is an affordable oil-based clay, that will not dry out and is reusable. Klean Klay is sold in a variety of colors. Buy an equal amount of two colors and use one color with tin-based mold projects and another color with platinum-based mold projects.

Color-coding makes it easier to keep the clays separate. Any clay that contains sulfur should be avoided at all costs because the sulfur will inhibit the cure of silicone. You can tell when an oil-based clay has sulfur in it by the smell. Roma Plastilina is popular with sculptors, but it contains sulfur and should not be used with mold making.

Do not use water-based clays because they contain silica and will bond with tin-based silicone. Water-based clay will also dry out and is not reusable, so don't bother with it.

Can I use dish soap as a mold soap?

I recommend staying with one soap. Polyurethane parting compound is the best I have ever worked with and is not expensive. The parting compound is a sealer and a release agent in the same mix. The sealer function performed by the parting compound is critical when molding porous objects like wood. Many suppliers will try to sell you both a sealer and a release agent separately. Don't waste your money. Using sealers or soaps from hardware stores is not a good idea. Household soaps can contain perfumes or elements that could inhibit the cure of silicone. Remember, the cost of silicone is far more than the cost of a proper soap.

What is the proper way to soap a model?

Soaping seals the surface to prepare it for the application of a material that you don't want to be absorbed. What you use depends on the material used in the model. If the model material is porous, such as wood or plaster, use two layers of parting compound. Brush the first layer on with a brush, but do not use a lot of soap. (If the soap is lathering up, you have put on too much.) Allow the parting compound to absorb into the model for five or ten minutes. Then wipe off any excess parting compound with a paper towel. Let the model sit for 15 minutes and repeat the process. Do not let any pools of parting compound to accumulate on the model because they can inhibit the cure of silicone or at the very least cause a loss of detail.

Remember, parting compound has wax in it. If you brush it on a smooth model, the brush marks will remain on the surface of the model. Always buff the brush marks off the model with a soft cloth or paper towel. Polyurethane parting compound is not food safe and so must be thoroughly washed from the molds that have come in contact with it.

I have never worked with plaster before. What do I need to know?

1. Never waste your money by buying plaster at a hobby store. It is not the right material, and it is ridiculously expensive. A few pounds in a craft store will cost you $10 or more. (Hopefully, a more appropriate selection will be made available at craft stores in the future.)

2. Buy your plaster from a construction supplier or plaster house. Look up USG (United States Gypsum) or Industrial Gypsum on the Internet. Find a distributor near you. Get ready, the bags are sold in 50 lb. and 100 lb. sacks. If you can't lift that, take some clean 5-gallon pales (with lids) and fill the buckets at the site. Take a dust mask. A hundred-pound bag of Hydrocal should cost around $30-$40. Keep it away from moisture and it will last you a long time.

3. For master molds, you can use almost any dense plaster. Dental plasters are excellent, but they are expensive. There are dozens of types of Hydrocal available. For simplicity, try using White Hydrocal or FGR95. They are durable and work well for master molds.

4. Mix Hydrocal to the manufacturers recommended ratio. A simple formula to remember is 1 pound water to every 3 pounds gypsum. Always put the water into the bucket first and then add the dry plaster.

5. See the plaster mixing section of the appendix for more instruction.

How do I extend the life of urethane materials after they are opened?

The shelf life (length of time the material is usable after opening) of urethane can be greatly increased by taking one simple step. Every time you use the urethane, remember to spray a nitrogen air blanket inside the container just before closing it. (Sounds complicated, but it is not.) Many suppliers sell this product (sold in a spray can) under various names such as Dri-Purge™ or XTEND-IT™. Both are nitrogen air blankets.

To understand how they work, it is important first to know that urethanes (not silicones) are moisture sensitive. Once you open a container of urethane resin (or rubber), the material is exposed to air. The air has moisture in it. Over time, moisture will ruin the urethane by making it crusty or thick. To prevent this, the urethane must be kept dry.

A half-full container of resin contains half resin and half air. The air in a closed container contains enough moisture to ruin the material. Spraying a small amount of nitrogen into the container (before closing it) will prevent the moisture from coming into contact with the resin. This works because nitrogen is heavier than oxygen. A microfilm of nitrogen will settle directly on top of the resin. Urethane stored in this manor can last for over a year. If you are going to invest in the cost of urethane resin, spend a little more on a can of nitrogen air blanket.

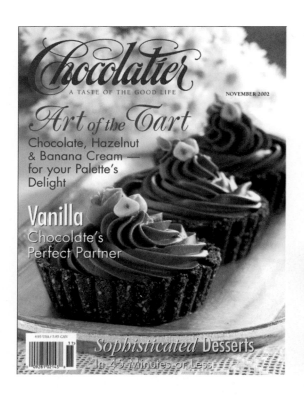

INTERNATIONAL SCHOOL OF CONFECTIONERY ARTS

THE INTERNATIONAL SCHOOL OF
CONFECTIONERY ARTS KEEPS YOU
IN STEP WITH THE CUTTING EDGE
OF THE CULINARY WORLD.
LEARN WITH WORLD RENOWNED
INSTRUCTORS LIKE:

OLIVIER BAJARD:
MEILLEUR OUVRIER DE FRANCE—
WORLD CHAMPION 1995

SUE MCMAHON:
FOOD EDITOR FOR WOMENS WEEKLY
MAGAZINE IN GREAT BRITAIN AND
A SPECIALIST OF TRADITIONAL
WEDDING CAKE DECORATION

NORMAN LOVE:
OWNER OF GANACHE CHOCOLATE AND
CO-FOUNDER OF THE WORLD PASTRY
TEAM CHAMPIONSHIP

COLETTE PETERS:
OWNER OF
THE DISTINGUISHED CAKE SHOP
COLETTE'S CAKES IN NEW YORK AND
AUTHOR OF MANY FINE BOOKS.

THESE ARE A FEW GUEST
INSTRUCTORS AS WELL AS OTHER
PRESTIGIOUS INSTRUCTORS FROM
AROUND THE WORLD

THESE ARE SOME OF THE FINE
CLASSES THAT ARE OFFERED BY
THE SCHOOL:

SUGAR DECORATION
CHOCOLATE DECORATION
PASTILLAGE DECORATION
SUGAR; CELEBRATION OF
COLOR AND SHAPE
CHOCOLATE OBESSION
WEDDING CAKE DECORATION
GUM PASTE FLOWERS

Ewald Notter, Founder and Owner of the International School of Confectionery Arts, is known worldwide for his exquisite craftsmanship and unique teaching style. Some of his most recent accomplishments include:

*2003 Winner of 5-Star Diamond Award from the American Academy of Hospitality Sciences for "**One of the finest Confectionary Chefs World Wide.**"*

Member of the winning Coupe du Monde Team for the United States in Lyon, France.

Ewald now focuses on teaching and sharing his world pastry experiences and skill with the pastry chefs of the world, as well as culinary enthusiasts. His classes are hands-on with limited class size to assure that each student receives the most out of each course.

International School of Confectionery Arts
9209 Gaither Rd.   Fax: 301 869 7669
Gaithersburg Maryland 20877   Email: Esnotter@Aol.Com
Phone: 301 963 9077   Web Site: Notterschool.Com

FRESH INGREDIENTS

UNIQUE FLAVORS & FILLINGS

NO PRESERVATIVES

HANDMADE WITH LOVE

WWW.GANCHECHOCOLOTES.COM

Experience the sensation of Ganache Chocolates all-natural handmade confections. Crafted from the finest chocolate, butter and cream, infused with the intense flavors of fruit purées, juices, fresh spices and nuts.

Choose from Darks, Milks, Whites, and Truffles. Each unique piece is an edible work of art that will arouse all your senses.

View our full collection of confections at our website:

www.ganachechocolates.com

GANACHE CHOCOLATES
239.561.7317

Carymax, LLC

PROUDLY PRESENTS

For more information visit our websites

WWW.WORLDPASTRYFORUM.COM

WWW.PASTRYCHAMPIONSHIP.COM

BIOGRAPHIES

Chef Sebastien Canonne

Master Pastry Chef/Instructor/Owner/Founder of the French Pastry School

Before joining Jacquy Pfeiffer and opening the doors at the French Pastry School, Inc., Sebastien Canonne had already completed a culinary journey that included cooking for the French President, working in the kitchens of several three-star Michelin chefs and apprenticing at the most famous pastry shops in Paris. Now, partners Canonne and Pfeiffer serve as co-owners of the French Pastry School, Inc., Chef Instructors, and Food Consultants. Presently, Sebastien is based in South America (Caracas, Venezuela) to open a new branch of the French Pastry School.

Not only has Sebastien Canonne achieved high goals, he has attained prestigious awards along the way. He won the Beaver Creek 2000 National Pastry Team Championship; the "1996 U.S. Pastry Cup" and led the 1997 U.S. Pastry Cup World Team to a silver medal finish at the finals in Lyon, France, against chefs from 16 other countries. His winning creations included an array of desserts and surrealistic sculptures made from sugar and chocolate. He was named one of the "Top 10 Pastry Chefs in America in 1996 and 1997" by Chocolatier Magazine and Pastry Art & Design, and was crowned as "1995 Champagne Taittinger Pastry Chef of the Year in America." Chef Canonne was received at the "Academie Culinaire de France" in 2000.

Canonne began his career in 1983 at the young age of 15, when he studied at the Ecole Hoteliere de Rouen in Normandy, France, for two years. In 1985, he apprenticed at the renowned Paris pastry shop, Gaston Lenotre, where he was first exposed to the complete pastry field. He then worked at the famous La Cote St. Jacques Restaurant in Burgundy, alongside three-star Michelin Chef Michel Lorain. In 1987, Canonne continued to practice his skills at the legendary Beau Rivage Palace in Geneva, Switzerland, and, subsequently, at the Hotel Palace Euler in Basel.

Two years later, his skills were put to the ultimate test when he cooked for French President Francois Mitterand at the Palais de Elysee in Paris. During this time, Sebastien worked under Master Chef Joel Normand, who had earned the prestigious honor of "Meilleur Ouvrier de France." With Master Chef Normand, Canonne assisted in the preparation for countless receptions held for over 40 visiting international political dignitaries, among them United States President George Bush, who visited France during the Bicentennial celebrations in 1989. Following several culinary promotions in Europe and around the world, Canonne moved to the United States in 1992 and became Executive Pastry Chef at the Ritz-Carlton Hotel in Chicago. He was responsible for all the desserts in the award-winning Dining Room, The Café, The Greenhouse, and Carlton Club, as well as for room service and banquets. During his five years at the Ritz-Carlton Hotel, it was twice named the best hotel in the U.S. and one of the top hotels in the world.

Now, Sebastien Canonne and partner Jacquy Pfeiffer, are co-owners of the French Pastry School, Inc. in Chicago where they focus on spreading their vast knowledge through teaching, not only in their school, but also in the world's most prestigious academies. As food consultants, they have been hired exclusively to work for the Chicago Symphony Orchestra for the opening of its new restaurant Rhapsody and, also, to consult with hotels and restaurants in the Bahamas and Mexico. Recently, Canonne and Pfeiffer were selected to develop a line of pastries for the Atlantis Hotel and attended the grand opening celebrations, where they made desserts and room amenities for numerous celebrities, including Michael Jordan, Michael Jackson, and Oprah Winfrey. The French Pastry School, Inc. is the exclusive pastry consultant for the re-opening of Jean Banchet's restaurant Le Français.

Chef Canonne is based in Caracas, Venezuela. This year, we are proud to announce that the French Pastry School was just voted "2002 Best Culinary School in the Midwest" and that chef Canonne was just awarded the pastry title of "2002 World Champion", at the Las Vegas World Pastry Forum and Competition in his role as coaching and leading the US team to the world title.

Chef Keegan Gerhard

Executive Pastry Chef, Four Seasons Hotel Chicago

Keegan Gerhard's passion for the Culinary Arts began modestly, almost as an after thought. He was training for the 1992 Olympic Games as a track cyclist when he realized that if he could cook, he could support himself regardless of where his training might dictate that he live. Once his pursuit of cycling was complete he put that same passion and competitive spirit into cooking which was clearly his new career. He found himself the Executive Chef of Piret's French Bistro in La Jolla, California, with a difficult decision to make. The pastry chef wasn't up to par. "Let them go and make it happen", was his decision as a replacement had not yet been found. This decision changed his life. Finally a field he could put all his energy and personality into. A professional pastry chef is, what he realized, he must be. He also realized he had a lot to learn.

Fortunately for Keegan, one of the best Pastry Chefs in the world was willing to give him a chance. In the fall of 1992 he began his apprenticeship with Jacquy Pfeiffer. Here the foundation was set and his eyes opened to the possibilities that the world of pastry could offer. Just as Jacquy Pfeiffer told Keegan it was time to go it alone, Andrew MacLauchlan invited him to join the team at Charlie Trotter's. Keegan took over as pastry chef when Andrew went on to work with Mark Miller.

At Charlie Trotter's, Keegan toured with Chef Trotter in support of his first book. During this same time he helped to achieve desserts for the Charlie Trotter Vegetable Cookbook. Charlie also invited Keegan to attend two James Beard Dinners as well as support for the hosting of the James Beard Awards. His time at Trotters also afforded him the opportunity to design a custom chocolate line for Hawaiian Vintage Chocolate Company.

What do you do to follow Charlie Trotter's? New York City of course. Keegan moved to Manhattan to become the Pastry Chef at The Waldorf-Astoria. This property gave him the chance to engage in all the various disciplines of baking and pastry on a world-class level. The Waldorf brought along opportunities not just for plated desserts and banquets but also for sugar and chocolate showpiece making, competitions, as well as specialty cakes and desserts for the many celebrities on The Waldorf's guest list. While at the Waldorf, Keegan made President Clinton's 50th birthday cake as well as birthday cakes for Madeline Albright, Lady Diana, Dr. Ruth and Phil Collins, just to name a few.

After the Waldorf, Keegan joined Norman Love, Corporate Pastry Chef for the Ritz-Carlton Hotel Company. The Ritz-Carlton Naples, Florida, is the home base for Norman and a training ground for Ritz-Carlton worldwide. Keegan assisted Chef Love with several openings as well as the Coupe du Monde de la Patisserie. While at this five-star, five-diamond property, Keegan began to garner attention both for himself as well as the Hotel. He helped the Dining Room Restaurant achieve its fifth star. The Hotel was ranked #1 Resort in the United States and the hemisphere. Keegan has been featured in several episodes of Great Chefs of America on the Discovery Channel. Grand Finales pastry book series also featured Keegan in their most recent release, *A Neoclassic View of Plated Desserts*.

Chef Gerhard is currently the Executive Pastry Chef of the Four Seasons Hotel Chicago. This property is the only Five-Star, Five-Diamond Hotel in the Midwest. Keegan is a regularly featured chef in Epcot's Annual Food & Wine Festival. In 1997 and 1999, Keegan was chosen to be the assistant to the United States World Cup Pastry Team. Keegan was selected as Technical Advisor and Consultant to the 2001 World Cup Pastry Team when the United States team was finally able to bring home the Gold Medal. Keegan also works with CaryMax Inc. as an organizer and Master of Ceremony for the National and International Pastry Team Championships held each June in Las Vegas.

Most recently, Pastry Art & Design and Chocolatier magazines named Keegan Top Ten Best Pastry Chef in America for 2002. In 2003, Keegan was given the prestigious honor of being named the Pastry D.V.C. by Johnson & Wales University and was also nominated Celebrity Pastry Chef of the Year by the Jean Banchet Culinary Excellence Awards Committee.

Michael Joy

Master Mold Maker/Founder of The Chicago School for Mold Making and Casting for the Arts

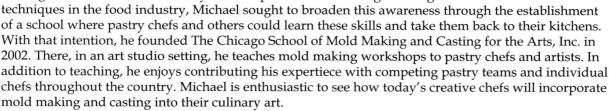

Michael Joy is a skilled mold maker and sculptor. Through his sculpture fabrication business, Chicago-based CLARO Art Studio, Inc., he undertakes a wide variety of commercial projects. Recognized for his commitment to superior craftsmanship, Michael's commissioned works range from monument restoration to making the re-designed master model of the Academy of Motion Pictures icon, the "Oscar."

Michael's mold making skills have found a new expression thanks to working with the great pastry chefs he has been fortunate enough to meet. Having become aware of the many creative possibilities of using molding techniques in the food industry, Michael sought to broaden this awareness through the establishment of a school where pastry chefs and others could learn these skills and take them back to their kitchens. With that intention, he founded The Chicago School of Mold Making and Casting for the Arts, Inc. in 2002. There, in an art studio setting, he teaches mold making workshops to pastry chefs and artists. In addition to teaching, he enjoys contributing his experiece with competing pastry teams and individual chefs throughout the country. Michael is enthusiastic to see how today's creative chefs will incorporate mold making and casting into their culinary art.

With 15 years' experience, Michael has accumulated a wealth of technical skills encompassing several industries. He is proficient in industrial tooling for casting ceramics, resin gift ware manufacturing, bronze casting, photographic model and prop making, chocolate and sugar molding, production tool design for casting sculptural reproductions, ornamental plastering and architectural restoration. His dedication to quality was recognized when the Frank Lloyd Wright Foundation called upon him to mold various ornamental architectural features on national and historic landmark buildings.

In addition to commercial applications of mold making and casting, Michael continues to produce his own sculpture whose playful themes and imagery are expressed in a unique surrealistic style. Through his sculpture, he has elevated an industrial process to an art form.

Michael is the author of several technical monographs and manuals for the mold making industry and is completing a series of books. The second book, titled, *The Art of Mold Making; A Pictorial Encyclopedia Of Mold Making And Casting Techniques For The Ceramicist*, will be published soon.

Chef John Kraus

French Pastry School / Chef Instructor

In August 2002, The French Pastry School proudly welcomed John Kraus as Chef Instructor. Chef Kraus began his pastry career in London, England at the Dorchester Hotel. Chef Kraus later contributed to the opening of the Michelin Star restaurant, Fleur de sel, under Chef Michel Perraud who has the title of Meilleur Ouvrier de Grande Bretagne.

Upon his return to the U.S., Chef Kraus worked with Chef Robert Waggoner at the famed five-star, five-diamond Wild Boar restaurant in Nashville, TN. He was then appointed Executive Pastry Chef at the exclusive Magnolia restaurant under Chef Emile Labrousse. In 1999, Chef Kraus was invited to join The French Pastry School in Chicago. Over the last three years he has worked diligently with his mentors, Chef Jacquy Pfeiffer and Sebastien Canonne, participating in major competitions and special events across the U.S. and France.

Chef Kraus' most recent awards include the prestigious 2002 Patisfrance Pastry Chef of the Year and the National Dessert Champion of 2002. Chef Kraus is best known for the innovative desserts he created while serving as the Pastry Chef at NoMI restaurant in the Park Hyatt Hotel Chicago. He has completed numerous stages which include Le Palais du Chocolat in Troyes, France, under Master Pastry Chef Pascal Caffet.

Chef Kraus' passion and vision for the art of pastry will be a great asset for the French Pastry School and its students.

Chef Ewald Notter

Instructor/Founder of the International School of Confectionery Arts

Ewald Notter is known worldwide for his exquisite craftsmanship and unique teaching style. He's worked and competed in over ten countries, winning fifteen gold medals including gold with distinction at the 1984 IKA Culinary Olympics in Germany and the Gold Medal with Diploma from the Foreign Minister of Japan at the International World Cake Fair in Yokoma, Japan.

In 1999, Notter won the gold medal at the first Beaver Creek Team Competition in Beaver Creek, CO, and in 2000, repeated the victory. In the Coupe du Mondeheld in 2001 in Lyon, France, Notter placed first with the highest score in sugar (699 out of 700 points) and helped the U.S. team achieve the first gold medal in the history of the prestigious competition. In addition to competing and teaching, Notter has published two books including "Sugar Pulling and Sugar Blowing" and "That's Sugar" as well as several instructional videos.

In 1992, Ewald Notter moved the International School of Confectionery Arts to Gaithersburg, Maryland, just outside Washington, DC. Traditional courses are offered in sugar and chocolate decoration in addition to production-based classes such as mold making and special holiday classes. Internationally renowned guest instructors are also invited to teach at the school on a regular basis.

Accomplishments

2003   Winner of 5-Star Diamond Award from the American Academy of Hospitality Sciences for "One of the finest Confectionary Chefs World Wide."

2001   Member of the winning Coupe du Monde Team for the United States in Lyon, France.

2000   Inducted into Pastry Art and Design Hall of Fame.
Beaver Creek Culinary Classic 1st Place winner with Jacquy Pfeiffer and Sebastien Canonne.

1999   Beaver Creek Culinary Classic 1st Place winner with Thaddeus Dubois.
Created Sugar Videos I & II with Culinary Institute of America.

1998   Created Chocolate Videos I & II with Culinary Institute of America.

1996   Judged the Culinary Olympics in Berlin, Germany.

1995   Distinguished Visiting Chef at Johnson and Wales University. Member of the International Judging Committee "Salon Culinare Mondial" in Basel, Switzerland.

1994   Received Gold Medal from the Academy of Gastronomy of Germany for book "That's Sugar."

1993   Member of International Judging Committee at "Salon Culinare Mondial" in Basel, Switzerland.

1992   Member of organizing committee for Union Helvetia National and International Competitions.

1990   Judged the International Pastry Competition in Wiesbaden, Germany.

1989   Winner of the Grande Prix at the "Concour Culinaire Exceptional" in Basel, Switzerland.

1988   Winner of the Gold Leaf at the Culinary Olympics in Berlin, Germany.

1987   Winner of 6 Gold Medals at the "Cuisine Artistique International" in Basel, Switzerland.

1986   Placed 1st at the "Alementaria" in Barcelona, Spain.
Winner of the Gold Medal at Expo Gast in Luxembourg.

1985   Authored the book "The Textbook of Sugar Pulling and Blowing."
Placed 2nd at the "International Pastry Competition" in Copenhagen, Denmark.

1984   Winner of the Gold Medal with distinction at the "Culinary Olympics" in Frankfurt, Germany.
Winner of the Gold Medal at the World Cake Fair Tokyo.

1983   Winner of the Silver and Bronze Medal at the "Pastry Competition" in Lausanne, Switzerland.

1982   Placed 1st at the "Exposition Gastronomique des Reconstres Professionnelles" in Epinal, France.

1981   Placed 1st at the "Club Propes Montagne Concours des Patissiers Confiseurs" in Switzerland.

Teaching Affiliations:

Richmont School, Master Bakers and Confectioners Association, Lucerne, Switzerland.
Master School, Cologne, Switzerland.
National Master School, Wolfenbuttel, Germany.
Madrid Confectionery School, Spain.
Nippon Kashi Senmon Gaya School, Tokyo, Japan.
Technic Slagelse Scole, Denmark.
National Confectionery and Pastry Scole, Ringstet, Denmark.
College of Art and Technology, Isle of Wight, England.
Confisier, Fazer, Finland.
Hotel Divan, Istanbul.
The Peninsula Group, Hong Kong.
The Portman Ritz-Carlton, Shanghai.

Chef Jacquy Pfeiffer

Master Pastry Chef/Instructor/Owner/Founder of the French Pastry School

Jacquy Pfeiffer is the owner and founder of the French Pastry School, Chicago, Illinois. His most recent awards include Manager/Coach of the 2002 World Pastry Team Champions and the winner of the prestigious Jean Banchet award for Best Culinary School.

- Born in Molsheim, France, Pfeiffer began his career at age 15 as an apprentice at Jean Clauss's Pastry Shop in Strasbourg, France where he worked from 1976-1978.

- In 1982, Pfeiffer was called to serve his country by being selected as the private pastry chef for an Admiral of the French Navy.

- In 1983, when he completed his commitment to the Navy, Pfeiffer earned positions at various highly regarded patisseries in Strasbourg. He then accepted a position in Riyadh, Saudi Arabia as the Executive Pastry Chef for the Royal Family.

- In 1984, Pfeiffer then accepted a position at Douce France in Palo Alto, California.

- In 1988, Pfeiffer was offered employment as the Pastry Chef for His Majesty, The Sultan of Brunei, the richest man in the world. After serving the Sultan for two years, Pfeiffer was selected to be the executive pastry chef at Hyatt Regency Hong Kong where he developed a new line of exclusive desserts and fine chocolates.

- In 1992, after two years of working in Hong Kong, Pfeiffer moved to the prestigious Fairmont Hotel in Chicago.

- In 1992, Pfeiffer competed in the National Pastry Chef Competition in New York where he was awarded the gold medal. In 1993, Pfeiffer was offered a position as the Executive Pastry Chef at the Sheraton Chicago Hotel and Towers where his state-of-the-art pastry shop catered to 1,200 guest rooms, five restaurants, and the largest ballroom in the Midwest, with a capacity of 4,000.

- Pfeiffer's numerous awards and accomplishments afforded him the opportunity in 1995 to compete as a U.S. team member in the Coupe du Monde de la Patisserie in Lyon, France where his team brought home the bronze medal. 1995 also saw Pfeiffer become the first person ever to win the National Chocolate Competition, Masters of Chocolate. Winning this competition allowed him to compete in Paris at the Grand Prix International de la Chocolaterie where he won first prize for presentation and second prize overall for his masterpiece, "Lore of Flight."

- In 1996, the year The French Pastry School was founded, Pfeiffer helped the U.S. team bring home the silver medal as captain of the 1996 U.S. team at the Coupe du Monde de la Patisserie. In 1996 and 1997, Chocolatier and Pastry Art & Design magazines awarded Pfeiffer the title of one of the Top Ten Pastry Chef's in the United States.

- Pfeiffer was one of seven U.S. pastry chefs invited to the White House in 1998 to create a confectionery showpiece for the White House Easter Egg Roll.

- In 1999, Pfeiffer and Sebastien Canonne consulted for the restaurant, Rhapsody, in Chicago and for the Atlantis Hotel in the Bahamas.

- Pfeiffer and Canonne were also placed on the Chicago Tribune's Good Eating Honor Roll. This award is given to those in the food industry who are making a difference in Chicago through their commitment, quality, vision and zeal.

Pfeiffer continues to share his knowledge, skills and vision with the students at the French Pastry School (www.FrenchPastrySchool.com) as he seeks to further the dynamic field of pastry.